Democracy, Multiculturalism, and the Community College

Critical Education Practice
(Vol. 5)
Garland Reference Library of Social Science
(Vol. 1081)

Critical Education Practice

Shirley R. Steinberg and Joe L. Kincheloe, Series Editors

Democracy, Multiculturalism, and the Community College
A Critical Perspective

Robert A. Rhoads
James R. Valadez

GARLAND PUBLISHING, INC.
New York & London
1996

Library of Congress Cataloging-in-Publication Data

Rhoads, Robert A.
  Democracy, multiculturalism, and the community college :
a critical perspective / Robert A. Rhoads, James R. Valadez.
      p.   cm. — (Garland reference library of social
science ; vol. 1081. Critical education practice ; vol. 5)
    Includes bibliographical references (p.   ) and index.
    ISBN 0-8153-2197-X (casebound).—ISBN 0-8153-2324-7 (pbk.)
    1. Community colleges—United States—Administration—Case
studies.   2. Pluralism (Social sciences)—United States—Case studies.   3. Community colleges—United States—Sociological aspects—
Case studies.   I. Valadez, James R.   II. Title.   III. Series: Garland
reference library of social science ; v. 1081.   IV. Series: Garland reference library of social science. Critical education practice ; vol. 5.
LB2328.15.U6R46   1996
378'.052'0973—dc20   95-48972
                                                         CIP

Paperback cover designed by Karin Badger.

The photograph for the cover was taken by Max Sa Leitao. Mr. Sa Leitao is the
winner of the Associated Collegiate Press Feature Picture of the Year (1995) and
is a graduate of Lansing Community College.

The work of Dr. Robert A. Rhoads was supported with funding from the Office of Educational Research and Improvement, U.S. Department of Education,
under project no. R117G10037. The work of Dr. James R. Valadez was supported by a Spencer Small Grant and a Spencer Postdoctoral Fellowship. The
opinions expressed in this book do not necessarily reflect the positions or policies of the funding sources.

Printed on acid-free, 250-year-life paper
Manufactured in the United States of America

Contents

Series Editor's Introduction

Robert Rhoads and James Valadez have written a dangerous book. *Democracy, Multiculturalism, and the Community College: A Critical Perspective* contends that American community colleges face an identity crisis. Burdened with so many tasks over the last several decades, community colleges have sometimes lost their organizational identity. Founded as open access venues of higher education, community colleges represent American education's commitment to democracy. It is this dangerous dynamic that Rhoads and Valadez seek to question. Around the democratic impulse the book takes shape.

Asserting that community colleges have too often failed the test of democracy, the authors delineate the institution's unsuccessful efforts to provide social/economic mobility to many of its students. Community college students from lower socioeconomic backgrounds continue to find low-pay, low-status jobs awaiting them after graduation. What changes are needed, Rhoads and Valadez ask, to make community colleges more democratic, more true to their egalitarian mission? What forces, what belief structures have impeded this attempt? At this point the explorations become especially hazardous. These questions are rarely asked in the public conversation about community colleges at the end of the twentieth century. Raising questions of democracy, Rhoads and Valadez become the bearers of the bad news, the dinner guests who broach the unspoken unpleasantry at the dining table. In an era where right-wing attacks on equal opportunity and various inclusionary practices have become the order of the day, such questions become even more "crass." In this social context too much talk about democracy is inappropriate; indeed, as the director of the National Endowment for the Humanities put it: "Too much democracy can be a bad thing."

How should community colleges deal with their identity crisis? How might they reaffirm their commitment to democracy? Rhoads and Valadez maintain that such tasks can be conceptualized around the discourse of critical multiculturalism. The term, multiculturalism, has been used by different groups to mean many different things. Understanding the lack of consensus about its meaning, the authors delineate a specific form of multiculturalism as the theoretical grounding for their effort to democratize the community college. Critical multiculturalism contends that representations of race, class, and gender are inseparable from larger social struggles. In this "power play" critical multiculturalists assume that multicultural curriculums attempt to transform the social, cultural, and institutional structures that produce these representations. Power operates, critical multiculturalists argue, by its ability to produce knowledge that shapes our understanding of the world. Mainstream science, the official curriculum, corporate advertising, and many other social dynamics *represent* reality in ways that benefit particular interests while undermining others. In the case of the community college and its students, power-driven representations of the world and its people are dramatic in their impact. For example, the representation of African-American, Puerto Rican, Mexican, or poor white students attending community colleges as unworthy or remedial students is damaging to the public commitment to community colleges in general and marginalizes students' self-concepts in particular. Critical multiculturalists point out these power-related issues and their relation to America's historical commitment to democratic values.

Thus, critical multiculturalists assume that issues of democracy and education must be analyzed in their relationship to power and privilege. Indeed, they assume that justice does *not* already exist and *only* needs to be distributed more fairly. In this context critical multiculturalists struggle with the definition of a just community, focusing their attention on competing conceptions of community as a homogeneous body and community as a heterogeneous body. Critical multiculturalists argue that community does not rest on a simplistic notion of consensus. In a racially and ethnically diverse society that respects but does not essentialize differences, great gains can be realized in the cultivation of critical thinking and moral reasoning. A homogeneous community grounded on consensus may be unable to criticize the injustice and exclusionary practices that undermine it. Criticism and reform of cultural pathology often come from the recognition of difference, from interaction with communities and individuals who do not suffer from the same injustices or who have dealt with them in different ways. Consciousness itself is spurred by difference in that we gain our first awareness of who we are when we become conscious that we exist independently of another or another's ways.

From this critical multicultural position Rhoads and Valadez challenge the tendency of contemporary community colleges to embrace what they call "an authoritarian view of knowledge and pedagogy." Such authoritarianism poses a special threat to students who fall outside the boundaries of white and upper-middle class contexts. Culture is irrelevant and student welfare is overlooked in the authoritarian curriculum's dismissal of their experiences and special needs. The authoritarian stance views the community college's pedagogical task as one of "adjusting" low-ability students to the workforce in a way that reflects the needs of business and industry regardless of the needs and best interests of the students involved. Too often community college leaders fail to question the purpose of career education in a domestic society. What skills do we want community college graduates to possess? What types of attitudes and behaviors? What understandings should students acquire that will help them to become better workers? Better citizens? How do factors of race, socioeconomic class, or gender affect various aspects of community college education?

The critical multicultural community college education that Rhoads and Valadez envision is grounded on the production of thoughtful worker-citizens. Such students understand the contradictions in their education and their work experiences; they appreciate the way power shapes their view of themselves and the world. Thus, the authors push us beyond narrow visions of careerism, working in the name of democracy to construct a new type of community college education that is grounded in the best traditions of America's sense of justice. A critical multicultural community college education empowers its students by cultivating their capacity for self-direction. Such an education grants students a sense of possibility, a sense that positive change can take place. Empowered com-

munity college students look for the footprints of power and domination in not only the construction of their own consciousness but
also in the curriculum and organization of their college. They question inequities, asking why the "mastery" of some forms of knowledge confers greater status than others. Acting on their own empowerment, they weigh existing social, economic, and educational
institutions against their own claims of integrity and democracy. In
this context they ask if the institutions that shape their lives expand
the possibilities of humanness.

Rhoads and Valadez are haunted by the questions: "Is it possible
to restructure community colleges around such issues?"; and, "If it is
how do we do it?" Maintaining that multiculturalism involves more
than merely offering courses on diverse peoples and cultures, the authors induce community college leaders to restructure their institutions so that all people are capable of input into decision making. If
critical multicultural institutions exist first and foremost as democracies, then a critical multicultural stance demands that innovation be
created within the culture of the college and its student and teacher
community. Thus, the authors conclude that in such a theoretical context, community college leadership ought to be reconceptualized. Critical multicultural educational leadership is not a quality found only
among college officials—leadership from the authors' perspective is
an ability possessed by a wide variety of institutional participants. The
authors provide important insights into the nature of democratic leadership: Leading involves not as much commanding as it does helping
institutional participants make sense of the multiple dynamics shaping the college and its relationship to the larger society.

The ability to make meaning is a primary theme of the book—
and the understanding of social context and the power of culture to
shape educational life is central to the authors' project. In the effort
to reclaim the democratic origins of the community college, understanding the cultural identities of its students cannot be ignored. All
members of the college community must understand the various
ways these cultural dynamics operate. When such understandings
are grasped by all parties involved, the community college is prepared to address issues that have traditionally undermined institutional effectiveness. An appreciation of cultural dynamics allows faculty, staff, and administration insight into the fact that student

performance has more to do with cultural difference and social interaction than most other factors. In this context Rhoads and Valadez
address assessment strategies, advising, and placement tests. Placement tests in particular have victimized several generations of community college students. To label and categorize students on the basis
of tests that often measure familiarity with industrialized modernist
ways of seeing the world (in other words, dominant cultural capital)
is a consequence of the absence of cultural contextualization. The
authors are keenly aware of the pernicious ways such "technologies"
of dominant power subvert the progress of students from outside
mainstream culture.

When we know that over half the students who attend community colleges are non-white, our view of community college pedagogy should change. Non-white and economically disadvantaged
students are saddled with an entirely different set of problems than
most students at four-year colleges and universities. Such students
bring a very different set of skills to the community college table—
skills that teachers and administrative officials view in sometimes
negative ways. Marginalized students who are intelligent and creative are convinced of their intellectual inferiority because educators
fail to understand the socioeconomic context in which they have
come of age. Such class-based and ethnic issues often do not "play"
well in American society where many argue *there are no social or
economic classes.* In a context dominated by such belief structures,
raising these issues subjects one to charges of demagoguery and unnecessary agitation. The use of racial and class analysis has never
been more important than in the 1990s with the massive redistribu-
tion of wealth from the poor to the well-to-do. Indeed, the attempt
to dismiss class as an American political and educational issue must
be exposed for what it is—an instrumental fiction designed to perpetuate the inequitable status quo by pointing out the poor and
culturally differents' own incompetence as the cause of their poverty. Suffice it to say that the authors of *The Bell Curve,* Charles
Murray and the late Richard Herrnstein, will not enjoy this book.

Rhoads and Valadez know that too many community colleges
are not equipped to take advantage of the skills and understandings
that marginalized students bring to the classroom. They know that
such students are handicapped when they run into problems tied to

their inadequate understanding of how to negotiate the culture of the college or how to "work" its impersonal bureaucracy. Such inabilities are not manifestations of low ability—they are marks of cultural differences and should not be confused with anything else. While the path to empowerment involves the ability to move beyond victimization and take charge of one's own destiny, this is not to be undertaken by the denial of socioeconomic context.

A strange alchemy occurs when the cultural baggage carried by marginalized students intersects with the middle-class dynamics of the community colleges. A pattern of alienation is created that frequently results in the failure of the student. Educational sociologists have for decades reported the cold and impersonal ways lower socioeconomic and marginalized students are treated, how they are made to feel like intruders who don't belong. School is at times like a jealous lover who demands that marginalized students choose between their culture and the school—that is, if school is chosen then one must give up her or his culture and adopt the identity of a school achiever. Rhoads and Valadez appreciate these painful cultural dynamics and dedicate *Democracy, Multiculturalism, and the Community College* to exposing them. To assert that no student is deficient or unknowledgeable and can benefit from the community college experience is to forsake the safe path.

Indeed, this book is hazardous to the status quo.

Joe L. Kincheloe
Penn State University

Acknowledgments

We wish to thank Lorrice Bedard and Barbara Scott for their editorial assistance and Estela Bensimon, Barb Gibson-Benninger, Nevin Robbins, and Sylvia Solorzano for their feedback on various aspects of this project.

Introduction

In this book, we examine community college efforts to serve an increasingly diverse student population. We focus on the multiple roles community colleges enact to serve the needs of a diverse clientele. More specifically, community colleges have struggled to meet the demands of students who vary by race, class, gender, and age, all while embracing three primary roles: transfer, vocational, and community education. One by-product of facing multiple commitments is the lack of a clear sense of organizational identity, which some writers characterize as the chaotic state of the community college. We argue that solutions lie not in simplifying the mission of the community college. Instead, solutions rest with the ability of community colleges to embrace organizational multiplicity—the idea that organizations, like individuals, have plural or multiple identities. We suggest throughout this book that multiculturalism provides a connective thread that enables community colleges to embrace an organizational complexity characterized by multiplicity.

Although the lack of a well-defined organizational identity afflicts many community colleges, this is not the sole challenge they face. Another concern relates to the basic foundation of the community college and how education is enacted. We contend that community colleges, more so than other postsecondary institutions in the United States, are deeply entrenched within a mentality characterized by an authoritarian view of knowledge and pedagogy. Such a view situates certain understandings and ways of knowing above others. This is problematic for most educational institutions, but for those serving large numbers of culturally diverse students, who often bring different understandings and diverse forms of knowledge to the educational setting, it is especially insidious. We suggest that multiculturalism, with its commitment to democratic educational processes, offers solutions to problems associated with authoritarianism as well as to problems presented by organizational multiplicity.

Thus, two different but related narratives form the foci of our research and theorizing. The first narrative discusses the multiple missions of the community college and the lack of a clear organizational identity. The other narrative describes the diverse students community colleges are expected to serve and the problem that authoritarian educational practices pose to embracing cultural diversity. We weave in and out of these two narratives the idea of multiculturalism. Our hope is to create a singular, coherent image of community college education as the practice of democracy in which organizational multiplicity is seen not as a problem to be solved but instead as a central aspect of organizational life.

This book is based on three years of organizational research conducted at five community colleges. Sites were selected because of their student diversity as well as their variety of program offerings. The colleges studied do not necessarily reflect ideal types in the strict Weberian sense. At some sites, the institutions have struggled with cultural diversity and have succeeded in creating multicultural organizational structures. At other sites, the success has been more limited. But, even in these latter cases, there is much to learn about multicultural education.

The general outline of the book follows. Chapter 1 outlines the theoretical framework as well as current observations of researchers and educators in the field. In chapter 2, we focus on the multiple roles community colleges enact and relate the discussion to multiculturalism. We also review the methodology used in conducting our research. In chapters 3 through 7, we present case studies of five community colleges. We use theoretical insights related to multiculturalism to frame our analysis. In chapter 3, we examine how the organizational culture of a rural community college contributes to the production of a narrow sense of students' identity centering on their role as workers. Chapter 4 focuses on how student diversity might be treated in a more celebratory manner as we highlight an urban community college education center organized to serve Spanish-speaking immigrants. In chapter 5, our focus centers on issues of community responsiveness as we examine a community college high school developed primarily to serve urban African-American students. Chapter 6 explores issues related to cultural capital and border knowledge as we examine developmental education at a rural community college. In chapter 7, we use a case study of an urban community college to clarify our idea of organizational multiplicity and to suggest ways that multiculturalism might help community colleges to deal with their complex, multiple roles. We conclude with chapter 8 by offering a comprehensive analysis of our findings and by suggesting some characteristics that a more democratic community college might exhibit. We also re-emphasize how educational practice is fundamentally linked to culture and identity issues.

Democracy, Multiculturalism, and the Community College

Chapter One
Multiculturalism and Border Knowledge in Higher Education

In this chapter, we expand upon our conception of multiculturalism and discuss what is sometimes described as *critical multiculturalism.* We relate critical multiculturalism to issues of culture and identity, which are vital to understanding the role of community college education. Our intent is to clarify a view of multiculturalism and the challenge it presents to authoritarian views of knowledge embraced most clearly in the idea of the canon. We introduce the notion of *border knowledge* and discuss its relationship to cultural diversity. Our discussion of border knowledge and the canon is linked to what has been termed the *politics of identity.*

This chapter provides the theoretical framework around which the remainder of this book is structured. Consequently, while the remaining chapters specifically focus on community colleges and community college issues, this chapter focuses on broader concerns within higher education in the United States. We see a need to situate discussions of community college education within an emerging theoretical wave led by feminism, critical theory, and postmodernism. In chapter 2 and subsequent case-study chapters, we refocus our analysis on the community college as we apply the theoretical perspective suggested here.

Campus Divisiveness or Cultural Diversity?

In debates about U.S. higher education a dualism is often posited between the traditions of past excellence and calls for greater access and equity. Idyllic images of professors and students framed by a shared language and culture, engaged in the pursuit of knowledge for knowledge's sake, are contrasted with portraits of campus divisiveness and curricula resembling more an *à la carte* menu than any coherent educational philosophy. There is little doubt that cultural diversity has pulled at the fabric that has structured higher education in this country for quite a few years.

But professors and students engaged in deep philosophical discourse have been the exception and not the rule, and enduring images are often reflections of the "good old days" that never were. Campus divisiveness is nothing new. At Harvard and Yale between 1745 and 1771, students frequently protested "the manner by which education was imparted" in what has been described as the "war with the tutors" (Moore, 1978, p. 125). Student revolts in the early 1800s were commonplace as students rebelled against the authority of the "old-time" college and what many perceived as "political indoctrination" at the hands of federalist-leaning professors and clergy who sought to uphold "religion, morality, civilization, authority, and order" (Novak, 1977, p. 72). And there seems always to have been disruptions caused by student social clubs emerging with or without official institutional support (Horowitz, 1987). Frequently, student resistance has focused on the learning process, evidenced by Lyman Bagg's (1871) discussion of how the more socially oriented students at Yale disliked the "grinds"—those students "digging and grinding for a stand [a good grade], existing all unconscious of the peculiar and delightful life about [them]" (p. 702). Clearly, students have for years found a multitude of ways to subvert the educational enterprise despite the best-laid plans of faculty and administrators.

Divisiveness is hardly new, but it has taken on a somewhat different tenor. Instead of complaints about upper-division students disrupting the lives of first-year students, or students forming allegiances against faculty, or the socials sabotaging the grinds, issues of race, gender, class, and sexual orientation have become central to what some see as fragmentation within today's academy. Several recent developments support our point. In protest of a decision by the college's trustees to admit men, students at Mills College, a women's college founded over a century ago, went on strike and effectively halted the school's operations (McCurdy, 1990). "Their spirited exchanges and passionate commitment showed the world that what they appreciate first about women's colleges is the empowerment they experience in institutions that place women students at the center of their educational mission" (Hartman, 1990, p. A40). At the University of California at Los Angeles, 99 students were arrested in demonstrations held to protest the university's refusal to grant Chicano Studies full academic status. Chicano students believed achieving departmental standing was a step toward strengthening the identity of the Chicano community (McCurdy, 1993). At the University of California at Berkeley, a coalition of Asian-American, Black, Latino, American Indian, and lesbian, gay, and bisexual students demonstrated over the lack of minority students and faculty, as well as the need to establish a Gay Studies department (Fifty-six Protesters, 1990). African-American students at Pennsylvania State University organized a student takeover of the university's communications tower. The demonstration was held to protest the university's lack of commitment to improving the campus environment for African-American students (DeLoughry, 1989). And finally, African-American students at Rutgers University halted and then forced the postponement of a highly anticipated Atlantic Ten basketball game in protest of degrading statements about African Americans made by the Rutgers president.

Multiple interpretations exist as to the causes and outcomes of campus disharmony. For example, what appears in much of the higher education literature, often in the form of innuendo, is that cultural diversity is the major cause of both campus divisiveness as well as incoherent curricula. Open access and efforts to achieve equal opportunity often come under attack from conservative critics such as Dinesh D'Souza (1991) and Roger Kimball (1990), who see inclusionary practices as threats to the best traditions of U.S. higher education and as indications of how ideology has come to corrupt the academy. Another example comes from a recent meeting of the American Educational Research Association at which Sheldon Hackney, director of the National Endowment for the Humanities and former president of the University of Pennsylvania, talked about cultural diversity and the declining sense of a common national identity. Hackney spoke about how fragmentation within our culture has become a source of tension. He discussed the 1960s as the watershed period bridging our current detachment from common connections and civility. As evidence of today's fragmentation and hostility, Hackney called upon studies that point to declining church attendance, decreased participation in Boy Scouts, and decreased interactions among neighbors. Implicit throughout his speech was the need to return to the spirit of the 1950s, which is often characterized as a period of strong family values and neighborliness despite the many Jim Crow laws and pervasiveness of patriarchy. One of the authors of this book suggested to Hackney that what he was describing as fragmentation and a declining sense of common identity may in fact be "democracy playing itself out" as marginalized peoples have finally achieved enough power to voice their concerns publicly. Yes, they have disrupted "neighborliness," but it was a false sense of neighborliness obtained through the silencing of many voices and the suppression of democracy. Rhoads went on to say, "It seems odd to me that just when various minority groups have gained enough voice to point out the inequities inherent in our society, those in power now call for common ground." Hackney's response was something to the effect that "too much democracy can be a bad thing." Bell hooks (1994b) speaks to this kind of reaction: "What we are witnessing today in our everyday life is not an eagerness on the part of neighbors and strangers to develop a world perspective but a return to narrow nationalism, isolationisms, and xenophobia. These shifts are usually explained in New Right and neoconservative terms as attempts to bring order to chaos, to return to an (idealized) past" (p. 28). Their fear, as hooks goes on to note, is that "any de-centering of Western civilizations, of the white male canon, is really an act of cultural genocide" (p. 32).

Hooks and others suggest a different interpretation than that offered by D'Souza, Kimball, and Hackney: The divisiveness witnessed on numerous campuses reflects what might be seen as a lack of institutional responsiveness. The principal reason postsecondary institutions have dragged their feet is because responding to cultural diversity through the implementation of a multicultural curriculum and organization threatens the canonical knowledge upon which the dominant forces in higher education are positioned. As the rug begins to be pulled out from under the feet of those who benefit from the elevated position of traditional knowledge, these same individuals resort to calls for a return to common ground. Their calls are intended to stabilize the resistance of those most silenced by hierarchical views of knowledge evident in the traditional canon.

The canon separates that which is deemed important from that which is not. The canon elevates certain aspects of a society's culture over others. It both centers and marginalizes types, ways, and sources of understanding. It tells us that art situated in a museum is superior to street art; classical music is superior to rap; and the writings of Shakespeare and Chaucer are superior to the work of Bebe Moore Campbell and Rudolfo Anaya. The canon tells us that scientific knowledge is superior to spiritual or emotional understanding, and that knowledge produced by white European males is superior to the knowledge of women and people of color. In short, the hierarchical nature of the canon silences cultural diversity. Multiculturalism offers a response.

Multiculturalism and the Canonization of Knowledge

That which is selected to be part of the canon involves value judgments about the quality or aesthetics of specific works, ideas, ways of knowing, and forms of knowledge. For this reason, the canon should be understood as a form of ideology that suppresses *border knowledge*—knowledge that resides outside of the canon, outside of the cultural mainstream. Border knowledge is essentially a form of cultural capital unworthy of exchange in mainstream educational settings. Border knowledge, of course, most often is embraced by those situated on society's margins. And because race, class, gender, sexual orientation, and age all contribute to marginality, it is hardly surprising that members of diverse cultural groups face the most serious challenges in negotiating college and university settings.

Although debates about the canon are oftentimes voiced in discussions of general education requirements at four-year colleges, we contend throughout this work that the canon—that which is deemed as appropriate knowledge to be attained by all educated people of a society—has major implications for how we structure community colleges. We need to be clear here. Community colleges are supposedly open-access institutions and, in an idealized sense, represent higher education's commitment to democracy. As such, they attract a great diversity of students. Because of the border knowledge culturally diverse students bring with them, understanding the shortcomings of the canonization of knowledge is imperative to constructing democratic community colleges.

Furthermore, we argue that achieving greater equity in higher education is compatible with the goals of academic excellence. However, the manner in which excellence gets defined needs to be brought into question. This implies that the canon and traditional views of knowledge acquisition must be challenged. Our intent is to create conceptions of academic excellence around the ideals of multiculturalism.

Multiculturalism is a central topic in today's debates about educational policy. To some, multiculturalism poses a threat to the best of what U.S. education has to offer—the values, beliefs, and traditions of Western civilization. For example, Diane Ravitch (1990) assails what she describes as particularistic multiculturalism for its criticism of a Eurocentric educational system and its attempt to "raise the self-esteem and academic achievement of children from racial and ethnic minority backgrounds" (p. 340). Ravitch argues that education in general and the curriculum in particular play an insignificant role in enhancing a student's self-esteem. Instead, educators ought to instill common values amongst all students regardless of their cultural heritage.

To others, multiculturalism is a means to achieve greater tolerance for diverse peoples. By offering courses and educational experiences that expose students to a wide range of cultures and worldviews, both the majority and the minority will gain from increased understanding of the other. The assumption is that with increased awareness will come greater toleration for difference. Estela Bensimon (1994) criticizes this view of multiculturalism and describes it as the human relations perspective: "The human relations vision downplays 'differences,' because it is primarily concerned with the reduction of tension and conflict among different groups. Accordingly, curricular change that is framed in human relations terms will focus on the development of more accepting attitudes" (p. 13). This is the most common expression of multiculturalism on today's college campuses and involves the study of topics related to various ethnic and racial groups, gender and sexual identity differences, international issues, non-Western cultures, and issues pertaining to the physically challenged (Gaff, 1992, p. 32).

"Multiculturalism without a transformative political agenda can just be another form of accommodation to the larger social order"

(McLaren, 1995, p. 126). The human relations view of multiculturalism, which we term "mainstream multiculturalism," fails to transform monocultural institutions into multicultural democratic communities because it situates cultural diversity as subject matter to be learned and not as ways of thinking and doing that fundamentally challenge Eurocentrically conceived institutions. As Patrick Hill (1991) maintains, "We would not have changed much if all we achieve is a sprinkling of multicultural courses in the departments. . . . Marginalization will be perpetuated . . . if new voices and perspectives are added while the priorities and core of the organization remain unchanged" (pp. 44–45). Mainstream multiculturalism has a limited impact because it is easily assimilated through its compartmentalization within the curriculum.

Still others see multiculturalism as much more than learning about diverse cultures and cultural groups. In contrast to mainstream multiculturalism is *critical multiculturalism*, which combines the conditions of cultural diversity with the emancipatory vision of a critical educational practice borrowing from feminism, postmodernism, and critical theory. Critical multiculturalism seeks to transform educational institutions from monolithic centers of power to democratic constellations in which organizational structures reflect diverse cultures and perspectives. From this point of view, multiculturalism reaches into the depths of what educational institutions *are* with the hope of creating what *ought* to be. Bensimon (1994) elaborates: "We must recognize that the perspective of multiculturalism, the struggle to create a more democratic, pluralistic education system in this country, is part of the struggle to empower people. . . . Such an education seeks not to inform but to transform" (p. 7). Peter McLaren (1995) speaks of critical multiculturalism in the following manner:

I am developing the idea of critical multiculturalism from the perspective of a resistance post-structuralist approach to meaning, and emphasizing the role that language and representation play in the construction of meaning and identity. The post-structuralist insight that I am relying on is located within the larger context of postmodern social theory . . . and asserts that signs and significations are essentially unstable and shifting and can only be temporarily fixed, depending on how they are ar-

ticulated within particular discursive and historical struggles. The per-
spective of what I am calling critical multiculturalism understands rep-
resentations of race, class, and gender as the result of larger social struggles
over signs and meanings, and in this way emphasizes not simply textual
play or metaphorical displacement as a form of resistance but stresses the
central task of transforming the social, cultural, and institutional rela-
tions in which meanings are generated. (p. 126)

For the remainder of this book, when we use the term multiculturalism, we imply a critical multicultural perspective akin to that
described by Bensimon and McLaren.

Multiculturalism is often pitted against the canon, for good reason. The canon calls forth a common culture—a culture that we all
share as members of the same society. And herein lies part of the
problem. The cultural experiences of people residing in the United
States are so diverse that common connections are not easily ob-
served, nor are they easily achieved. Invoking a common culture, a
canon, reinforces the cultural knowledge some possess, while at the
same time indoctrinating others to this cultural knowledge. Critical
multiculturalism encourages resistance against the superior-inferior
dualism so prevalent in pedagogical treatments of culture. As McLaren
(1995) maintains, critical multiculturalism examines identity and
difference as radical politics positioned against romanticized visions
of a common experience. For example, critical multiculturalism resists the superior status accorded to Western civilization, as well as
to knowledge produced by the upper and middle classes, whites,
and men.

What is at stake is respect for and celebration of cultural difference. The canon encourages homogenization of society through assimilation on the part of culturally diverse peoples. The canon is
antidemocratic because it silences those on culture's borders. Resistance to the canon is not the decline of higher education, as some
conservatives might have us believe. Instead, resistance may be interpreted as a sign of rising democracy. Edmund Gordan and
Maitrayee Bhattacharyya (1992) argue that "The need to celebrate
uniqueness in our society, interestingly enough, is at issue not because it is necessarily a new phenomenon, but is due in part to the
progress the society has made toward democratization" (p. 407).

Democracy is rarely neat and clean. The cacophony that many conservatives and liberals hear ringing in their ears may in fact be progress toward greater inclusion and voice on the part of marginalized members of our society. In a democratic society, harmony is not to be achieved through silencing tactics.

Gordan and Bhattacharyya point out that increased resistance may be explained by various groups achieving greater voice throughout our society as small advances are made toward democratization. Additionally, resistance also may reflect the changing demographics of U.S. society. A growing population of minorities may in fact have reached a critical mass in which their voices can no longer effectively be silenced. Understanding the changing demographics therefore is important to our ability to comprehend the historical, political, and cultural implications of debates about multiculturalism and the canon.

Cultural Diversity and Higher Education

The ascendancy of multiculturalism, of course, parallels the changing demographics of U.S. society and those who participate in higher education. In light of changing demographics, multiculturalism, as a theoretical and political strategy, may be seen as a response supporting greater cultural diversity.

At no time in the history of U.S. higher education has the student population been as culturally diverse as it is today. For example, Elaine El-Khawas (1992) reports that during the academic year 1991–92, more than half of the 411 colleges and universities surveyed by the American Council on Education increased their enrollment of African-American students. At the same time, nearly half of these same institutions increased their enrollment of Hispanic and Asian-American students. Approximately one fourth of the institutions increased their enrollment of Native American students. And sixty percent of the institutions reported increases in the number of students who are twenty-five or older.

Immigration has been a major factor in these changing demographics. During the 1970s, the U.S. experienced the highest percentage of population growth accounted for by immigration since the period between 1900 and 1920: The foreign-born population accounted for over nineteen percent of the total population growth, some 4.46 million people. The foreign-born population continued to grow throughout the 1980s as more than six million people migrated to the United States. In terms of geography, the majority of recent immigrants to the U.S. have come from Asia or Latin America (La Belle & Ward, 1994). This trend is expected to continue throughout the 1990s.

Demographic projections suggest that by the year 2000, one third of all school-age children will be from minority groups and that forty-two percent of all public school children will be from minority or lower socioeconomic backgrounds (American Council on Education, 1988). And, of course, only a few years later, many of these students will be participating in postsecondary education.

Recent findings from *The Almanac* (1994) published annually by *The Chronicle of Higher Education* also are revealing. For example, we know that nearly twenty-three percent of all students attending college are from minority groups. Furthermore, women outnumber men by nearly a million and a half and constitute roughly fifty-five percent of the student body. In relation to community colleges, *The Almanac* points out that student enrollment at two-year colleges amounts to nearly half of the overall U.S. undergraduate population. Of special significance to our work is the fact that fifty-three percent of African-American, Hispanic, and Native American undergraduates attend two-year colleges, whereas the percentage of White undergraduates who attend these same institutions is forty-three percent. Compare this to the fact that seventy-seven percent of the undergraduates who attend four-year institutions are white, and only eighteen percent are African-American, Hispanic, or Native American students. The disproportionate representation of minority students at two-year colleges makes issues of multiculturalism that much more relevant to community college settings.

The diversity of today's student body poses a challenge to postsecondary institutions. Frances Stage and Kathleen Manning (1992) argue that cultural diversity has made educational practice more complex than ever and call for revised policies and procedures. They highlight six weaknesses of traditional approaches to working with students: (1) assuming that culturally diverse students must change; (2) making culturally diverse students, faculty, and administrators already in the institution responsible for socializing other new students from similar backgrounds; (3) encouraging culturally diverse students to adapt to the dominant culture; (4) helping only identifiable diverse students; (5) failing to provide equitable educational opportunities to all students admitted to the institution; and (6) failing to educate those of the dominant culture about their culturally diverse colleagues.

The fundamental flaw of today's colleges and universities, as Stage and Manning argue, is that they continue to operate from a monocultural view. More specifically, U.S. social institutions, including schools, are predominantly based on Eurocentric cultural norms. They argue that a weakness of monoculturalism is its inability to consider other cultural traditions and perspectives. Monoculturalism, which is akin to the canon, projects one culture as superior to all others and is reflected in organizational structures and practices. If U.S. colleges and universities are to survive in an increasingly diverse society, Stage and Manning (1992) believe they "must change from a monoculturalist to multiculturalist perspective" (p. 16).

Authors such as Stage and Manning call attention to the fact that barriers to enacting multicultural academic communities involve confronting not only the canonization of the curriculum, but also the canonization of organizational beliefs and practices. Revising the curriculum without altering the underlying organizational fabric is akin to renovating a house by painting it, but doing nothing to alter its underlying structure. Hence, conservative and mainstream multicultural strategies often reflect mere housekeeping efforts in which students are required to take a "diversity" or "diversity enhanced" course, which in many cases they do begrudgingly. Little is changed as multiculturalism is effectively assimilated into the traditional structures of the institution. In the end, the power of multiculturalism to transform the academy is lost, and the hopes that rest upon it are betrayed.

The question that we pursue throughout this book concerns how community colleges might move from a monocultural perspective to a multicultural organizational framework. Our focus is both on the underlying organizational culture or structure (the frame and foundation of the house) as well as its most visible representation— the curriculum. To understand where our work must head, we need to come to terms with the effects of the canonization of knowledge.

Border Knowledge and the Canon

The concept of border knowledge is central to our work. Students who possess the proper knowledge, that which relates to the canon, tend to do well. These students are able to exchange their knowledge for academic (and later economic) returns. Pierre Bourdieu's (1986) notion of "cultural capital" is another way of understanding this exchange. Instead of money being traded for goods, cultural knowledge is exchanged for academic success. Those with the "wrong" cultural capital, those possessing border knowledge, tend to do poorly. Because the academy is predominantly framed by a European white male, middle- and upper-class perspective, women, members of diverse racial groups, and the lower and working classes are inherently disadvantaged. They possess forms of knowledge that, for the most part, are not rewarded in traditional academic settings.

Border knowledge is not as exchangeable as mainstream knowledge or canonized knowledge. Students from diverse cultural backgrounds are in effect penalized for their cultural identities because the acquisition of border knowledge derives from one's cultural background. For this reason, issues of culture and identity must be central to discussions of how colleges and universities ought to be structured, and how the curriculum ought to be shaped. For example, educational researchers and theorists have long pointed out the inequalities involved in traditional methods and perspectives (especially standardized measures) used to assess intelligence and educational achievement (Belenky, Clinchy, Goldberger & Tarule, 1986; Dawes, 1993; Ferguson, 1991; Magolda, 1992; Sternberg, 1988). The idea that cultural backgrounds privilege some and marginalize others is by no means a new argument. Our contribution to this argument lies in what follows—in how these issues relate to community colleges and their challenge to serve diverse students. Although similar arguments have been made before, we must revisit them in order to make our position clear.

On the one hand, conservative critics such as Allan Bloom (1987) and E.D. Hirsch (1987) see the problem quite simply: Schools are not doing a very good job of conveying to students the kind of knowledge they need to succeed in U.S. society. And, of course, the type of knowledge needed is the language and cultural base of middle- and upper-class, white, male America. Progressive educators, on the other hand, maintain that the canon, as it is traditionally constituted, ignores the cultural backgrounds and experiences diverse students bring to the schooling process. For democratic educators such as Paulo Freire and Henry Giroux, the requirement of a common core of knowledge is nothing more than an assimilationist strategy used to silence cultural difference and stifle democracy. The canon promotes a unitary and simplistic view of culture and strives to produce and reproduce a homogeneous society.

The core or the canon is about *cultural capital*—that knowledge needed to succeed within U. S. social, economic, and political systems. Somewhat surprisingly, scholars such as Harold Bloom (1994) question whether the concept has any relevance: "Is there, has there ever been, any 'cultural capital' in the United States of America?" (p. 518). He goes on to describe multiculturalists as members of the School of Resentment "who wish to overthrow the Canon in order to advance their supposed (and nonexistent) programs for social change" (p. 4). His statement is inaccurate. Yes, multiculturalists raise questions about the canon. Not only do they question what gets included as relevant knowledge, they also question a process that enables some educators to make such choices while others go unheard. Furthermore, multiculturalists take issue with the notion that knowledge is static and therefore can be grouped into coherent texts and passed on to students as if they were simply the receptacles of a society's relevant knowledge. Multiculturalists stress education as the process of engaging in critical thought and discussion about the construction of knowledge. Knowledge is seen as dynamic. From such a perspective, the teacher is viewed no longer as the keeper of relevant facts and information, but as the facilitator of student inquiry and debate about what gets defined as knowledge. In a very real sense, the social program multiculturalists offer involves a restructuring of education in which the teacher-and-student relationship exists on a more level plane where authority is no longer the central fiber connecting one to the other. Knowledge is seen as contested terrain. Students are seen to possess a whole range of knowledge, experience, and understanding that they bring with them to the classroom, and which is worth sharing with other students and teachers. This is a more democratic view of education and one that we discuss further in chapter 2 and throughout this text.

Harold Bloom (1994), however, argues that certain texts are aesthetically superior to others and that such texts should constitute the canon. What he fails to acknowledge is that even questions of aesthetics involve value judgments, judgments that are inherently ideological. While Bloom finds Goethe aesthetically pleasing and thus includes his work as part of the canon, a multicultural educator might prefer to discuss a work such as *I, Rigoberto Menchu,* because of the story of cultural identity and human struggle expressed in its unique narrative. Bloom argues from an ideology of aesthetics. Multiculturalists argue from an ideology founded on equality, justice, and freedom. Neither position is neutral, although clearly one is democratic and the other authoritarian.

Multiculturalists restructure educational settings around democratic ideals that encourage inclusiveness. Bloom (1994) fails to see the connection between education and democracy and instead resorts to a hierarchical view of knowledge and understanding. This is never more clear than in his discussion of poetry and its accessibility: "The strongest poetry is cognitively and imaginatively too difficult to be read deeply by more than a relative few of any social class, gender, race, or ethnic origin" (p. 520).

Bloom's vision of intelligence and cognitive complexity reflects a modernist perspective in which intelligence and creativity are seen as static and innate qualities of a privileged few. As Joe Kincheloe (1995) argues, "Intelligence . . . is not a static, innate dimension of human beings; it is always interactive with the environment, always in the process of being reshaped and reformed. We are not simply victims of genetically determined, cognitive predispositions" (p. 141). Multiculturalists see the literary complexities of poetry as something open to everyone and refuse to situate poetry, music, art, theorizing, and other forms of cultural production within rigid hierarchies that only serve to marginalize the multiple ways people have of making sense of their worlds. The objective of multiculturalists is to create educational settings in which authoritarian views of culture, knowledge, and identity are challenged. Because democracy lies at the center, no one should be excluded from participation. Henry Giroux (1993) writes about the need to develop pedagogical practices that create opportunities "for students to take up subject positions con-

sistent with the principles of equality, justice, and freedom ra
than with interests and practices supportive of hierarchies, oppre
sion, and exploitation" (p. 55). Traditionalist claims to a common
culture or a canon of knowledge are merely efforts to reposition
certain individuals and structures as the gatekeepers and gates of
academe and necessarily the prime lenders of cultural capital. We
draw from Giroux once again: "Lacking the courage to rework dominant traditions in light of a changing present and future, conservatives continue to develop 'imaginary unities' aimed at creating rigid
cultural boundaries that serve to seize upon fear and cultural racism" (p. 69).

Achieving inclusionary colleges and universities committed to
the principles of equality, justice, and freedom involves significant
change in the way we think about the educational process. Such
change involves recognizing and understanding the significance of
border knowledge and its relationship to culture and identity. From
the perspective of multiculturalism, the central problem faced by
higher education institutions within the United States relates to
matters of culture and identity. Whether through disagreements about
recruiting diverse faculty, or debates about admission criteria and
the need to diversify the student body, or curriculum debates over
the relevance of cultural knowledge, or concerns over increasing the
supply of women engineering graduates, or discussions of declining
SAT scores, the theme is clear: race, class, gender, sexual orientation,
and age matter. The ever-increasing diversity that students bring to
classrooms continues to produce mass confusion about whom to
teach, how to teach, and what to teach.

Part of a multicultural critique of education investigates not
only what gets taught and what gets defined as relevant knowledge,
but also the very nature of teaching itself. Traditionalists, on the one
hand, tend to view education as the transmission of knowledge.
Teachers convey knowledge to the student in the form of factoids
(small isolated pieces of knowledge), which are to be memorized
one by one. The student becomes a consumer of factoids much like
PAC-Man consumes dots in the once-popular video game. Standardized teaching and learning plans dictate the sequence and direction of the students' consumption as they become passive recipients
in the educational process (Kincheloe, 1995).

…er hand, multiculturalists argue that education should
…uch on transferring information and facts as on chal-
…s to engage as full participants in both education and
…means structuring the classroom in such a way that
…and willing to enter into dialogue with professors
…ts. The educational goals of multiculturalists and
…different. Because traditionalists envision knowl-
…given body of facts, principles, and information that accu-
mulates as knowledge is advanced, the goal for students is to acquire
as much knowledge as is necessary to function effectively in U.S.
society. And, of course, to function effectively typically gets defined
in terms of vocationalism and fitting in to the U.S. labor force.
Multiculturalists focus more on process. They see the goal of education as more than the accumulation of knowledge. They view education as the development of the ability to think critically and independently. Those who develop this ability are better equipped to
engage as full participants in a democratic society—not just in economic terms, but as participants in governance and cultural politics
as well.

Significantly different outcomes result from these disparate goals.
Because the goal of traditionalists is to pass on knowledge from one
generation to the next, through the relationship of teacher as expert
and student as neophyte, students become for the most part passive
recipients of the best of what society has produced—the canon. As a
result, the values, beliefs, customs, and practices of a society, which
are inherently part of the canon, get reproduced. Simply stated, since
students are not encouraged to be critics of what gets defined as
knowledge, questions about the way things are often do not get raised.

Because multiculturalists concern themselves with creating a
classroom and an educational environment where students actively
engage in discussion and in decision making, students become active participants in the schooling process. Education viewed in this
manner is guided by visions of social justice in which equality and
the right to be heard are vital concerns. We draw from Iris Marion
Young (1990): "A goal of social justice. . . is social equality. Equality
refers not primarily to the distribution of goods, though distribu-
tions are certainly entailed by social equality. It refers primarily to
the full participation and inclusion of everyone in a society's major

institutions, and the socially substantive opportunity for all to develop and exercise their capacities and realize their choices" (p. 173). As active participants in the educational process, students are better able to form opinions and make informed choices about their culture and society and where they fit in the larger scheme of things. Because the ideals of equality, justice, and freedom are central to the educational process, current structures and social arrangements that impinge upon democratic ideals are more likely to be challenged. Social and cultural change becomes possible, if not inevitable.

Again, issues of culture and identity are paramount. If the status quo gets reproduced, those situated on society's borders remain marginalized. The idea of a common culture and a common body of relevant knowledge promotes the colonization of culturally diverse peoples and the suppression of their cultural identities. This form of educational practice necessarily leads to cultural hierarchies contained in notions of the privileged and the deprived, the insider and the outsider, the dominant and the subjugated. As hooks (1994a) writes, "Structures of class privilege [such as cultural capital] prevent those who are not materially privileged from having access to those forms of education for critical consciousness that are essential to the decolonization process" (p. 5).

Critical multiculturalism calls attention to the role of education as a powerful force in situating student identities as privileged or marginalized. La Belle and Ward (1994), for example, discuss multiculturalism as a concept that heightens our understanding of intergroup relations and conflict not only over power and resources, but in terms of social identities as well. They argue that multiculturalism is not so much about learning about a particular culture or cultural group, nor is it about which cultural groups ought to be represented in the curriculum. Instead, multiculturalism is first and foremost about the "struggle for power, control, and access to opportunities" (p. 186) on the part of groups historically situated on the margins of our society. What we are moving toward here is a discussion of what some describe as the "the politics of identity."

The Politics of Identity

In recent years, issues of culture and identity have become increasingly vital to educational theory and research. Schools play a pivotal role in identity formation, and both reflect and shape the cultural borders within which they operate. Penelope Eckert (1989), Jay MacLeod (1987), Peter McLaren (1986, 1989), and Paul Willis (1977) reveal how social class contributes to students' sense of self and the resistance they offer to the schooling process. Michelle Fine (1991) demonstrates how issues of race, class, and gender relate to persistence among urban high school students. And Angela McRobbie (1978) describes how notions of femininity get reproduced among working-class girls in school settings.

Research on colleges and universities also reveals the interconnections between schooling and issues of culture and identity. For example, Dorothy Holland and Margaret Eisenhart (1990) uncover a "culture of romance" that contributes to a lowering of career aspirations among groups of college women. William Tierney (1992) explores how Native American students oftentimes are forced to leave behind their own cultural heritage in order to be successful in mainstream colleges and universities. Robert Rhoads (1994) examines the struggles gay students face as they "come out" in a university setting whose culture is largely hostile to lesbian, gay, and bisexual identities. And finally, Lois Weis (1985) contributes to this growing body of literature through her study of African-American students attending an urban community college. She highlights the problems students face when the culture they produce is incongruent with the culture of the institution.

In all of the preceding works, many of which are ethnographic in nature, issues of culture and identity are central to how students experience the educational process. Emerging from this body of research and corresponding to notions generated largely by postmodernism and feminism is a heightened awareness of how culturally diverse students and people are situated within educational institutions and depicted in research and writing. Such depictions are often discussed in terms of issues of representation or representational practice. Just as feminism and postmodernism have challenged what gets defined as truth and as knowledge, they also have raised concerns about how cultural identities get situated within social hierarchies that relegate some to superior and others to subordinate status.

Postmodernism and feminism pose a challenge to the sanctity of knowledge and truth. In a touch of irony, Jean-François Lyotard

(1984) calls all truisms fallacious. He argues that science offers only one interpretation of knowledge: "It has always existed in addition to, and in competition and conflict with, another kind of knowledge, which I will call narrative" (p. 7). Lyotard's work and that of other postmodernists and feminists is helpful in that they situate knowledge within the context of power and domination (McNeil, 1993; Nicholson, 1990; Tierney & Rhoads, 1993b). Recognition of the theoretical and practical connections between knowledge and power is especially pertinent to understanding issues of culture and identity within the context of educational settings: "As old borders and zones of cultural difference become more porous or eventually collapse, questions of culture increasingly become interlaced with issues of power, representation, and identity" (Giroux, 1993, p. 90).

For Lyotard, there is only narrative—context-specific understandings of social life. Lyotard highlights the relational quality of postmodern understanding. A similar idea is conveyed by feminist scholars who speak of "relational standpointism." Maureen Cain (1993) explains, "The gist of the argument is that anyone producing knowledge occupies a relational and historical site in the social world which is likely to shape and set limits to the knowledge formulations produced" (p. 88). Consequently, understandings of knowledge must be situated within the historical, cultural, and political context of educational settings in which individuals enact strategies to establish or resist definitional processes.

Postmodernism and feminism call attention to the idea that knowledge is relational. Normativity is displaced by multiplicity— a theoretical notion depicting social and cultural phenomena more in terms of complexity and difference than simplicity and similarity. The rise of such notions of knowledge and truth helps to demonstrate that truth claims do not exist on their own; they must be grounded in specific positions and assumptions. As Michel Foucault (1978, 1980) points out, that which is determined to be true is largely the product of who has the power to assert and insert a specific discourse into public consciousness. In support of Foucault, Laurel Richardson notes, "Wherever truth is claimed, so is power; the claim to truth is a claim to power" (1991, p. 173). And Steven Seidman adds, "Concealed in the will to truth is a will to power" (1991, p. 135).

Like notions of knowledge and truth, cultural identities also are framed by discourses contingent to a large degree on power relations. Power is evident through the ability to control the discourse or the language of identity. Stuart Hall (1990) elaborates on this point: "Cultural identities are the points of identification, the unstable points of identification or suture, which are made, within the discourses of history and culture. Not an essence but a *positioning*. Hence, there is always a politics of identity, a politics of position, which has no absolute guarantee in an unproblematic, transcendental 'law of origin'" (p. 226).

To further understand the politics of identity in relation to schooling, one must make sense of culture. Culture is an often-used expression that conveys the values, beliefs, norms, and attitudes understood by a group of people. It is a concept that can be applied to a wide array of human groups, as large as whole societies, as small as dyads. Culture provides a framework for interaction within social groups. For example, when a student interacts with his or her professor, knowledge about the professor's role and the student's role frames how such interactions ought to occur. Indeed, those students who lack the cultural capital related to student-and-professor interactions are less likely to leave such interactions satisfied. They may walk away without having obtained an understanding of the homework assignment, the grading procedure, or the attendance policy. Most of us can recall instances when our interactions with others, oftentimes people in positions of authority over us, were dissatisfying. Perhaps we left someone's office confused and unsure of what the discussion was all about. For students from diverse cultural backgrounds, navigating one's way through academe can be full of confused and ambiguous interactions.

Although culture provides a guiding framework for interactions, culture is continuously revised through those same interactions (Geertz, 1973). And here is why we speak of culture and identity in terms of politics. Because culture and social interaction have a reciprocal relationship, it is possible through contestation and struggle to engage culture with the hope of transformation. At the risk of oversimplification, let us return to the issue of the canonization of knowledge versus multicultural education.

To promote the canon is to promote one vision of culture. William Bennett (1984) describes the humanities as "the best that has been said, thought, written, and otherwise expressed about the human experience" (p. 3). To exclude Shakespeare's *Macbeth*, Plato's *Republic*, or Mark Twain's *The Adventures of Huckleberry Finn* from the canon is to deny students the opportunity of inheriting the best of what our culture has to offer. Of course, the underlying assumption is that such forms of cultural production need to be perpetuated. Such a notion is clearly revealed in another passage from Bennett: "Great souls do not express themselves by the written word only; they also paint, sculpt, build, and compose. An educated person should be able not only to recognize some of their works, but also to understand why they embody the best of our culture" (p. 11). One cannot help but wonder to whose culture Bennett refers when he writes about "our culture." Clearly, the music of Bach and Mozart are part of "our" culture, and just as clear is the fact that the current work of Salt-n-Pepa and Nine Inch Nails is not.

Multiculturalists take issue with the elevation of some cultural forms over others based on vague notions of aesthetic value. Multiculturalists argue that all forms of cultural production exist within social relations framed by power. Classical music is held in higher regard than rap because those who prefer classical have the power to define it as superior. Most important to what multiculturalists seek to accomplish is the fact that just as a culture gets ranked as superior or subordinate, social identities become categorized in a similar manner.

To reject the canon and instead provide a diversity of learning experiences designed to engage students and teachers in a critique of knowledge and cultural production is to take issue with the hierarchical nature of social identities. The goal is not only to understand cultural identities different from our own, but to move beyond classifications that seek to marginalize and disempower. We are not talking about cultural relativism, as conservative critics often assert. The underlying values of justice, equality, and freedom guide multicultural pedagogy. This is by no means relativistic. In essence, multiculturalists seek to overthrow claims to political neutrality underlying an ideology of aesthetics with a more open and forthright commitment to democratic ideals.

Culture not only provides the parameters for our social interactions, it also provides a framework for how we define ourselves in relation to others. Culture offers representations of people. These representations contribute to how identities are understood. The politics of identity involves raising questions about how people are represented through culture. Such questions in the end serve as challenges to the very means our society has used to define knowledge and truth. As Trinh Minh-ha (1991) maintains, "To raise the question of representing the Other is . . . to reopen endlessly the fundamental issue of science and art; documentary and fiction; masculine and feminine; outsider and insider" (p. 65).

But the politics of identity moves beyond merely understanding how forms of cultural production have named and situated otherness. The politics of identity both interrogates the intent behind representations and attempts to create newer self-representations. For people who exist on culture's borders, the struggle to create one's own representations is necessarily a struggle to seize power. Cornell West (1993a) writes about this issue in his discussion of the "new cultural politics of difference," primarily in reference to black struggle: "The intellectual challenge—usually cast as methodological debate in these days in which academicist forms of expression have a monopoly on intellectual life—is how to think about representational practices in terms of history, culture and society. How does one understand, analyze and enact such practices today?" (p. 5). For West, this question cannot be answered unless one first comes to terms with previous struggles to create more honest and empowering self-representations. Understanding the role history, culture, and society have played in situating people's lives is crucial to moving toward newer forms of representation.

But history, culture, and society are not static concepts; they are theoretical constructs that serve as vehicles to engage oneself and others in the process of constructing, deconstructing, and reconstructing knowledge and truth. The goal, as West (1993a) explains, involves more than merely expanding access and contesting stereotypes: "Black cultural workers must constitute and sustain discursive and institutional networks that deconstruct earlier modern black strategies for identity-formation, demystify power relations that incorporate class, patriarchal and homophobic biases, and construct more multivalent and multidimensional responses that articulate the complexity and diversity of black practices in the modern and postmodern world" (p. 20).

West calls attention to the fact that ongoing agency—social action grounded in emancipatory theory and self-reflection—is crucial to successful engagement in the politics of identity. Agency, of course, is grounded in the hope of a more just and equitable society. Multiculturalism situates agency at the center of its educational goals and objectives. The hope, of course, is a society where those currently situated on society's borders have a voice in a truly democratic process. The vision calls for social transformation, as hooks (1992) highlights in her discussion of representations of race:

The issue is really one of standpoint. From what political perspective do we dream, look, create, and take action? For those of us who dare to desire differently, who seek to look away from the conventional ways of seeing blackness and ourselves, the issue of race and representation is not just a question of critiquing the status quo. It is also about transforming the image, creating alternatives, asking ourselves questions about what types of images subvert, pose critical alternatives, and transform our world views and move us away from dualistic thinking about good and bad. Making a space for the transgressive image, the outlaw rebel vision, is essential to any effort to create a context for transformation. And even then little progress is made if we transform images without shifting paradigms, changing perspectives, ways of looking. (p. 4)

Hooks moves us closer to the crux of our argument. Educational institutions are composed of people who make representations of others to themselves, to colleagues, to the public, and to students. The representations we adopt may not be revealed through our discourse because a variety of sensitivities have taught us to conceal and in effect enact a symbolic form of discrimination—symbolic not because it is not real, but because it is hidden in actions that have underlying meanings that must be interpreted. Despite an acquired proficiency for hiding prejudice and disdain of the other, representations oftentimes emerge in the context of educational programs and pedagogical practices. In other words, the assumptions we have of the other are revealed through the educational endeavors we adopt in relation to our students. When we create educational structures that prepare students from lower socioeconomic classes for nonprofessional careers without stressing their potential to assume leadership positions in social, political, and economic institutions, a representation of class is made. When we provide inner-city Chicano students opportunities to acquire vocational skills, but close the door to other possibilities, the racial representations educators adopt about those students is apparent. When we channel women away from science and mathematics programs because the demands are too great, a representation of gender gets reproduced. By the same token, when we offer upper- and middle-class White males the education and training enabling them to assume positions of corporate and political power, representations of those students are apparent as well.

This leads us to the following questions: How do we structure community colleges in a way that diverse social identities are celebrated instead of silenced, and honored instead of scorned? How can we ensure that the knowledge and experiences brought by diverse students is shared instead of suppressed? What will the community college look like when critical multiculturalism forms the basis of our actions?

As we see it, a fundamental goal of educational institutions, including community colleges, is to contribute to changing the relations of representations. Understanding issues related to culture and identity are central to how we go about this task. Perhaps nowhere is this more true than in community college settings where nearly half of all students come from underrepresented backgrounds. Our objective in this book is to explore community college settings with issues of culture and identity in mind as we seek to build multicultural educational centers. We argue that cultural diversity influences educational institutions in both broad and specific ways—ways that we have yet to fully understand. For example, can community colleges prepare low-income students for vocational careers and at the same time instill critical thinking skills that contribute to a student's sense of civic and social responsibility? How can we expect community colleges to increase the educational attainment of students from underrepresented groups (and thus encourage transfer to four-year colleges) when many of these very students exist at or near the poverty level (and thus have as a preeminent concern the immediate economic return that a vocational career may offer)? How can we provide not-for-credit remedial education for community college students whose economic limitations often restrict their ability to pursue additional credits and thus attain a degree? How can we expect community colleges to educate immigrants and non-English-speaking populations when these colleges are already overburdened with multiple functions and responsibilities? These are questions we explore as we delineate what it means to build a multicultural community college around democratic principles.

The central challenge faced by community colleges is to serve a culturally diverse student clientele. By necessity, this involves two important facets: enacting multiple organizational roles and embracing multiple forms of cultural knowledge—border knowledge. Both produce a community college characterized by multiplicity. We argue throughout this book that multiculturalism offers solutions to the complex problems inherent in organizational multiplicity.

In the next chapter, we explore the many roles that community colleges embrace. We highlight the organizational incongruence that often results from such varied missions and argue that multiculturalism offers a connective thread grounded in education as the practice of democracy. Also highlighted are the methods used to collect data for this book.

Chapter Two
The Many Faces of the Community College

Every weekday at 5 A.M. Alicia Fernandez[1] drags herself out of bed in order to open a nearby restaurant where she has been employed since her junior year in high school. Alicia works from 6 A.M. until the breakfast rush is over, which typically slows to a lull at around 11 A.M. Then she hurries off to class at the local community college where she has taken classes part-time for the last three years. On weekends, Alicia puts in eight-to-ten hour days working the lunch and dinner shifts. Despite her hectic work schedule and helping out around home, Alicia has maintained a 3.5 grade point average. She takes only academic courses because her goal is to transfer after completing her associate's degree. Alicia dreams of studying at Harvard or Stanford, but finds it hard to imagine herself too far from her family. Her college plans sometimes frighten her mother, who dreads the thought of Alicia leaving for some far-away college. She wants Alicia to attend the nearby state university so that she can continue living at home. Alicia's father is supportive of her educational plans, but even he fears her leaving. Alicia often prays for the wisdom and courage to do what is right for herself and her family.

Bill Jenson grew up in a rural community in the southeastern United States. Although his father had a steady income working as a construction worker, there was not enough money for Bill to give college any serious thought. College was for the "rich boys" from the other side of town. If the kids of the working stiffs ever left town, it was to join the service, which is exactly what Bill did after dropping out of high school at the age of seventeen. What he was taught in high school never made much sense to Bill and his grades reflected this attitude. His interactions with his teachers also were never very positive. When his stint in the Army was up, Bill got a job with his father working construction. A few years later, he got married and eventually had two children. Life for Bill was pretty much like he had envisioned as a schoolboy until he had a disabling accident at work and had to quit his job. As the years passed, Bill considered going to college and acquiring some skills, but all the negative experiences he recalled from his high school days made him fearful of additional education. College was so foreign to him. Nonetheless, he decided to visit the local community college. He liked what he heard, and after taking some developmental courses to raise his basic skills, he enrolled in an architectural technology program. Last semester Bill Jenson made the dean's list and surprised not only his family, but himself as well.

Corrine Bolanos dropped out of high school when she was 16. She was typical of a large number of school-age youth in the urban community she grew up in, as only about half graduated from high school and only a few went on to college. Getting a high school diploma was not only difficult for someone with poor English skills, but it also made little sense to her because the kinds of jobs she envisioned herself getting required very minimal education. Corrine took a job with a local fast-food restaurant: "It was not a good period in my life. I was very unhappy." A few years went by before Corrine found out about a bilingual GED program offered by a nearby community college. "I saw it as a chance for me to do something more with my life. Getting my GED was a stepping-stone." After taking courses for almost a year, Corrine passed the GED examinations and eventually enrolled in the same community college.

The Multiple Roles of the Community College

The stories of Alicia, Bill, and Corrine are based on real-life stories told to us by three of our student informants. Although their educational histories are unique, they nonetheless shed light on some broad issues that community colleges face. For example, their stories highlight the multiple roles that community colleges often are expected to fulfill in terms of transfer, vocational, and community education. Furthermore, Alicia, Bill, and Corrine also highlight the diverse backgrounds community college students often bring to the college setting. None of these students fit definitions of traditional college students. Bill and Corrine are over thirty, Alicia and Corrine are part-time students and full-time employees, Bill is married and Corrine is divorced. Alicia identifies as Chicana, Corrine as a Hispanic, and Bill is white; all three are from lower socioeconomic backgrounds. They all bring diverse cultural experiences to their college settings.

Community colleges have traditionally served three essential roles. Alicia's story highlights the role community colleges play in providing general education and preparation for students to transfer to four-year institutions. Bill's highlights the role community colleges play in providing vocational training. Bill has no plans to go on to get a baccalaureate degree—he just wants to acquire marketable skills so he can get a job and help to support his family. Corrine's story calls attention to the community education responsibilities that community colleges have. In the urban area where Corrine lives, dropping out of high school is practically the norm. The local community college saw a need and helped to meet that need by providing GED courses.

Transfer education—providing students with a general education that fulfills the requirements of the first two years of college—is central to the historical identity of the community college. As Kevin Dougherty (1994) explains, "When they first appeared around the turn of the century, community colleges were largely liberal-arts-oriented institutions, providing many students with the first leg of their baccalaureate preparation and others with a terminal general education" (p. 191). In recent years, however, the transfer role has come under increased scrutiny, largely because of the professed desire to improve underrepresented student participation in and graduation from four-year colleges and the perceived ineffectiveness of two-year colleges as catalysts in this process (American Council on Education, 1991; Eaton, 1994b; Grubb, 1991; Palmer, Ludwig, & Stapleton, 1994).

However, many see community colleges as something more than suppliers for public and private four-year institutions; community colleges also have the role of preparing students for immediate entry into the labor market. This is often thought of as the vocational education component of the community college. Although technical training was evident in many of the earliest community colleges (Ratcliff, 1994), it was during the 1920s that vocationalism began to play an increasingly important role in shaping community college offerings (Brint & Karabel, 1989). Arthur Cohen and Florence

Brawer (1989) point out that from the first meeting of the American Association of Junior Colleges and subsequent meetings throughout the 1920s and 1930s, discussions of occupational education were central (p. 199). The vocational movement gained even more strength during the 1960s and 1970s as the federal government increased its funding for vocational education from $13 million in 1965 to $173 million in 1981 (Dougherty, 1994, p. 231). The vocationalization of the community college became so prevalent that at the end of the 1984–85 academic year, over seventy percent of the associate's degrees awarded went to students in occupational areas (Cohen & Brawer, 1989, p. 210).

Some argue that the growth of vocational programs has been at the expense of liberal arts and general education offerings. In assessing recent decades, Judith Eaton (1994c) notes that, "Some of the humanities disciplines were abandoned and second-year courses became increasingly rare" (p. 30). Cohen and Brawer (1989) add that, "Many liberal arts advocates have become understandably apprehensive about the future of their area, fearful that the higher favor enjoyed by career education will mean the further slighting of their disciplines" (p. 222). Weakening liberal arts and general education curricula, of course, poses a threat to an institution's ability to support student transfer. "The shift toward more vocational programs has been one of the dominant explanations of declining transfer as well as evidence for those who have attacked the community college for restricting opportunity" (Grubb, 1991, p. 202).

While vocational education began to displace to a large degree transfer education, another community college mission gained strength. Steven Zwerling (1980) argues that during the 1950s and 1960s, the comprehensive mission of the community college came not only to mean a balance between transfer and vocational education; community education became increasingly important as well. As the preponderance of adult part-time students grew throughout the 1970s, Zwerling explains, the movement toward the community education function gained even greater strength.

Although the transfer and vocational community college roles require a wide range of curricular offerings, they cannot begin to match the diversity of offerings designed to meet community needs. Community education encompasses a whole host of possibilities, which include (for our purposes) remedial and adult education. For example, the following educational programs were offered during one semester at one of the urban community colleges included in our study: programs on foster care parenting; independent living skills programs for foster youth; teen pregnancy programs; citizenship education for recent legal immigrants; life and social skills courses for undocumented immigrants who arrived in the U.S. prior to 1982 (part of the Amnesty Program); workfare and job training opportunities for welfare recipients; and even instructional programs for local elementary, middle school, and senior high students.

Clearly, much is demanded of the community college. We were not surprised by the fact that so many of the administrators and faculty with whom we spoke during the course of our research often talked about their institutions as "having multiple personalities" or "lacking a clear vision." "So great is the multiplicity of function of community colleges, and so great the eclecticism and diversity, that they can hardly be intelligibly described as single institutions at all," write Dennis McGrath and Martin Spear (1991, p. 66). They go on to argue that the most common organizational feature of community colleges is that they lack a center: "They are not driven by any unitary view of what education, especially nontraditional education, is all about" (p. 66).

McGrath and Spear call attention to the lack of organizational identity that today's community colleges tend to exhibit. Stephen Mittelstet (1994) raises a similar concern when he argues that the central challenge facing today's community colleges is the quest to build community: "One of the interesting ironies regarding community colleges is that, all too often, they lack many aspects of community" (p. 549). Mittelstet suggests building campus communities around an ethic of caring, an idea consistent with multiculturalism: "Caring is not one of the ways in which we can act as we attempt to educate; it is an essential, integral aspect of education" (p. 562). Others, such as Eaton (1994a), also maintain that community colleges are torn between multiple and competing visions. For example, Eaton highlights four visions that community colleges are expected to maintain: providing access, sustaining transfer and liberal arts programs, offering occupational education, and meeting community needs.

Although Eaton discusses providing access as an additional vision, we tend to think of access as more of a fundamental quality that ought to shape the other three roles of the community college. However, when we use the term *access*, we imply much more than simply an open admissions policy. Access also relates to opportunities that an education ought to produce. In other words, the outcomes of a community college education ought to increase a student's ability to participate in various economic, political, and social institutions. To merely open the doors to students without any serious attempt at creating opportunities for their full participation in America's social life in all its forms is really not access at all. We suggest throughout this book that access ought to be grounded in the democratic ideals of participative citizenship—a fundamental goal of critical multiculturalism.

The democratic vision of the community college we espouse is epitomized by John Dewey (1916, 1927). For Dewey, education, as a social institution, plays a critical role in the establishment and maintenance of democracy. However, he saw democracy as much more than merely every citizen's right to vote; a democratic society provides all citizens with opportunities to participate in forming the values and beliefs that shape social life. Dewey (1916) elaborates the connection between education and social life:

Since education is a social process, and there are many kinds of societies, a criterion for educational criticism and construction implies a particular social idea. The two points selected by which to measure the worth of a form of social life are the extent in which the interests of a group are shared by all members, and the fullness and freedom with which it interacts with other groups. An undesirable society, in other words, is one which internally and externally sets up barriers to free intercourse and communication of experience. A society which makes provision for participation in its good of all its members on equal terms and which secures flexible readjustments of its institutions through interaction of the different forms of associated life is in so far democratic. (p. 105)

Dewey's vision of education, which has been taken up by critical theorists of education such as Henry Giroux, Peter McLaren, and William Tierney, involves the creation of educational institutions in which all members have opportunities to contribute to the values and beliefs—the culture—that guides the educational process. We return to a discussion of education as the practice of democracy later in this chapter. For now, we build our argument upon the debates about the confusing and sometimes contradictory roles of the community college.

Debates about the Roles of the Community College

Although multiple roles are commonplace in today's community college, there is much debate about which roles ought to take precedence and about the effectiveness of community colleges in fulfilling these various roles (Vaughan, 1980). Eaton (1994a) maintains that the reality of multiple missions and roles is hardly a recent trend: "The two-year college has functioned as a multipurpose institution from its earliest days. Although the liberal arts and transfer function dominated the early two-year college, the occupational function was alive and well" (p. 13). Eaton goes on to suggest that some of the other roles community colleges have taken on, namely community service roles such as providing remedial education, threaten the community college environment by diluting the quality of the curriculum. These added-on roles pose a threat to student transfer, as resources may be spread across too many curricular commitments. She argues for the creation of the "collegiate community college" in which high academic standards are maintained and remedial programs are eliminated:

While the community college must retain its commitment to access and to assisting underprepared students, it makes a fundamental error when it honors this commitment by diluting its curricula and academic standards to something less than college-level work. The collegiate community college is academically demanding and there is a limit to the extent to which it can serve the underprepared. Community colleges can and should acknowledge this limit. (1994a, p. 12)

Hence, for Eaton, community colleges should not be open access after all. Instead, they should follow the lead of the elite colleges and universities and pursue what she terms a *collegiate function*—a structured liberal arts education as well as career education with an academic emphasis.

Eaton's idea of the collegiate community college is somewhat surprising. Her suggestion that community colleges should close their doors to the underprepared supports a form of institutionalized racism and classism because clearly many of the underprepared come from diverse cultural groups and lower socioeconomic backgrounds. Selectivity based on previous educational performance or achievement is something many have come to accept in four-year institutions, but to suggest that community colleges become more selective violates the fundamental identity of the institution itself.

In fairness to Eaton, she does suggest an alternative path for underprepared students in the form of "transition schools"—educational centers apart from the community college that focus on precollege reading, writing, and mathematics instruction (1994a, p. 155). Eaton's idea that an additional layer of educational institutions be added in order to protect the community college from having to serve underprepared students seems rooted in a concern for institutional status grounded in elitist assumptions about postsecondary education. Her solution also seems to ignore responsibilities to the local communities in which community colleges reside. This too seems to reject a fundamental aspect of community college identity as an institution responsive to its local citizenry.

Although Eaton sees transfer and liberal arts education as the ideal of what community colleges ought to accomplish, others disagree. In fact, some are quite skeptical about what the community college is really intended to accomplish in the first place. A criticism often leveled against the community college is that it serves a "cooling-out" function, whereby students' aspirations are redirected toward more easily obtainable vocational careers (Clark, 1960). Brint and Karabel (1989) discuss the vocationalization of the junior college that began to take root in the 1920s and 1930s under the leadership of Leonard Koos, Walter Eells, and Doak Campbell, described by Gregory Goodwin (1971) as the "generals in the field" (p. 115). The movement toward vocationalization was in effect a way of both leveling student aspirations as well as capturing an organizational niche unclaimed by four-year institutions. Brint and Karabel expand on this notion:

*Noting that there were only a limited number of professional and upper
management positions and that far more junior college students aspired
to these positions than could ever attain them, such men as Koos, Eells,
and Campbell saw the two-year college's task as the firm but gentle re-
channeling of these students toward middle-level jobs commensurate with
their presumed abilities and past accomplishments. Seen through this
prism, the educational and occupational aspirations of most junior college students were "excessive" and therefore in need of "adjustment." The
appeal of the leadership's vocationalization project resided in its promise
to provide "latent terminal" students with at least short-range upward
mobility at the same time that it would satisfy the junior college's organizational interests by capturing for them the best training markets still
unoccupied by their four-year competitors. (1989, pp. 208–209)*

Brint and Karabel argue that the vocationalization of the two-year
college was a strategic decision by institutional leaders and not a
response to student demand. The demand was, in effect, created by
the two-year colleges to ensure their survival.

The argument follows that through vocational tracking the community college contributes to the ongoing race and class stratification within U.S. society (because vocational education graduates often
assume lower-paying, nonprofessional positions). Additionally, the
community college serves to protect four-year colleges and universities from having to admit underprepared students, and thus enables
four-year institutions to continue elitist policies (Brint & Karabel,
1989). Although there is much debate about the outcomes of the
vocationalization movement, what is clear is that vocational education has taken on major importance if not preeminence in many of
today's community colleges, as evidenced by the low transfer rates
and the high percentage of students involved in vocational tracks
(Cohen & Brawer, 1989; Dougherty, 1994).

How can we make sense of these debates? In one sense, the
community college, through its open-door policy, represents a democratic ideal in which all people have the opportunity to achieve the
American dream. This is the egalitarian vision defended in the work
of Marlene Griffith and Ann Connor (1994), who describe the community college system as "democracy's open door." If a four-year
degree is a ticket to the professional sphere, and higher-paying

careers, and if community colleges are meant to be vehicles for so-cial mobility, then as "democracy's open door" an emphasis on transfer over vocational education seems well placed. However, the Ameri-can dream eludes significant numbers of community college stu-dents, and the reality is that a community college education has not produced economic return for many of its graduates. This is the basic idea Brint and Karabel (1989) put forth when they argued that "in the popular mind" the central role of the early junior colleges was to democratize U.S. higher education by providing opportuni-ties to students previously excluded from higher learning. At the same time, however, the junior colleges faced pressure to limit the number of students who pursued the baccalaureate because of a lim-ited number of professional positions. Brint and Karabel explain the dilemma: "Poised between a burgeoning system of secondary edu-cation and a highly stratified structure of economic opportunity, the junior college was located at the very point where the aspirations generated by American democracy clashed head on with the realities of its class structure" (p. 9).

Other perspectives exist as well. Zwerling (1986) maintains that community colleges have second-class status and have done little to contribute to social mobility: "There has been little change in people's relative position in the social hierarchy, in spite of the democratization of higher education. The society is just as inequi-table as at the turn of the century" (p. 55). Zwerling argues that the educational system ritualizes competition for position and ad-vantage within society. The ritualization serves the hidden pur-pose of convincing those who participate in postsecondary educa-tion that the resulting rewards have been fairly distributed, since schooling has supposedly been fair. Joe Kincheloe (1995) makes a similar point when he points out that education in the U.S. is based on an individualist view of human capital—the belief that anyone can be successful as long as they have a degree of ability and are willing to work hard. As Kincheloe argues, the myth is that education ensures that all students have access to the ladder of socioeconomic mobility. "If they fail, they have no one to blame but themselves" (p. 15). A partial solution to this educational my-thology is, for Zwerling, the elimination of the community col-lege, which he argues would enable students from lower socioeconomic backgrounds to attend four-year colleges directly, instead of having to scale the many barriers to transfer.

Norton Grubb (1991) rejects the notion that vocationalism is the principal cause of the decline of student transfer. Grubb argues that "the problem of declining transfer rates has been one of 'death by a thousand cuts,' rather than a single mortal blow; a large number of causes rather than one single explanation, explain the decline" (p. 213). He points to several contributing causes: changing demographic backgrounds, declining achievement during high school, a collapse of career counseling in high school, an increase in students who are merely experimenting with college, the weakening of the academic associate's degree, and the shift from academic to vocational programs. Although vocationalism may not be the sole culprit in the decline of the transfer role, Grubb nonetheless warns of the dangers of vocationalism. He argues that because vocationalism has a number of short-term benefits for specific constituents—students see improved job opportunities, businesses envision better trained workers, and educators see increased enrollments—decision makers ignore the potentially damaging long-term drawbacks. Grubb points to three problems: projections of the number of jobs available tend to be exaggerated, specific training fails to prepare students in the general math and science skills necessary for further learning, and vocational jobs perpetuate patterns of inequality because they do not have the same economic rewards as careers associated with the baccalaureate.

Despite much criticism directed at vocationalism, other community college writers call for an increase in vocational education as a means to better serve students and ensure organizational survival. For example, David Breneman and Susan Nelson (1981) support a division of labor among postsecondary institutions "that would result in the community colleges enrolling fewer full-time academic transfer students of traditional college age and retaining a dominant position in those activities that four-year institutions have not undertaken traditionally and are likely to do less well" (pp. 211–212). Similarly, Darrel Clowes and Bernard Levin (1989) argue that "The only viable core function for most community colleges is career education. This is a function the society needs and supports, it is a function the institution can and does provide, and it can serve as the essential element, the core function . . . about which community colleges may be restructured for a viable future" (p. 353).

Part of the problem in analyzing the conflicting positions concerning the community college is the fact that critics and proponents are often comparing apples to oranges. Critics tend to focus on outcomes or achievement of students, while supporters tend to focus on opportunity and the ideals of open access (Eaton, 1994a). Critics raise the argument that open access has no meaning if most students are unable to transfer in order to achieve the baccalaureate degree and obtain meaningful employment. Proponents counter that open access provides students with the opportunity to achieve a four-year degree; and even though many do not succeed, many others do. Grubb (1989) notes that there is perhaps a bit of truth in both perspectives: "The differentiation of higher education through the expansion of community colleges may increase the education of some students who would have otherwise stopped at high school. It may enroll and 'cool out' others who might have gone to a four-year institution and completed a B.A." (p. 351).

The most complete analysis of the community college debate and all its contradictory problems is a recent work by Kevin Dougherty (1994), which is appropriately entitled *The Contradictory College*. Dougherty suggests that one way of envisioning these multiple and seemingly contradictory debates is first to examine the theoretical positions of the combatants. He argues that three general perspectives deriving from sociology and political science frame discussions about the community college: functionalism, instrumentalist Marxism, and institutionalism.

Functionalists tend to come to the defense of the community college by describing several vital social needs that are served by this social institution: to provide college opportunity, to train middle-level workers, and to preserve the academic excellence of four-year colleges and universities. Functionalists argue that community colleges democratize college access through their open-door policies, vocational options, and lower prices. Leland Medsker (1960) and, more recently, Cohen and Brawer (1989) perhaps offer the most sustained functionalist analysis.

Instrumentalist Marxist critics argue that "The community college's real social role is to reproduce the class inequalities of capitalist society" (Dougherty, 1994, p. 18). Dougherty highlights three critiques offered by instrumentalist Marxists. First, community colleges provide workers who have developed the necessary skills and docility to be successful employees within a capitalist framework. Second, community colleges serve a diversionary role in protecting the elite four-year institutions from having to admit underprepared students, thereby preserving the integrity of a four-year degree for a capitalist class of students. And third, community colleges maintain class inequality by channeling working-class children into working-class jobs. Notable scholars reflecting this perspective include Samuel Bowles and Herbert Gintis (1976), Fred Pincus (1980, 1983, 1986), and Steven Zwerling (1976).

The institutionalist critique has its most sustained expression in the work of Brint and Karabel (1989). Institutionalists, like instrumentalist Marxists, believe that community colleges serve to divert student aspirations and reproduce social inequality. However, instead of placing the blame on capitalism, institutionalists blame the structure of U.S. higher education, whose hierarchical nature encourages monumental inequities in status and resources. Community colleges, of course, occupy the bottom rungs of such a hierarchy and the message of second-class status gets conveyed to students in a variety of ways. Ira Shor (1987) supports such a view when he describes the "drab physical reality" of most community colleges that sends an ideological message about nonelite students and their relative importance (p. 49). A similar point is conveyed in Howard London's (1978) ethnographic study of an urban community college. More to the point, London criticizes "cooling-out" interpretations that fail to uncover how "the wounds of blocked opportunity fester rather than heal" (p. 153). London adds, "To say that students repress such unpleasant thoughts is perhaps a bit of wishful unawareness by those who would subscribe to the harmlessness of the 'cooling-out' function. To the contrary, stress and anomie and deviant behavior were evident in the students' resistance to their schoolwork, in their absenteeism, in their 'assaults' on teachers, and in their self-criticisms" (p. 153).

Dougherty argues that there is some truth in all three positions. On the one hand, instrumentalist and institutional critics are correct when they point out that community colleges are ineffective in helping baccalaureate aspirants succeed. On the other hand, functionalist supporters may be correct when they argue that community colleges serve a democratizing role in that they allow many students to attend college who may not gain acceptance to four-year institutions, and they also serve students who aspire to something less than a four-year degree. All three camps seem to be correct in pointing out that community colleges help to protect selective admissions policies at elite colleges and universities. Functionalists tend to see the latter outcome as positive because community colleges preserve the academic excellence of four-year colleges and thereby serve the larger higher education system. Institutionalists and instrumentalists, however, see such an outcome as inherently discriminatory.

The problem, as Dougherty sees it, is retaining the democratizing effects of the community college that functionalists point to, while at the same time improving the success rate of baccalaureate aspirants as instrumentalists and institutionalists recommend. Functionalists such as Eaton (1994a) also call for improving the transfer role of the community college.

Improving transfer education, however, poses a significant dilemma: How can community colleges as open-door institutions supposedly committed to serving the needs of the less privileged provide opportunities and resources that promote student transfer and, at the same time, meet the needs of nonbaccalaureate aspirants (who are likely to be the majority)? In other words, how can community colleges stress academic integrity, defined in terms of traditional views of liberal learning and general education, and at the same time serve the needs of a majority of students who seek vocational, remedial, and adult education? We have come full circle and are back to the original question: What vision should community colleges embrace?

Dougherty argues that resolving this dilemma is unlikely under today's community college structure. He maintains that the solution to the complex problems of access and social mobility is either to transform community colleges into four-year colleges or two-year branches of the state universities. Transforming community colleges into four-year colleges would make acquiring the baccalaureate degree easier because hurdling all the obstacles posed by transfer would no longer be necessary. Despite the obvious advantage, Dougherty highlights significant criticisms that have been leveled against such a strategy, which was suggested two decades ago by Zwerling (1976). One objection relates to the idea of institutional prestige: Merely changing a two-year community college to a four-year college may not alter its place in the higher education hierarchy, and thus even a four-year degree from a once-upon-a-time community college may not lead to increased career and social mobility. A second objection is the incredible expense that transforming community colleges into four-year colleges would incur. A third objection is that too many bachelor's degree holders might result, possibly fueling educational inflation. A fourth concern is that the needs of the majority of community college students will not be served, as most students seek vocational, remedial, or adult education. And finally, a fifth objection is that transforming community colleges to four-year institutions is politically unlikely. Simply put, too much resistance would arise from both community and four-year colleges.

Perhaps a more realistic alternative suggested by Dougherty is to transform community colleges into branch campuses of state universities. The change from community college to branch campus entails the following advantages. First, potential baccalaureate students are less likely to be swayed by vocational education, because less emphasis is typically placed on vocationalism at university branches. A second advantage is that a branch campus makes it easier to gain admission and transfer credits to a four-year institution, in this case the state university. And third, students who transfer from branch campuses encounter fewer problems than those who transfer from community colleges. For example, Dougherty notes that students are less likely to run into problems over financial aid because university systems typically operate unified aid programs.

The problem we have with Dougherty's work is certainly not the amount of serious thought he has given to the data and the debates. Dougherty points out that changing community colleges to four-year institutions would threaten community and vocational education, but he does not see that same threat in the movement from community colleges to branch campuses. What obligation do branch campuses of state universities have to their local communities? The answer to this question is that branch campuses have some responsibility, but much less than the traditional community col-

lege has. This is the fundamental problem with Dougherty's suggestion. Transforming community colleges into branch campuses effectively removes the "community" from the local community college. Here, we agree with Edmund Gleazer's (1980) view of the
community college as the "community's college": "It is through the
cooperative [author's emphasis] mode that the community college
achieves its distinctiveness. It is to serve the community and it is to
do more than that. It is to be creatively occupied with the community. It is the community's college, a vital part of an integrated system of community services" (p. 38). From our perspective, transforming community colleges into branch campuses is not the
solution.

Where do we stand? We agree with many of the critics and defenders who argue that vocationalism has taken on too large a role at
many community colleges. We also agree that transfer education
needs to be strengthened. But strengthening transfer education should
not come at the expense of equal opportunity as Eaton (1994a) suggests, nor should improved transfer programs involve sacrificing community responsiveness as Dougherty's solution implies.

We agree with many of the writers and critics who point to
the lack of organizational identity of the community college as a
significant problem. Yet, we question the position that community colleges are stretched too thin by their multiple roles. We recognize the need for a better balance between general education to
support student transfer and vocational education to provide training for specific careers. In fact, we give much credence to Eaton's
point about the need to stress academic career education. But to
eliminate vocational education or community education, or to
weaken them to such a degree that they are no longer part of the
central mission of the community college, is a mistake. It is a mistake because such efforts fail to consider the diversity of students
who enter the community college and thus fail to serve the community and its citizenry.

We reject the idea that community colleges need to develop a
more narrow vision and decide among transfer, vocational, and community education. Indeed, in today's postmodern world, organizations often take on multiple roles, serve diverse constituencies, and
manage contradictions on a daily basis (Burrell, 1988; Cooper, 1989;

Cooper & Burrell, 1988; Gergen, 1992; Reed & Hughes, 1992). The challenge is developing and maintaining a sense of organizational identity in spite of the multiplicity inherent in postmodern life. While critics such as Eaton (and Dougherty to a much lesser degree) seek clarity in terms of the community college's mission, we suggest instead an organization defined by multiplicity—an organization in which multiple roles and missions are seen as the norm. Despite an emphasis on multiplicity, organizations nonetheless must be held together by some connective thread. We argue throughout the remainder of this text that multiculturalism provides such a thread and, at the same time, offers solutions to some of the problems of educational access and equity that are part of the democratic vision of the community college.

Multiculturalism as Connective Thread

The shortcomings of today's community colleges extend beyond achieving the proper mix between transfer, vocational, and community education. Other problems encompass an underlying issue that is seldom addressed in the community college literature—the lack of democratic practice inherent in pedagogical and administrative processes. Critical multiculturalism, deriving its critical component from critical pedagogy, offers solutions to the authoritarian emphasis of the community college.

Critical pedagogy challenges the authoritarian and one-directional relationship between the teacher and the student. As we note in chapter 1, a critical multicultural pedagogy rejects a view of the teacher as knowledge broker and student as passive recipient of that knowledge. This is the "banking" concept of educational practice rejected in the work of Paulo Freire (1970). As Freire details, such a view of education includes the following:

1. the teacher teaches and the students are taught;
2. the teacher knows everything and the students know nothing;
3. the teacher thinks and the students are thought about;
4. the teacher talks and the students listen—meekly;
5. the teacher disciplines and the students are disciplined;
6. the teacher chooses and enforces his choice, and the students comply;

7.   the teacher acts and the students have the illusion of acting through the action of the teacher;

8.   the teacher chooses the program content, and the students (who were not consulted) adapt to it;

9.   the teacher confuses the authority of knowledge with his own professional authority, which he sets in opposition to the freedom of the students;

10.   the teacher is the Subject of the learning process, while the pupils are mere objects. (1970, p. 59)

Freire goes on to note, "It is not surprising that the banking concept of education regards men as adaptable, manageable beings. The more students work at storing the deposits entrusted to them, the less they develop the critical consciousness which would result from their intervention in the world as transformers of that world" (p. 60).

Thus, a critical education not only calls for a reconceptualization of the role between the teacher and the student, it also challenges students to understand how society has situated their lives and how they might transform society (Giroux, 1983). A multicultural curriculum founded on critical pedagogy seeks to engage students in the historical, political, and cultural forces that frame their lives. At the same time, such a curriculum focuses attention on the roles individuals and groups might play in reshaping social life. Critical pedagogy is grounded in the emancipatory role of a dialectical and dialogical education that seeks to reconstitute representational relations. "Critical education prepares students to be their own agents for social change, their own creators of democratic culture" (Shor, 1987, p. 48).

A critical multicultural pedagogy does not oppose incorporating vocational opportunities for students into the community college curriculum. For obvious reasons, many students from lower socioeconomic backgrounds have a greater need to enter into a career as soon as possible; community colleges often provide opportunities for these students. When students engage in the struggle to understand the social complexities that help to shape them as individuals, and as members of specific social groups within a specific historical and cultural context, decisions about vocations can be made in a more informed manner. They might come to reject vocationalism altogether. As Pincus (1980) argues, if community college educators really desire to assist working-class and underrepresented students, "They should provide them with a historical and political context from which to understand the dismal choices they face. Vocational education students might then begin to raise some fundamental questions about the legitimacy of educational, political, and economic institutions in the United States" (p. 356). Perhaps Pincus touches on the hidden curriculum of the community college—maintenance of the economic, social, and political status quo. Along this line, Zwerling (1976) talks about "heating-up" students instead of the "cooling-out" idea. By heating up he refers to helping students to understand the relevance of their own histories and cultures:

Another important function of affective learning is to help students validate their own prior experiences. The academic world reflects upper-middle class values and values upper-middle class culture. Lower-class people feel put down or alienated by this kind of exclusive collegiate environment. Validating working-class culture via affective learning in community colleges does not mean a different kind of exclusiveness: it means a cultural balance within which all people can have a chance to feel good about themselves. By validating the experiences and feelings of the students, we tell them in essence that they do know something. (pp. 188–189)

Zwerling directs attention to our earlier discussion of border knowledge—the knowledge and ways of knowing culturally diverse students bring to the educational setting. When students engage in discussions that increase their understanding of their position in today's world, they can better make informed decisions about careers and where they see themselves in relation to others. Vocational education without a critical multicultural component is exploitative. The same is true of transfer and community education that does not seek to help students seriously reflect on the forces acting upon their lives. An organization grounded in critical multiculturalism is one that offers students opportunities to actively participate in discussions and decisions affecting social life in the institution and in the broader society. To make informed decisions, one must have a depth of understanding of the social complexities contributing to social life. Critical multiculturalism offers such a vehicle.

Our contention is that a commitment to democratic education, encompassed in the idea of a critical multicultural pedagogy, offers a cultural thread connecting the multiple functions of the community college. Multiculturalism, hence, is not an additional role to perform. Instead, it serves as a link among the multiple functions community colleges adopt. For example, preparing students to transfer to four-year colleges, providing vocational training, or implementing continuing education programs all have the similar goal of offering students educational opportunities ideally leading to increased economic prosperity and social mobility. Although on the surface there may be little connection among these multiple roles, when these three responsibilities are structured around an educational process in which issues of history, politics, and culture are linked to transfer, vocational, and community education, a common connection is formed through an organizational commitment to democracy. In this way, transfer, vocational, and community education take on a similar component—a critical component built on naming and then challenging social forces that hinder the development of a society committed to social justice and equality. What we are suggesting then is not a major revision of mission, but more a restructuring of how that mission gets enacted.

Our concern in this book is with how we structure, or in some cases restructure, community colleges along the lines of the democratic ideals embraced by multiculturalism. As we have already noted, multiculturalism is more than merely offering courses on diverse peoples and cultures. Multiculturalism involves restructuring educational institutions so that all people play a significant role in decision making. Creating multicultural institutions involves rethinking the goals of education so that issues of citizenship, social responsibility, and democratic participation become central. Estela Bensimon and William Tierney (1992/1993) elaborate this view of multiculturalism:

Multiculturalism is a complex set of relationships framed around issues of race, gender, class, sexual orientation, and power. One of the struggles in multicultural organizations is to understand the commonalities and differences among underrepresented groups, and to develop an appreciation of how an understanding of these characteristics might create alli-

*ances for change. Thus we need to respect the differences among diverse
groups and at the same time work to develop institutions whose central
organizing concept is the creation of multicultural excellence based upon
a democratic acceptance of both the commonalities and the differences of
all groups on campus. (p. 5)*

Seen in this light, multiculturalism may be interpreted as an organizing concept around which colleges and universities might work
to achieve greater justice, equality, and freedom. Central to
multicultural organizational struggle are the notions of commonality and difference.

A modernist view of culture suggests that all cultures and cultural groups are bound together by common threads. These threads
derive from various elements of culture, which may relate to shared
values, beliefs, attitudes, or norms. In today's complex societies, the
common connections are more difficult to maintain as difference
becomes a prevailing feature of social life. In postmodern societies
and organizations, few in fact may buy into the same values or beliefs, and few may adopt similar attitudes. Cultural differences stretch
the cultural fabric and threaten group cohesion. In cultures characterized as homogeneous, difference is less likely to surface and harmony tends to prevail. In heterogeneous cultures, differences are
common and group conflicts persist.

From a modernist perspective, homogeneous cultures are portrayed as the norm, the ideal. Thus, organizations and social groups
have tended to strive toward the norm of homogeneity, in which the
goal is to silence disputes and differences in favor of harmony. The
traditional canon, for example, depends on homogeneity. The reality, however, is that we live in an increasingly diverse society where
traditionalist goals of harmony and like-mindedness are not only
next to impossible to achieve, but are silencing as well. What is the
alternative?

In his book entitled *Building Communities of Difference,* Tierney
(1993) talks about communities organized around difference instead
of commonality: "It is curious perhaps that I am suggesting that we
build the idea of community around the concept of diversity, for
communities generally suggest commonality. Such communities,
however, have inevitably silenced those of us on the borders" (p.

25). Tierney suggests that academic communities need to embrace cultural differences by forging dialogues across "border zones." Border zones refer to cultural differences such as race, class, gender, and sexual orientation. By stressing dialogues across difference (across border zones), Tierney is not suggesting that differences be silenced or whitewashed. Instead, what is suggested is a respect for cultural difference; yet, at the same time, we cannot allow difference to interfere with important dialogues over common social concerns such as justice and equality.

The challenge then for the multicultural organization is to create an environment where cultural difference is respected and at the same time to provide opportunities for diverse groups to come together to engage in cultural struggle over important organizational and social issues. As Giroux (1993) notes, "There is more at stake than simply developing an empathy for difference or an appreciation of the pleasure that can be produced in the discourse and relations of difference; there is also the need to struggle collectively around a politics of hope" (p. 81). A politics of hope refers to what Nancy Fraser (1990) describes as "the possibility of a society in which social equality and cultural diversity co-exist with participatory democracy" (p. 69).

We find it striking that of all postsecondary institutions, community colleges are the least involved in multicultural organizational innovation (Eaton, 1994a; El-Khawas, 1992; Levine & Cureton, 1992), and that community college educators are the least involved in debates about multiculturalism (Eaton, 1994a). This book represents an effort to move the community college as an institution toward the creation of multicultural community colleges. We offer five case studies that focus on specific organizational issues related to enacting multicultural structures. These case studies are only examples of how some institutions have dealt with cultural diversity. In some cases, the institutions have been relatively successful, and in others they have not. There is much to learn in either case.

Although we believe the organizational scenarios and our analyses are informative, we make no claims that these case studies are inclusive of all the complex issues community colleges face. Before proceeding to the case studies to be presented in chapters three through seven, we first explain the methodology used in collecting and analyzing our data.

Case Study Methodology

The data for this book derive from organizational case studies conducted at five community colleges over the past three years. Three of the community colleges are situated in urban settings, and two are rural. Two colleges are in the southeast, one is in the south, one is in the midwest, and one is in the west. Colleges were purposely selected in order to examine organizational structures designed to improve the educational experiences of students from diverse cultural groups. For example, one community college was selected because of its middle college–high school program designed primarily to serve African-American students. Another community college was selected because of its community education program geared for Spanish-speaking immigrants. And a third was chosen because of its remedial education offerings oriented toward students from lower socio-economic backgrounds.

Case study methodology is "an empirical inquiry that: investigates a contemporary phenomenon within its real-life context; when the boundaries between phenomenon and context are not clearly evident; and in which multiple sources of evidence are used" (Yin, 1989, p. 23). In the case of our work, the boundaries between specific organizational structures—the college itself, the local community, and the higher education context—are all quite fluid and demand multiple methods for understanding. Relatedly, we relied upon many of the data collection tools typically associated with qualitative research methods: formal and informal interviews, participant observation, and document analysis. Over two hundred students, faculty, and staff participated in formal structured interviews that typically lasted from one to two hours. Interviews either were tape-recorded and transcribed verbatim or shorthand notes were kept and transcribed at a later date. Countless other informal interviews were conducted, oftentimes lasting only a few minutes. Participant observation also was a primary data collection tool and provided an opportunity to double-check the behaviors that individuals reported during interviews. For example, one instructor described his teaching style as "very collaborative" during an interview, but classroom observations raised questions about how collaborative the instructor actually is. The use of multiple data collection methods amounts to what Norman Denzin (1989) describes as "triangulation," and provides for greater corroboration of evidence.

Site visits were repeated as a means to increase reliability and to control for findings that might be time-specific. Case study reports were produced and read by organizational participants. This relates to what Yvonna Lincoln and Egon Guba (1986) describe as "member checks"—the idea that research participants have the right to participate in the production of findings. Member checks contribute to a study's "authenticity," a term used by qualitative researchers that roughly is akin to the traditional social science notion of "rigor."

The central concern of our case studies is summarized by the following research question: How does a community college organize itself to meet the many demands of a culturally diverse student population? In pursuing this question, we relied upon theories of culture and identity deriving from critical multiculturalism to inform our observations and analyses. And, of course, we explain the main components of our theoretical position in chapter 1.

In addition to the theoretical ideas we discuss in the opening chapter, we also rely on a number of theoretical constructs derived from organizational theory. In particular, we borrow heavily from theories of organizational culture. We find such perspectives most compatible with efforts to make sense of cultural diversity and multiculturalism. Some of the organizational concepts we discuss include celebratory socialization, boundary spanning, restructuring, leadership, and multiplicity.

The strength of case study research is that it enables researchers to develop a depth of cultural knowledge within specific organizational settings. The weakness is that generalizations based on findings are sometimes tentative. This is where theory plays a vital role. Theoretical constructs help to link particular qualitative findings that may be site-specific to the larger context. In this case, findings at one of our sites may have limited significance to other institutions unless theoretical connections can be made between such findings and the larger community college scene. Multiculturalism and related theoretical perspectives on culture and identity help us to link localized findings to larger issues pertaining to cultural diversity and community colleges.

Data analysis amounted to what some describe as "cultural analysis." For Clifford Geertz (1973), cultural analysis is a systematic process that involves "guessing at meanings, assessing the guesses, and drawing explanatory conclusions from the better guesses" (p. 103). At the risk of forfeiting our social science credentials, Geertz's description very closely describes the process we employed. The process is self-reflective in that a great deal of interpretation and reinterpretation is involved. Such a strategy involves revising questions as well as theories as one progresses toward the conclusion of a study. A strength of the data analysis is the fact that each of us had opportunities to critique the analysis and interpretations of the other. This added-feedback mechanism increased the strength of the case study chapters.

In conducting our analyses, we searched for themes that might help us make sense of the data gathered. Themes formed in two ways. Some themes reflect the theoretical positioning we brought to our study and the responses to specific questions asked of our research participants. Examples of these themes include the following: the nature of the organizational culture, the nature of student-faculty interactions, characteristics of faculty and student culture, and the general characteristics of the local community. Other themes came to mind after reading and rereading the data. This latter type of analysis relates to Michael Patton's (1980) notion that the grouping of data is an inductively derived process whereby salient patterns emerge from the data. Examples of these themes include the following: the kinds of community partnerships formed, the different pedagogical practices enacted in classrooms, various curricular debates evidenced at the colleges, and the diverse management styles of administrative staffs.

What Follows

In chapter 3, we introduce our first case study as we examine a rural community college referred to as Vocational Community College. The discussion focuses on how the culture of the college centers on vocationalism and contributes to a student's sense of identity as a prospective worker. Kincheloe's (1995) theorizing about "good work" highlights how vocational education might be reconstituted within a community college setting in a way that challenges dominant conceptions of work and worker identity. We suggest a broader vision of students, encompassing not only their role as workers but also their role as citizens.

Chapter 4 focuses on an immigrant education program designed to serve Spanish-speaking immigrants situated at an urban community college—Outreach Community College. Central to the discussion is what we term *celebratory socialization*—the idea that the culture, forms of knowledge, and ways of knowing that students bring with them to educational settings ought to be embraced within the organizational context. Such an idea resists the canonization of knowledge and elevates the relevance of border knowledge. As we point out, such a process is crucial to the creation of educational institutions committed to multiculturalism.

In chapter 5, our case study focuses on an example of community responsiveness as we explore a middle college–high school program introduced at an urban community college—Divided Community College. The program was created primarily to serve African-American high school students. Our focus is twofold. First, we examine how middle college high school as a multicultural innovation has helped to enhance the learning opportunities of African-American students. Second, we examine multicultural innovation in relation to issues of organizational restructuring and leadership. The debate that has sprung up around the adoption of the middle college–high school program is used to highlight leadership problems at Divided and the need for more democratic strategies.

In chapter 6, a rural community college referred to as Remedial Community College is examined. The focus is on Remedial's efforts to develop effective developmental education programs for underprepared lower- and working-class students. We rely on theoretical issues related to cultural capital and border knowledge to highlight how the community college limits student opportunity by the way knowledge and culture are situated within the classroom and the curriculum. We suggest that successful remediation must come to terms with the multiple forms of knowledge and experiences culturally diverse students bring to the community college.

Chapter 7 highlights Perplexity Community College's efforts to balance its multiple roles and meet the many needs of a culturally diverse student body. We examine how responsibilities related to providing transfer, vocational, and community education create confusion for faculty and staff at the college. We focus on the idea of organizational multiplicity and how postmodern theories of organizational life might help educators to come to terms with organizational complexity and enable community colleges to embrace multicultural education.

Finally, we conclude our book by returning to a discussion of community college education as the practice of democracy. Critical multiculturalism is used to translate localized case study findings to the wider arena of community college education. We introduce a fictional community college known as Democratic Community College as a means to situate some of the issues we raise throughout the text. Some general principles are offered as guides for the creation of critical multicultural community colleges committed to a democratic educational vision.

Notes

1.   All names of individuals and institutions participating in this study are pseudonyms.

Chapter Three
Organizational Culture and Worker Identity
A Case Study of Vocational Education

This chapter focuses on the interaction between the organizational culture of Vocational Community College (VCC) and students' emerging sense of identity. We examine how an organizational commitment to vocationalism influences students' choices and career opportunities. At the same time, we acknowledge and seek to uncover the role students play in this complex interactional process. The idea of resistance is central to our analysis as we discuss how vocationalism often leads to student apathy about learning. Joe Kincheloe's (1995) notion of "good work" is key to our discussion of how community college education might be restructured so that students have opportunities to advance their careers and at the same time be challenged as democratic citizens. We highlight how a pedagogy centered on good work is compatible with the critical multicultural perspective adopted throughout this book.

As we note in chapter 2, education is often viewed as a democratizing force in U.S. society. It is part of American ideology that students, regardless of race, gender, or social class, can study hard and rise as far as their ambitions and abilities will take them. This vision of American education is based largely upon a belief that the educational system provides equal opportunity for all students. We know, however, that not all schools are equal, and that students who attend school in some of our urban centers or rural communities are not afforded the same opportunities available in affluent suburban school districts (Kozol, 1991; Orfield & Ashkinaze, 1991).

A similar argument can be made about the U.S. system of higher learning. Critics of the community college describe a two-tiered system of higher education with community colleges at the bottom and elite four-year institutions at the top. These critics view the community college as an institution that serves society by perpetuating the social class system of the United States. As the critics explain, the community college has opened its doors to the masses of American people; but, rather than providing the opportunity for social mobility, the community college "cools out" the ambitions of lower- and working-class students by channeling them toward vocational majors and eventually working-class jobs. Meanwhile, higher-status majors and more lucrative professional careers are reserved for middle- and upper-class students.

Defenders of the community college, on the other hand, champion the open-door policy and proclaim that the community college is the most egalitarian of higher education institutions. The community college indeed has opened its doors to a broad range of people. As a result, the community college is more heavily working-class, minority, and female than four-year institutions (Adelman, 1992; Dougherty, 1994). For example, twenty-two percent of community college students are minority (compared to eighteen percent in four-year schools), ten percent have family incomes below $15,000 annually (compared to six percent in four-year institutions), and thirty-seven percent of the students are over thirty years of age (compared to twenty-five percent in four-year schools) (Dougherty, 1994).

As Kevin Dougherty (1994) explains, the idea that community colleges are portrayed by some as democracy's colleges and at the same time are seen by others as agents in the reproduction of class inequality is part of the contradictory organizational persona of the community college. The contradictory message is compounded by the fact that minority and lower- and working-class students have had limited success in the community college. Indicators such as graduation and transfer rates (to four-year colleges) remain low for minority and lower- and working-class students when compared with middle-class white students. The disparate graduation and transfer rates lead many critics to conclude that the community college has failed in its promise to provide social mobility for less privileged students (Brint & Karabel, 1989; Nora, 1993; Nora & Rendon, 1988; Olivas, 1979; Rendon, 1993; Rendon & Valadez, 1993; Velez, 1985).

Explanations for the wide differences in educational attainment, particularly college transfer, between working-class students and middle-class white students have centered on the sorting of students into academic or occupational tracks (Brint & Karabel, 1989; Karabel, 1972, 1986; Pincus, 1980; Velez, 1985). The analysis has primarily been at the macro level where state and national data on community college transfer rates have been useful in highlighting the problem. This type of analysis, although useful in identifying the educational inequities associated with educational tracking, tends to neglect the role faculty and staff play in daily interactions with students. We need to advance this kind of structural account of educational inequity by focusing on the lived experiences of students and faculty as they interact in community college settings. Jennifer Gore (1993) speaks to the kind of analyses suggested here:

Much of the educational production of knowledge takes place at the very private, personal level of teacher and student, and therefore cannot all be explained (away) with structuralism or structuralist politics. It seems to me that there is something about the educational enterprise that leads to the local, partial, and multiple foci of poststructural theories; there is something about the lives of those in classrooms, as well as the lives of (social) "classes," that requires the phenomenological, personal accounts of multiplicity and contradiction. (p. 49)

Our concern throughout the research, analysis, and writing of this book relates to Gore's call for a phenomenological analysis of many of the kinds of problems highlighted by structuralist critiques of the community college.

A structural analysis also fails to capture the role students play in making decisions about their careers and their futures. What is needed is an analysis of how faculty and staff attitudes, beliefs, and values influence the decision making of students and how students at times offer resistance to organizational initiatives. What we are talking about is a closer examination of how the organizational culture of a community college gets translated to the student experience. More to the point, how does the culture influence a student's sense of identity?

Our analyses follows work by Howard London (1978), Linda Valli (1986), Lois Weis (1985, 1990), and Paul Willis (1977), who examine how school culture contributes to the reproduction of working-class consciousness. London (1978), in particular, examined the impact of community college culture on the academic achievement of working-class students. He detailed the cultural conflict between students' struggle to make sense of their lives and their educational experiences in light of the culture of an urban community college.

Students created a perspective that diminished the possibility of success as defined by their middle-class, gate-keeping teachers. Indeed, the self-doubts of students, so intimately linked with social class, created a double bind: Suspecting their abilities to work with ideas led them to suspect the worth of working with ideas, yet mind and intelligence were held to be important indicators of worth and character. The students' problem, then, was to define an unfamiliar institution, an institution that, on the one hand, might be a vehicle for a critical opportunity, but, on the other hand, might injure them further. (p. 27)

Like London, we focus on cultural aspects of community college settings as we examine students' experiences as they become intertwined with the working lives of community college faculty and staff. We also include an analysis of students' experiences within and responses to the structures throughout the overall educational system, of which the community college is a fundamental part. Thus, our analysis places issues of student identity and organizational culture at the center of explanations about social and cultural reproduction.

In focusing on the interaction between organizational culture and student identity, we acknowledge the role individuals play both wittingly and unwittingly in their own social reproduction. Such an explanation acknowledges that culture as well as social systems are reproduced through the mutual interaction between social actors and the structural arrangements of institutions (Giddens, 1991). We emphasize that in any relationship, even one of unequal power, people have some degree of power and influence over others (Burbules, 1986). This is true of educational settings like the community college. Because individuals have a degree of power in all social interactions, resistance to another's course of action is always an alternative. This is true for the students at Vocational Community College, who at times openly resist the values and beliefs projected by faculty and staff. For example, instructors often complain about failed attempts to persuade students of the value of particular subjects such as history or speech. One instructor stated, "I can only do so much to convince them that this is useful." Students see little connection between studying history or learning to communicate better and their lived experiences. As a result, the classroom becomes the site of a cultural struggle where instructors must defend the logic of their course offerings, and where students often resist or argue against what appears to be irrelevant to their lives and to their identities as members of the lower and working classes.

In what follows, we present a description of Vocational Community College and its surrounding community. We highlight the problems of students and faculty as they struggle over a vocational curriculum that faculty believe provides students with the knowledge and opportunity to secure jobs leading to improved economic standing. As we will point out, however, there are many problems inherently rooted in how job-oriented education has come to be conceptualized at Vocational. We offer Kincheloe's (1995) conception of "good work" as a solution to how education ought to be shaped at Vocational. As Kincheloe explains, a critical postmodern pedagogy of work challenges educators to restructure vocational education around a more dignified and democratic view of work. Narrowly defined jobs that restrict a worker to perform simplistic and repetitive tasks are to be rejected. And because the workplace is democratic, a wide range of perspectives are brought to bear on the production of work as worker creativity becomes a vital resource. Work education based on democratic principles also envisions students as something more than merely prospective employees—they are seen as citizens and community members as well. Kincheloe argues that, "The idea of democracy as a political benchmark that guides the interrelated educational goals of individual development and civic commitment has been missing from the conversation about work education. When political leaders have discussed job training and the relationship between schooling and work, they rarely ask what type of citizens do we want to produce or what kind of society do we want to build" (p. 24). We keep Kincheloe's work in mind as we analyze Vocational Community College.

Organizational Background

Vocational Community College is located in a rural area in the southeastern region of the United States. The college is part of a rapidly growing system of fifty-eight community colleges. Vocational was founded as an industrial training center in 1957 and by 1967 had evolved into a comprehensive community college. Currently there are 2,400 students taking courses in a wide variety of programs, including one-year vocational, two-year technical, and a college transfer program leading to an associate's degree.

The community colleges in the state are largely autonomous institutions under the control of a local board of trustees. The board works closely with college administrators to hire personnel, maintain the facility, and raise local funds to support educational programs. The college receives most of its funding from the state (seventy percent) and derives the balance of its budget from federal and local sources.

There are 138 full-time faculty at Vocational. In terms of the highest degree achieved, five hold a doctorate, eighty-six have achieved a master's degree, and thirty-seven have as their highest degree a baccalaureate. A few of the full-time vocational instructors do not have baccalaureate degrees, but have received diplomas or certificates in their areas of specialization.

The student body is typical of many of the rural community colleges in this southeastern state. The students are predominantly white (sixty-seven percent), but a sizable proportion of the students are African American (twenty-nine percent). The remaining four percent of the students are either Latino/a, Native American, or Asian.

Most of the faculty and administrators at Vocational are white: ninety-one percent are white, and only eight percent are African American. At the senior administrative level (deans, vice presidents, president), the situation is similar. Six of the eight (seventy-five percent) senior administrators are white, and two are African Americans. Only one woman is a member of the senior administration team.

The administration of the college recognizes that the overrepresentation of whites, and particularly white males, in the administrative ranks is a problem. The administration is also attempting to understand the disparity in educational achievement and graduation rates between its African-American and white students. The college continues to expand its Upward Bound program in order to recruit and improve support services for African-American students from local high schools. As a staff member with Upward Bound said, "We need to reach out to the high schools. There are students there who need to be thinking about us."

The Local Community

Vocational Community College is situated in a rural county where business and industry centers around agriculture. VCC lies in the heart of tobacco country, and the crop dominates the local economy. Other crops such as cotton, corn, and grains are also harvested for large markets. Livestock production, particularly hogs and poultry, are important commodities in the county. In addition to agriculture, manufacturing remains an important feature of the local economy. However, the relative importance of manufacturing has diminished in recent years because several large employers have left the state and relocated to Mexico. The remaining industries employ workers in the production of furniture, textiles, footwear, and foundry products.

The county has not experienced the explosive growth that has been common to the urban centers of the state. As a result, the population has remained stable with 104,000 residents. Sixty-six percent of the population is white, and thirty-two percent is African American (Bureau of the Census, 1990). There is a large disparity in income and educational attainment among the African-American and white residents. White families have a median income of $26,000 compared with African-American families whose median income is $17,160 (Bureau of the Census, 1990). As far as educational attainment is concerned, seventy-five percent of the whites in the county over twenty-five years of age have achieved at least a high school diploma, compared with sixty-five percent of the African-American residents who have done so.

Using common indicators of educational achievement such as math and reading achievement test scores, county students rank below the state average. Local educators have cited declining SAT scores as a disturbing trend. The declining SAT scores are particularly bothersome because the rest of the state has experienced steady gains over the past ten years. In 1984, students in the county scored seventeen points below the state mean. By 1994, the gap widened to fifty-five points on the combined math and verbal components of the exam.

The picture presented of Vocational's surrounding county is not unlike other rural counties in the state. In the midst of unprecedented growth and prosperity in the urban areas of the state, many rural areas have been left behind economically. Consequently, Vocational Community College, as well as other rural community colleges in the state, is faced with many difficult problems. As a center of educational and cultural activities, VCC is seen as a vital county resource. The college is expected to provide more than education and job training; many community members view Vocational as a catalyst for economic development.

VCC takes its commitment to the county and its residents seriously and places great emphasis on providing skilled employees for county and statewide businesses and industries. Thus, Vocational Community College hopes to contribute to the economic development of the area by providing an attractive and well-trained labor force. In what follows, we contextualize the college's commitment to vocational education as well as the experiences of its students as they pass through the halls of Vocational Community College.

The Findings

In order to understand who the students are at Vocational, and why they come to the institution, we examine key elements of the day-to-day practices of the college as a means to better understand the organizational culture. Our goal is to move beyond structural accounts of social reproduction and focus on some of the underlying strains and points of tension within a community college setting as students both comply and resist the educational process. As Dougherty (1994) points out, critics of the community college have viewed its structural arrangements as a powerful determinant of what students choose for their academic and vocational futures. In this rather deterministic analysis, a criticism often voiced is that many community college students are sorted into vocational tracks in which their social mobility is limited (Brint & Karabel, 1989; Clark, 1960;

Karabel, 1972, 1986; Pincus, 1980, 1983). The problem with such an analysis is that it fails to consider the complexity of student decisions about their futures and the resistance they sometimes exhibit. For example, what kinds of knowledge do community college students seek? What are their aspirations about social mobility? How much do students know about the economic conditions of our society, and what are their perceptions of the occupations and careers available to them? And finally, what types of responses do students offer when they recognize the limitations society places upon them?

In what follows, we present three significant themes that characterize the cultural context of Vocational Community College. First, we describe the messages the institution sends to students concerning their instruction and preparation for work. We follow with a discussion about how students define and claim the knowledge they need to prepare for the world of work. Lastly, we discuss the economic and social contexts that contribute to the college's emphasis on vocationalism. We describe how an evolving economy affects the way students envision their future and make decisions about their education and their lives.

Delivering the Message Vocational Community College, like most community colleges, faces multiple challenges. A central challenge embraced by Vocational is its commitment to local employers and to providing career opportunities for its students. Many students enter Vocational with a desire to gain appropriate skills for entering the work force. Along with the skills learned in vocational courses, students are also challenged to internalize the values that go along with being a good employee and a good worker. Deeply embedded in the philosophy of instruction at Vocational is the idea that students need to learn the values and attitudes required for a smooth transition from school to work. The college catalog provides a statement about the instructional philosophy:

Instruction in the college is based on attaining student competency rather than imparting knowledge. . . . Instruction is accomplished in three stages. The first is to identify the actual activities on the job in industry. This step is accomplished by making direct contact with people in industry and doing a task analysis. The second is to organize the curriculum to include the tasks necessary for effective learning. The third step is to establish appropriate assessment.

The instructional philosophy is closely tied to the needs of the business community, and reflects the predominant attitude of administration and faculty. In fact, the purpose of the college is described in writing as follows: (1) to provide all students with marketable skills, and (2) to provide the training needs of local business and industry.

There is a sense among faculty that the college's performance is evaluated on how well students are prepared for the work force, and the college actively seeks feedback from employers about the performance of their students. A current initiative in Vocational's home state is to identify "critical success factors." The concept of critical success factors was developed for application in a business setting by the Massachusetts Institute of Technology; but, according to a recent state publication, the notion of critical success factors is applicable to other organizations. The state's primary concern about community college education is employer satisfaction with community college graduates. The connection to local and regional employers is evident in comments from a senior administrator at Vocational:

Our philosophy is based on our students achieving competencies. We have gotten significant feedback from employers. This is true for several of our programs. In childcare, for example, we have specific competencies we want our students to achieve. It's a checklist, and students are evaluated based on how they achieve each of those skills. We have found that employers are pleased with the students we send them.

Students at Vocational Community College acquire specific skills so that they are marketable and can function in a specific work setting. Students also learn the values and attitudes that the college believes are necessary for the workplace. Talcott Parsons' (1959) notion that the function of schools is to help students internalize such qualities as responsibility, cooperativeness, respect, and other characteristics important for the world of work is consistent with the beliefs of the faculty and staff at Vocational. In fact, some faculty became quite animated when discussing the values they were attempting to instill in their students: "There is value in knowing that you have to come to class on time. You've got to come prepared. It all comes down to learning responsibilities associated with the workplace and doing what is expected."

At Vocational, the values associated with the world of work are usually transmitted to students in the classroom. One faculty member talked about the integration of the competencies involved in the workplace into her classroom: "Competency-based education has shown us how to transform the external demands of the workplace into the internal setting of the classroom." Transmission occurs through both the content and the pedagogical style as specific work tasks are delineated and then discussed as part of the course design.

Along with the content of the course work, instructors believe they must instill the values of the workplace, including timeliness, attention to instructions, and personal responsibility. An instructor said, "I'm strict when it comes to handing in assignments or following directions. If they misread the directions or if they're late, I will take off points. I know people say I'm too strict, but I tell you, I've had people come back and tell me they learned valuable lessons in my classes." Another instructor talked about kicking students out of his class if they failed to come prepared or if they were late. This instructor believes that he is instilling the same kind of values students will need in the workplace; values that he feels students are not getting at home.

The classroom is not the only place where the attitudes, values, and beliefs that faculty and staff hold about the world of work and what constitutes good work are transmitted to students; programs such as orientation and motivational workshops are also designed to convey the organization's wisdom on work. One of the college's programs targets students who dropped out of high school or who have experienced extended periods of unemployment. The goal of the program, as one staff member noted, is to "turn people's lives around." This staff member believes that Vocational must change students' values and attitudes as a means to make them more employable. "We talk to them about interviews. We show them how to dress. How to act. How to respond to questions. I've had people say after they've gone through our program, 'No wonder I never got a job.'" The message conveyed to students is that they need to adapt to the requirements of the employer and to understand the culture of the workplace. This staff member went on to note that the program is not for everyone: "If it's not for them, then I tell them not to come back." He added that some students resist the message at the outset, but come around later: "It doesn't hit them until many months down the road."

Students respond to Vocational's messages about the world of work in a variety of ways. A consistent theme conveyed by students is that "education is valuable." They believe that "education will get them a better job" or "without education they will be stuck in dead-end jobs." Every student interviewed, whether white or African American, male or female, mentioned that education was a means for improving their lives. The students were also clear about the kind of knowledge they believed they needed for finding good work.

For example, Sammy Klinger, a twenty-five-year-old white male student, found the learning experiences at Vocational to be quite helpful. Sammy was enrolled in a two-year program that would qualify him to become an electronics technician. He was already employed at a local company and was looking forward to working full-time. Sammy said, "Once I finish this degree I can work full-time. The company has been great. Giving me a part-time job and a scholarship to come to school. I've got to work full-time. My wife works, but we need two incomes."

Another student, Margaret Willmont, achieved her goals by attending Vocational. For a while, Margaret depended on welfare to support herself and her two young children. She enrolled in school through a government program that paid her fees, provided childcare, and offered transportation. She completed the requirements for a Graduate Equivalency Diploma; and then enrolled in a one-year nurse's aid program. "That didn't pay much, only minimum wage, maybe a little higher." Margaret returned to school because she wanted to become a registered nurse. She commented about her improved economic circumstances: "Now I can make close to $50,000 a year with my overtime." Margaret's instructors talk about her being a role model for other students; she is frequently asked to come back to Vocational and speak to students about her life.

Other students expressed sentiments similar to those of Sammy and Margaret. They set goals for finding work, and they looked to Vocational as the institution that was going to provide them with the skills and knowledge they needed. But not all students embraced the culture of work as delivered through the messages of Vocational faculty and staff. Some students sought to claim their own forms of knowledge and understanding about work and education.

Claiming Knowledge The teaching philosophy at Vocational, which is tied closely to the needs of business and industry, is also viewed as an efficient way to deliver information. An instructor commented that it is easier to get students to learn the content of the course if they can "relate the skills to specific job functions." Students expressed the idea that what they wanted to learn needed to be relevant. Evelyn Johnson, a student in the cosmetology program, spoke about her experience in a speech class: "I was in speech class and I didn't want to be there. There's no reason I could think of for having to learn how to give a speech. The instructor talked about how important it was for cosmetologists to learn communication skills, so I sort of agreed that maybe it might make some sense."

These types of challenges to instructors occurred frequently at the college. Students complained to their advisors or their instructors about having to take what they saw as irrelevant courses. Such resistance often took the form of hostility in the classroom with students arriving late, or sometimes refusing to cooperate. Evelyn commented, "I didn't want to be there, but I knew I had to go to graduate; but I just didn't like the class."

The students had strong and definite ideas about the courses they believed were relevant and necessary to prepare themselves for the world of work. They were seeking skills that enabled them to qualify for jobs, and they often rejected or resisted the idea of taking courses that had little meaning to them in their preparation for finding a job. Students were more willing to accept a course if the instructor could place the learning within the context of the job they wanted to perform, even if the learning objectives seemed menial and rote.

Instructors felt frustration from what they believed was the students' refusal to learn. Comments from faculty reflected their frustration: "These students are not motivated." Or, "They don't have any goals." Faculty directed most of their criticism at younger students—those who were just out of high school—because, as one faculty member noted, "They don't know why they are here or where

they are going." Another instructor commented on what he perceived as student indifference to learning: "Some of them are just
here for the check. You see them lined up for their Pell Grants, and
then you don't see them for the rest of the quarter."

An academic administrator reflected on the differences between
older students who were goal-oriented and younger students who
seemed to be unmotivated. She praised returning adult students,
who seemed to know exactly what they wanted from their education at Vocational: "Older students are a delight. They have definite goals. They have other responsibilities. Sometimes they have
kids, a job, and they have considerably less time than the younger
students. They are often a pleasure to work with because you know
they are serious."

Many students entered vocational programs to find a way out
of the cycle of low-skilled, low-paying factory or service jobs and
unemployment. They believed that by returning to school they could
improve their lives. One student, a twenty-nine-year-old African-
American woman had been out of school for ten years. She had
been cleaning houses and working in restaurants after high school.
She was entering the business education program because, "You can
get seven or eight dollars an hour to start."

Some students did indeed choose their paths out of poverty
through vocational education. They expressed a desire to get a good
job, but the completion rates in many of the vocational programs
had been low, particularly among the younger students. As we noted
earlier, faculty characterized younger students as lacking direction
or as less serious than older students. Faculty cited disruptive behavior, lack of attention, and hostile attitudes as evidence that younger
students lacked commitment. The following is excerpted from our
field notes and concerns a student in a communication course. The
student, Morris, is a twenty-year-old African-American male:

*Morris sits in his chair with the desk turned around and his back is to
the teacher. He seems invisible to the other students. His head is down
on his desk. He raises his head from time to time to look around and
then returns to his resting position. In the middle of the lecture, Morris
raises his hand and says to the instructor as he rises from his chair: "I've
got to go." Morris leaves the classroom and does not return.*

From the point of view of faculty and staff, Morris' behavior demonstrates a lack of respect for the instructor and disinterest in the class activities. Students, however, have a different interpretation. One student in the class said, "The teacher is really boring. I don't think this is for me." Others bragged about the number of times they have cut the class because it is such a "waste of time." We encounter this type of resistance to the educational process when students cannot connect the information conveyed in the classrooms to their lives and as a result become bored and disconnected in the process. The instructor explained, "The skills presented in the course had relevance to any setting." But Morris and many of his classmates resisted the message and the knowledge offered by the instructor.

For older students who returned to Vocational, there seems to be a different level of motivation and interest. Faculty and staff expressed pleasure over the dedication of the older students. One older student, a white male in his late twenties, commented on his motivation for returning: "My last job was washing dishes. I need to get a better job." The fact that the job they were being trained for paid little more than minimum wage seemed to have little impact. Older students appeared eager to learn the specific skills being taught in the nurse's aid course that would qualify them for placement in a hospital or nursing home. Their eager acceptance of the ideology of the institution and their compliance with the instructor's directions were in direct contrast with the behaviors and attitudes of some of the younger students such as Morris. Older students' views of the institution were largely uncritical and complimentary of the faculty and the staff. Notions of racism, classism, or the inequity of opportunity did not enter their analysis of employment opportunities. Rather, they returned to a familiar refrain: "I've got to get a job."

Younger students, on the other hand, often complained about the lack of job opportunities they faced regardless of whether they get a degree from Vocational. Several of the African-American students in particular talked about the racist attitudes of some of their instructors and the demeaning way in which they were sometimes addressed. An African-American woman in the nursing program, which has a ratio of fifteen White students for every one African-

American student, complained that she is oftentimes ignored by her instructors: "The faculty don't seem to care if I need advice or information. The professors make me feel like I don't know anything." Another African-American student noted a similar feeling: "The faculty have the attitude that all we [African-American students] want to do is get the check [Pell Grants]. They don't have to say anything. I can tell by their attitude that they don't think we want to learn anything. They have a bad attitude toward us because we're Black and we're poor." The fact that younger students were not only critical of the educational experience at Vocational but also of faculty attitudes relating to racial matters highlights an interesting and perplexing difference between younger students and older students. We return to this issue later in this chapter.

Up to this point, we have examined the ideological messages delivered by the college, and the varying degrees of resistance to and acceptance of such messages by the students. In the next section, we discuss how students analyze the economic conditions of their community in making choices about their careers.

The Changing Economy The fact that these are changing times also had an important impact on the students and the decisions they made about their working lives. As Lois Weis (1990) points out, the de-industrialization of America has changed the nature of the American economy:

The American economy has changed drastically within recent years and the jobs upon which the working class built their existence have severely eroded. What is important for current purposes is that the landscape of the American economy has changed and that this represents a permanent shift which affects not only the Traditional Proletariat but all Americans. (p. 6)

Similarly, Kincheloe (1995) suggests that in a postindustrial economy, the poor have a remote chance for ever achieving social mobility (under present economic and educational structures). He suggests that educational institutions will continue to face the consequences of students who have little to look forward to except absurdly low wages and low-skilled employment opportunities.

In Vocational's home county, tobacco was the dominant crop of the local economy, but the changing fortunes of the tobacco industry, and the decline of family farming in the area in general, have changed the face of the community. In addition to agriculture, the rural south was also home to the textile industry that provided large numbers of jobs for unskilled laborers. As the nation shifted from an industrial to a service economy, many factories closed or relocated to Mexico and other developing nations in search of cheap labor. Around the county, many factories have closed down, including a local shoe factory which had been a major employer. An administrator at Vocational commented:

When the shoe company closed its plant here and moved to Mexico, that left a lot of people unemployed. We had a program for displaced workers. The women who worked there, making slippers, they were all Black. Most of them had limited schooling. They were reading below the seventh grade level. They came back here for school. To get their GED.

With plant closings and the diminution of manufacturing jobs in general, a way of life has changed for the lower and working classes throughout the county. In the past, high school graduates, or even those with less than high school degrees, could count on finding a job on the shop floor. These jobs, of course, were low-skilled, low-paying factory jobs in deplorable working conditions. The idea of empowered workers participating in dignified work with opportunities for participation in the decisions of the company was a foreign concept in these rural manufacturing centers. The factory or mill town, once common in the south, is being quickly replaced with a late twentieth-century version. Now, low-paying service jobs dominate the employment opportunities in the area surrounding Vocational Community College. These jobs tend to be filled on a temporary basis and certainly do not seem suited for lifelong employment. Thus, the only constant in nearby communities is that workers continue to toil in dehumanizing and degrading labor.

Many students enter Vocational to help them find a way out of their economic quagmire. The students also face a critical decision regarding their futures. Because the community has not attracted the kind of industries that would support relatively high-paying mid-level technical work, the students must decide whether they want to leave the area or toil for very low wages. One of the deans at Vocational elaborated on this problem:

We can get the students motivated. We tell them how to get jobs, and we get them to enroll in the vocational programs. But there's got to be something for them when they get out. We need more than $4.25 an hour jobs for them to go to. If they get training here, they've got to move away, and a lot of them don't want to move.

What is reflected here is part of the struggle of Vocational Community College. Students want to improve their social conditions, and they would like to obtain a degree to qualify for better jobs. They face the reality, however, that they will not find good jobs in their communities and they must make the decision of whether or not to leave the area. A staff member offered the following comments about a student with whom he is concerned:

I know this student. He's an architectural assistant. Got his degree [at Vocational], but there weren't any openings here, so he got a job in the state capital. He makes a good wage, but he doesn't want to move. He commutes about one and half hours to work. He wants to move back, and he may open his own business here.

The students base their decisions to pursue vocational or technical degrees on tangible structural conditions concerning what is available in the labor market. The local economy supports a limited number of professional jobs, a dwindling number of low-skilled factory positions, a growing number of minimum-wage service jobs, and relatively few mid-level technical jobs. The state economy, however, is healthy; there are opportunities for students with postsecondary credentials. The students perceive the advantages in pursuing technical degrees, particularly in light of the economy and their own personal needs. Because many of these students experience a feeling of economic urgency to find work, any long-range plan for four-year degrees seems out of reach. When students were asked whether they considered a four-year degree, they often stated they considered it, but "maybe sometime down the line" they would return to school and continue their education.

Discussion

The evidence presented here suggests that students at Vocational make decisions about their careers based on a combination of factors. For example, students examine the employment conditions of the area in light of their personal needs. Many students cannot envision leaving the area as family and community ties keep them bound to local economic prospects. They are left to examine where they might fit into the local and regional labor market. And, of course, Vocational Community College plays a central role in shaping students' understandings of the labor market and setting expectations of what particular students might achieve and hence pursue as a vocational program. This suggests that the emergence of a sense of worker identity is the by-product of multiple forces, many of which are interactive. For example, the types of vocational programs offered by Vocational reflects to a significant degree the perceived job opportunities in the region. Also, faculty attitudes about student abilities get reflected in classroom expectations and in the career advice faculty offer to students. Faculty expectations of students and administrators' perceptions of work force opportunities become interconnected and form a significant part of the organizational culture of Vocational. Students experience the culture in conjunction with many of the qualities they bring to the institution. The result is a whole host of behaviors and attitudes ranging from compliance with institutional goals and objectives to the type of resistance evidenced by Morris.

The point is that students and their self-perceptions as workers do not develop in a vacuum; the institution plays a major role in how these perceptions get formed. As Weis (1990) points out, students are encouraged or constrained by a variety of institutional factors. And Willis (1977) highlights how students make decisions about their lives based on "penetrations"—experiences with educational and social institutions that shape understandings of where students believe they belong in society. In analyzing the student experience at Vocational, one must keep in mind that the culture of the institution promotes the development of a work force for the state's businesses and industries, and plays a major role in directing students to consider vocational and technical careers.

Students' aspirations are shaped through their experiences with their lived world, and they base their goals on what they believe is possible. The students find that the curricular organization and structural arrangements of Vocational Community College form pathways that lead from specific course offerings to specific job opportunities. The arrangements between Vocational and the local employment sector provide little flexibility for students; because of the emphasis on developing task competencies, students are prepared in the most narrow sense and in most cases are unable to transfer competencies to other career possibilities. The fact that the courses are arranged to match the job functions within the local economy provides students immediate job opportunities, but does little to broaden their overall skills or advance the notion of lifelong learning.

Vocational's organization is based on the idea that it is preparing students to enter the work force. The way the courses are organized and the manner in which the course material is delivered reflect the needs of business and industry. Course content is broken down to match specific competencies that employers desire from their employees. Knowledge in the classroom is fragmented into pieces whereby students are judged on how well they master the individual parts. This decontextualization of learning corresponds to much of the work available in the local economy. A holistic view of work seems unnecessary because employees are expected to become proficient at specific and repeatable tasks. The idea that institutions would teach students to think critically about the tasks they are performing, as one would expect in Kincheloe's (1995) conceptualization of good work, seems absurd in the present workplace. Students, after all, are being trained to perform specific tasks and there is little demand for individuals to be critical participants in high-tech assembly lines. In fact, judging by the way most faculty at Vocational structure their classrooms, faculty clearly believe employers prefer docile, compliant workers who just do what they are told. If docility is desired by employers, then community colleges such as Vocational are right in line with meeting the needs of prospective employers.

Vocational defines knowledge such that it corresponds directly with what students need to know to obtain a specific job. The convergence of faculty and staff expectations and the knowledge of what students need to qualify for a vocation leaves a deep impression on students and their perceptions of what constitutes the world of work. Students insist that the courses they take ought to have direct relevance to their career goals. They are much more eager to learn when instructors place the course material within an authentic job context. When knowledge seems to have little relevance to their lives and to the world of work, instructors have a more difficult time convincing students of its importance. Mathematics courses in particular seem distant to many of Vocational's students and their expectations of the work setting; the memorization of algorithms does not seem to have any connection to anything they expect to do in their lives. To add to the problem, faculty at Vocational have great difficulty in helping students make connections between classroom learning and life's broad experiences. In fact, most faculty and staff are so caught up in careerism that students are rarely thought of in a holistic sense; instead, students are seen mostly as prospective workers and the other facets of their lives remain invisible.

Interestingly, younger students in particular are the most intolerant of any forms of knowledge that appear marginal to their goals. Traditional-age students at Vocational are at a point in their lives where dreams of a better future meet the realities of economic opportunity for the lower and working classes. There is a sense among the younger students that the options Vocational offers are insufficient to meet their expectations and hopes for social mobility. Vocational's curricula, after all, prepares students for working-class careers in an economy that provides few options. For many of the younger students, the promise of Vocational Community College was falling short of their own visions as workers in our society. In a very real sense, their hopes for improved economic opportunities must be deposited at the doorway to Vocational Community College as the curriculum, the classrooms, and the expectations of faculty and staff limit the range of possibilities. The result is a leveling of aspirations. The frustration of having to lower one's aspirations left many of the younger students with low motivation and the desire to leave VCC altogether.

Older students tend to have different perceptions of their role in the work force and of social mobility. The messages conveyed by Vocational do not seem out of line with the expectations of many of these students. Little resistance is offered and for the most part the older students move passively through their vocational programs and into the labor force. The older students attribute their motivation to a need to find employment and to lift them out of their present economic conditions. Older students seem to turn a deaf ear to the economic inequalities they face and accept an unfair system and make the best of it. They see Vocational as an opportunity to avoid poverty and not so much as a ticket to social mobility, which is the hope of many of the younger students.

What seems clear in this case study is that the sorting and selecting of lower- and working-class students into working-class jobs by the institution, as suggested by previous critical analyses of education and the community college (Bowles & Gintis, 1976; Brint & Karabel, 1989), occurs through complex interactive processes that must be understood through a phenomenological case study approach. There is much that is explained by structural accounts of schooling. However, what is missing is an in-depth understanding of localized processes that contribute to shaping students' choices. Such understanding is key to efforts to alter educational contexts and structures. The types of responses and interpretations students offer to the educational processes they are confronted with are central to understanding how change might occur. Structural explanations fail to reveal how lower- and working-class students form understandings of their identities as students and as workers. The students at Vocational demonstrate how their perceptions are formed and influenced through their experiences and contact with the institution's culture. In the case of younger students at Vocational, many are disillusioned not only with education, but with the pitiful employment opportunities they expect to find once they finish college. Many believe the two or three years they spend at Vocational will be a waste of time because the kind of job they will get is something they could be trained for in a matter of weeks. For them, taking advanced mathematics or improving their communication and analytical skills makes little sense.

Vocational Community College is caught in its own double bind: It expects students to be excited and motivated about learning essential skills, such as those typically developed in mathematics and writing courses, and at the same time offers courses that involve nothing more than rote memorization of tasks as preparation for specific jobs that are hardly interesting to young people with dreams of having a better life than their parents. It is no wonder that many of the younger students resist both types of learning. One seems irrelevant and the other offers no challenge.

Implications for Multiculturalism

Vocational Community College is organized to facilitate what it believes is the best way to attend to the needs of its community. In the face of all the problems associated with rural communities in the state, it has organized itself to prepare students to enter the work force. This close connection with business and industry has influenced the culture of the institution as well as the curricular organization of the college. The relationship has also forged an ideological stance concerning what constitutes knowledge and what students need to internalize to become productive workers.

The idea that community colleges need to provide vocational education to their constituents is an essential part of the community college mission. Providing students with skills to enter the work force serves the needs of students and the community. What we suggest, however, is that community colleges need to move beyond the idea that they are merely providing job training and socialization to a particular work force. Community colleges need to envision a broader view of vocational education if they are truly to serve as a democratizing force. To expect students to spend two to three years of their lives developing specific skills for a position that may not exist five years down the road is an injustice to the lower-class, working-class, and minority students who attend such institutions.

Community colleges need to adopt a different vision of vocational education. A critical multicultural view of vocational education places emphasis on the validation of student knowledge. As Kincheloe (1995) maintains, this is particularly important for students of color and low-income students, whose sense of identity is often undermined and whose knowledge is ridiculed or dismissed by the dominant culture of education:

The dominant discourse of schooling teaches us that the difference in occupational and educational achievement is basically the consequence of ability variations among individuals. Educational experts induce students to believe that class and status-based divisions of students and workers are natural and necessary. Students from outside the mainstream, the non-white and the poor are entangled in the myths of cultural and academic inferiority. (p. 33)

A critical multicultural perspective opens the possibility for lower- and working-class students as well as culturally diverse students to share and build upon the stores of knowledge and abilities that they bring to campus by teachers who intentionally incorporate students' experiences into the pedagogical process.

Vocational Community College presents contrasting views of how students sought educational knowledge. Older students eagerly lay claim to knowledge they believe will help them find employment. Some of the younger students, however, resist the knowledge that the institution believes they need to be employable. This is particularly true when the institution offers skills that are not tied specifically to the workplace. Younger students have little motivation to learn math or speech because those skills are outside the realm defined by the institution as needed for a specific job function. Because the college and industry have defined work and knowledge in a narrow sense, a broad view of knowledge seems irrelevant to students. Students such as Morris sense the irrelevancy of math or communication to the workplace, reject the idea of learning it, and prefer rote memorization of specific tasks if given a choice. A broader view of good work incorporates the need for learning how to communicate, analyze problems, or compute. Such a view challenges employers to create more democratic work settings in which employees have the opportunity to participate in important aspects of the labor process. Workers prepared for a democratic workplace find that skills such as critical thinking, communication, and creativity are essential to being full participants of a working team.

Developing students to be democratic participants in the work force implies that community colleges must challenge prospective employers to establish more participatory work environments. From such a perspective, the community college does not merely exist to serve employers; it also serves the well-being of its students and community residents as it challenges companies and businesses to modify their structural arrangements as a means to improve employee conditions through a more democratic work space.

Of course, a critical multicultural vision of vocational education means adopting more democratic and transformative classrooms and pedagogies. Classrooms that incorporate the views and perspectives of lower- and working-class students also open up the conversation to include important discussions of race, class, gender, and their relations to power and social mobility. We know that community colleges predominantly serve lower- and working-class students and that many will choose working-class jobs. A critical multicultural classroom encourages discussion of the structures of society that influence students to make such decisions. The interrogation of the relationship of power, education, and the workplace increases the opportunities for students to explore these issues and leads to understanding and questioning of their positions in society. There is nothing inherently wrong with lower- and working-class students following working-class ideals, as long as they make such choices from an informed position in which they are knowledgeable of the other options available to them and free to make such choices. A true democracy allows for social mobility and thus prepares all students to be informed participants in not only the political and social life of a society, but its economic sectors as well.

Classrooms that are open to critical discussions and analyses of forces surrounding social mobility and the world of work offer a return to the Deweyan ideal of education that provides students with a sense of social understanding that propels them to become transformative individuals in a democratic society. Career education that incorporates a democratic spirit engages students and invites them to contribute their sources of knowledge and understanding. Democratic classrooms, therefore, are interested in students as whole persons and do not view students as mere objects to be modified or fitted into the economy. Students educated in democratic classrooms learn to become good workers who develop creative and analytical skills as well as a participatory spirit.

As we have indicated, Vocational Community College is structured to provide trained students to fill jobs in the local economy.

Instructors design courses to meet the expectations of employers. Students not only receive specific job training, but also learn the ideology of work to help them make the transition to the workplace. Students who learn the tasks well are rewarded and typically find employment related to their vocational preparation. Students who resist the ideology of the institution are sanctioned or lose favor with the institution. The trouble with this system is the exclusionary nature of the practices that are intolerant of dissension or that fail to explore the dissatisfaction of the students. In addition, the system is designed to train students to incorporate specific views and to learn specific job tasks. The problem is that the mastery of a task today becomes tomorrow's obsolete skill.

Because students learn only specific skills to fill specific positions, they have not been given the wherewithal to make adjustments that would allow them to adapt to other types of industries. The classrooms are designed to break tasks down into component parts and to drill students until they become adept at specific tasks. Students become masters at learning decontextualized skills, but lack the understanding of how these parts fit together. Education for good work encourages an analysis of the whole and exploration of the underlying theoretical concepts that apply to the job. As an example, students who learn how to repair automobiles may also learn the underlying concepts of chemistry, physics, and mathematics and how they are applied to auto mechanics. In this way, students learn mathematics and science through authentic activities and gain an understanding of how these concepts have connections to their everyday lives. Even if their current job is eliminated in the future, the students still have the theoretical constructs that can be applied in other settings.

A critical multicultural view encourages students to understand the society in which they live, their role in society, and the part they might play in shaping that role. Students need all the information they can get before they make decisions about their lives. Some of the students at Vocational Community College see through a social and economic structure that limits their opportunities and seeks to situate them firmly within working-class roles. Changing this opportunity structure requires a change in society. Such a change might begin with a restructuring of education so that students learn about democratic work and how to become democratic participants. This means that institutions must encourage students to become analytical and thoughtful about the structure of society in order to become contributing citizens in a democracy.

Summary

This chapter provides an analysis of the interactions between the organizational culture of Vocational Community College and students' emerging sense of worker identity. We examined the way knowledge, as defined by the institution, is organized, packaged, and delivered to vocational students and how students react to such pedagogical practices. Through an analysis of Vocational, we have examined the processes through which lower- and working-class students construct their identities as students and as workers. We have examined how students enter the community college and form identities and make career choices through their interactions in the community college.

Because knowledge is defined by the institution as information that students need to take with them into the world of work, students had a variety of reactions to the message delivered. The courses at Vocational were designed to integrate the specific job functions in the workplace into their classroom work. Students understood that they needed to master these specific objectives to become employable. When the institution offered knowledge that was outside the narrow band that was defined by the institution to include knowledge needed in the workplace, students tended to reject the message. This resistance to the message of the institution was interpreted by faculty to be hostility or a lack of commitment on the part of the student. Faculty and staff frequently cited the contrast between older and younger students, and complimented the work ethic and commitment of the older students.

The challenge Vocational faces is to reorganize itself to include a broader concept of what constitutes education for work. Vocational education that trains students to master specific job skills for specific jobs in the economy fails to activate the strengths of the students. Critical multiculturalism challenges community colleges to adopt a perspective that strives to include the strengths and the knowledge of the lower and working classes. In this way, students are more likely to become engaged participants in a democratic classroom, and are better prepared to become democratic workers.

Chapter Four
Education as Celebratory Socialization

A Case Study of an Immigrant Education Program

In this chapter we examine an immigrant education center situated at Outreach Community College. The program, known as Nuevos Horizontes (New Horizons), is an extension of Outreach and is located in a nearby suburb. We focus on how the program encourages immigrant students to learn about their new culture in the United States, while at the same time helping students retain the cultural heritage they bring to the college. In a very real sense, these students must learn to be bicultural.

Central to our discussion throughout this chapter is what we term "celebratory socialization." We borrow from John Van Maanen's (1983) work on organizational socialization in which he discusses socialization practices that involve welcoming and confirming ceremonies enacted to promote the development of attitudes and abilities new members bring to an organization. As Van Maanen notes, "Socialization agents may wish to take advantage of whatever attitudes and skills entering members already possess and, therefore, do what is possible to encourage recruits to exhibit and further refine such attributes. Socialization under these conditions is principally celebratory and benign, involving welcoming and confirming ceremonies" (p. 212).

Our view of celebratory socialization, however, extends beyond merely the abilities and attitudes new and diverse members may bring to an organization; organizations also need to consider the multiple forms of knowledge and ways of understanding diverse members might possess. In other words, celebratory socialization processes support a multicultural mission by embracing border knowledge. Unlike traditional views of socialization that seek to assimilate new members to the society or organization, and thereby erase cultural differences brought by entering members, celebratory socialization embraces cultural differences. And whereas traditional socialization processes silence border knowledge, celebratory socialization welcomes border knowledge as a means to transform and diversify the organizational culture.

What is suggested in this chapter is a bidirectional view of socialization in that both the new member and the organization are transformed by contact with the other. Such a view of organizational socialization is discussed by William Tierney and Robert Rhoads (1993) in their treatment of faculty socialization. They argue that socialization's purpose is twofold. On the one hand, socialization is a process that builds commitment and loyalty to an organization. Ideally, this occurs as new members learn more about an organization's culture. "On the other hand, since an organization's culture is interpretive and dynamic, as new members enter the institution it is resocialized. We are suggesting that since an organization's culture exists as a product of social relations, as new members engage the organization they are able to change it" (p. 22).

In examining the Nuevos Horizontes immigrant education center, we apply the concept of celebratory socialization to highlight how the cultural background of students is embraced by the center and its educational activities. We also use this concept to point out how colleges and universities need to think about how to create socialization processes that are bidirectional, and thus provide opportunities for diverse members to reshape the organization. However, before we discuss Nuevos Horizontes in relation to the preceding issues, we provide some background information about the college and the surrounding area.

Organizational Background

Outreach Community College is located in a major urban center in the midwestern region of the United States. Founded in 1964, the college serves twenty-three communities with a combined population of nearly 320,000. During a typical semester, Outreach provides services for 20,000 students. The college offers programs in continuing education, adult basic education, and career education, and awards associate's degrees in both the arts and sciences in thirty-five different majors. Outreach has established a transfer center to assist students in pursuing a four-year degree. All courses in the arts and sciences at Outreach have been approved for transfer to particular state universities and colleges within the state. The same, however, is not true of career education, where only some of the courses are transferable.

Issues of cultural diversity have become increasingly important to faculty and administrators at Outreach. Underrepresented students constitute approximately thirty-one percent of the student body. Eleven percent of the students at Outreach are Hispanic[1], a figure that represents nearly a threefold increase since 1984. Part of the reason for the increase in Outreach's Hispanic student population is due to immigration. Another factor is age: Over fifty percent of all Hispanics in the area are under the age of twenty-five. The breakdown of the Hispanic population in the area is as follows: sixty-nine percent Mexican American, seven percent Puerto Rican, seven percent South American, five percent Cuban, four percent Central American, and seven percent of other origin.

Despite a recent increase in the Hispanic student population, Outreach has been unsuccessful in forming a diverse faculty; as of 1993, only one out of 214 full-time instructors is Hispanic. The number of Hispanic faculty at Outreach is obviously a serious problem, especially in terms of creating a diverse campus environment where Hispanic students have role models and mentors to whom they might turn. The lack of a diverse faculty has become a concern among some at Outreach, and the most recent strategic planning document describes Strategic Goal # 3, which deals with the institutionalization of a student-oriented/staff development plan to create an effective organizational climate. A component of Strategic Goal # 3 is to develop a recruitment plan to increase the hirings of minorities.

Although the formal discourse of Outreach Community College speaks about the importance of minority recruitment efforts for faculty and staff, other discourses are contradictory. For example, we met with some key personnel at the college to discuss an instrument designed to assess an institution's commitment to multiculturalism. What we failed to understand going in to this meeting is that the instrument makes little sense if those using it are not committed to the goals of multiculturalism, which was clearly the case for these individuals. Others at the college, who *are* committed to multicultural educational efforts, expressed their concern about the lack of broad institutional support for multiculturalism. As one administrator mentioned: "I question how serious some members of the upper administration are to creating a more diverse faculty. It doesn't show in recent hirings."

In other areas, Outreach has done a far better job. For example, the college has recognized the need to provide specific services for its diverse constituents. In a recent college document, the president commented that, "The college population is in the process of evolution. . . . In order to reach the college's goals, in the next ten years, we need to reach out, to go to the community." The strategic plan talks about creating additional outreach centers in the district similar to Nuevos Horizontes. Many of the faculty and staff who were interviewed spoke about the plans to serve large pockets of African-American, Polish, and Hispanic residents. As one staff member noted, "The idea is to serve people who have either immigrated or who have had a poor experience with education. They may not understand how college works. The outreach centers give them the exposure they need, within their own community. That's the uniqueness of it—reaching people within their own communities."

The Local Community

Outreach Community College is located in a suburb (Montego Park) of a large metropolitan area, which serves as a hub between the eastern and western sections of the United States. The economy is characterized by its diversified enterprises, which include the production of steel, metal products, food products, chemicals, and communications and electronics equipment. The metropolitan area has attracted a significant population of immigrants originating primarily from Latin America, Eastern Europe, and Asia. The immigrant population adds to the cultural diversity of the area, which is considered by many to be a cultural center and is known for its jazz, blues, and classical music.

The demographic breakdown of the suburban district served by Outreach is as follows: seventy-five percent are white, sixteen percent are black, and eight percent are Hispanic. Although whites make up the largest group within Outreach's district, their numbers have decreased by fourteen percent since 1980 at the same time that the Hispanic population increased by eighty percent. Much of the increase can be attributed to immigration.

The growing size of the Hispanic population in the area is one reason that Outreach Community College has seen a need to provide special services for Hispanic residents. Another reason relates to educational achievement of Hispanics in the area. Forty percent of Hispanics within the district who are twenty-five years of age or older have not achieved a high school diploma. This compares to twenty-five percent for non-Hispanics. These figures compare to national findings that also reveal high attrition rates for Hispanic college students (Nora & Rendon, 1988), and low transfer rates for Hispanic community college students (Rendon, 1993). Unemployment rates for district Hispanics, male and female, are also higher than for non-Hispanics: The unemployment rate for male Hispanics is 6.7 percent compared to 5.2 percent for non-Hispanics, and the rate is 8.4 percent for female Hispanics and 4.4 percent for non-Hispanic females.

The demographic, educational achievement, and employment data all highlight a need to direct Outreach's resources toward programs for Hispanic residents. Nuevos Horizontes is the central organizational structure in Outreach's efforts to serve Hispanic residents, and the center symbolizes the college's commitment to reaching out to its constituent communities.

Although Nuevos Horizontes theoretically serves all the communities within Outreach's district, the reality is that most of its students and clients come from the local community of Montego Park. Montego Park has the highest percentage of Hispanic residents of all the communities in the district: twenty-three percent of all Hispanics in the district live in Montego Park, and thirty percent of Montego Park's residents are Hispanic. The overall per capita income of the community for all residents is $13,249 compared to $8,931 for Hispanic residents. Nearly eight percent of all residents in Montego Park exist below the poverty level, the great majority of whom are Hispanic (ninety-three percent).

The Findings

Nuevos Horizontes, also formally referred to as Outreach College Community Center, was founded in 1981 as an outreach center to provide educational opportunities to Outreach's diverse communities. The goal of Nuevos is threefold: (1) to promote and facilitate access to higher education among Hispanic and other students; (2) to provide educational programs and services to enable immigrant adults to become productive and responsible parents, employees, and citizens; and (3) to inform the community of educational and cultural opportunities available at Outreach.

The Center is located in a small building along the main thoroughfare of Montego Park. A large storefront sign written in both Spanish and English reflects the commitment of Nuevos to bilingual education. The "Nuevos Horizontes" sign adds to a host of businesses that clearly signify Montego Park's Hispanic influence. Other businesses include El Palacio de las Novias, Hardware Jimenez, La Casa Latina Grocery, La Esmeralda Super Carniceria, Los Amigos Supermarket, and Salinas Shoe Store: Zapatos Para Toda La Familia. The angled parking on both sides of the streets and the Spanish store signs give the main thoroughfare of Montego Park a Southwestern motif.

Maria Vasquez is the director of Nuevos Horizontes. She stands about five feet tall and is in constant motion. Maria moves from one task to the next with a clearness of purpose that is rare and has but one overarching concern guiding her work—improving the lives of the residents of Montego Park and the surrounding communities.

Maria is an immigrant herself, having come to the United States from Guatemala. She understands many of the problems local residents face in their adjustment to new cultural surroundings. "I know what it's like to have to learn a new language, new customs, and a new way of life. It's been difficult at times for me, but it's easier when you have a place to go or other people to turn to. That's one of the purposes we serve here at the center."

Maria adopts "Hispanic" as a self-identifier, although she acknowledges that many of the younger students (traditional college age) seem to prefer the term "Latino" or "Latina." For some younger people, Maria noted, "Saying Latino is a way of taking more pride in who we are." A female student involved in programs at Nuevos Horizontes explained, "Hispanic relates more to the language, whereas Latino highlights our culture. By preferring to call ourselves 'Latina' or 'Latino' we are trying to make a statement about what it means to be Hispanic. We take pride in our heritage. It's an effort to change our own attitudes as well as those of others."

Although much of Maria's activities are geared for Spanish-speaking residents, she is quite cognizant of the need to be inclusive regardless of one's cultural background. Nonetheless, because of the prominence of Hispanic residents, most of the programs and activities coordinated by Nuevos Horizontes reflect their needs. "Nuevos Horizontes is exciting. We get to do a lot of things for people. We feel we are a part of the community." She describes her vision of Nuevos Horizontes: "Our main goal is to help students to learn the system. Forty percent of our students every semester are new, and we want them to become independent. Most of our staff [both full-time and volunteers] are immigrants, so we know how overwhelming it is at times."

In terms of services, Nuevos Horizontes offers a variety of programs, classes, and workshops: Outreach Community College admission information; academic counseling; citizenship classes; community agency information; cultural events; English as a Second Language (ESL) classes; general education classes; free legal advice about immigration and naturalization policies; registration for ESL and GED classes; tax preparation assistance and classes; tutoring in Spanish literacy, English, and math; and a variety of workshops designed to meet the specific needs of Hispanic students, parents, and immigrants. One workshop offered by Nuevos Horizontes, the "Parents Education Program," deals with some of the communication problems immigrant parents have with their children, who often are immersed in English-speaking schools and U.S. student subcultures. Maria commented on advice she offers to immigrant parents: "Your children are now learning English and American culture. You also need to learn it, or you cannot communicate with your children. At the same time, it's your job to teach your heritage. No one else is going to do it. You have to."

A question that ought to be asked of all immigrant education programs relates to issues of cultural identity: How do people learn a new language or a new culture without losing their own sense of culture? The following response from Maria is helpful: "We want people who come here to see that the Center is part of the culture. We can keep our own culture. We can add another culture. We can add other languages. We cannot forget who we are. If we don't have our own identity, how are we going to grow?" Maria went on to add, "We never say, 'This is it. You are in the United States. Forget about your culture.' You can be bilingual." Maria's comments highlight a fundamental component of multicultural education: the celebration of cultural difference and diverse identities as opposed to the homogenization of cultural identities.

One way that Nuevos Horizontes helps students to learn English and at the same time maintain their beliefs and convictions about the diverse Latin American cultures is by offering a wide variety of reading materials dealing with Hispanic peoples and issues, but written in English. Nuevos Horizontes has its own modest library. Many of these works are written by Hispanic authors and have been translated into English. Staff at Nuevos Horizontes believe that helping students to recognize the strong literary tradition of Latin America is important because many of the local schools and colleges do not adequately deal with this literature.

Probably no single program signifies the commitment of Nuevos Horizontes to Hispanic cultures more than "HispanoFest." HispanoFest is a two-week cultural celebration coinciding with Hispanic Heritage Month. The culmination of the two-week celebration is a two-day festival held in Montego Park. HispanoFest originated in 1990 and attracts not only residents of Montego Park but residents from throughout the district. A Nuevos Horizontes staff member talked about the reasons behind the creation of HispanoFest:

We had an art and writing contest with the elementary school children. We got the local businesses involved. We could not believe the response. It was overwhelming. We had to form subcommittees to evaluate all the submissions. We gave prizes to each grade level—dictionaries and Outreach Community College sweatshirts donated by the president. More important though was what we learned. We noticed there was a lot of low self-esteem. Not only in the art work but in the writing too. We felt that we needed to do something on a larger scale to bring the community together, to let people in the Hispanic community share their culture with others so that the children learn that their culture is important, is special. And that it is good to share with others. Some of the children felt that they should not speak Spanish, that Spanish was inferior. So what we decided to do was to have a festival to celebrate our culture and our language. We came up with the idea of HispanoFest.

During the two-day festival that marks the culmination of HispanoFest, the main street of Montego Park is closed and booths are set up in which artists, musicians, and merchants share their goods and talents with visitors. Each year the event has grown. "We ask people from around the area to come and share *our* culture. To Hispanics who live here, we ask them to come and share '*your* culture' with others," explained Maria.

HispanoFest involves a great deal of collaboration with local business people. A local merchant commented on why he gets involved in HispanoFest, both in terms of his time and financial contributions: "It's more than the benefit we get as a business. It's an opportunity to give something back to my customers. Helping Nuevos Horizontes and HispanoFest is a way to say thank you." All proceeds generated by HispanoFest go to a student scholarship fund for deserving students of Hispanic origin. This past year four full-year scholarships to Outreach were awarded.

Efforts such as those behind HispanoFest are necessary to battle some of the resentment and discrimination faced by Hispanics in the area. Although there has been a significant increase in the Hispanic population of Montego Park, they are still the minority (recall that Hispanics constitute thirty percent of the population of Montego Park). Over recent years, much resentment has been stirred by the changing demographics of the area. For example, in a recent article published in a monthly publication funded by the Village of Montego Park, a local resident attacked the immigration policy of the U.S. and local policies dealing with illegal aliens. In Rush Limbaugh fashion, the article provides a whole host of refutable statistics that to acknowledge here would give them greater credence than they deserve. Clearly, the effort is to generate contempt for immigrants and policies pertaining to immigration. The real problem, however, is not the author's disdain for immigrants. What is particularly pernicious about the article is that it equates illegal immigrants with Hispanics, as if they are one and the same. No mention is made of any other cultural group. This type of discourse of hate that contributes to passage of legislation such as

California Proposition 187 is harmful to all Hispanics. Maria Vasquez was outraged by the article and took steps to organize a response from Hispanic residents of Montego Park. She found it reprehensible that a community-sponsored publication would not attempt to still such hostility.

HispanoFest as an activity symbolizes the commitment of Nuevos Horizontes to celebrating Hispanic cultures and heritage and to battling some of the negative stereotypes and hostilities directed at Hispanics in the area and around the country. The center's physical setting sends a similar message. Nuevos Horizontes is housed in a two-story building. On the first floor is a reception area, a reading room, and two offices. The second floor houses two classrooms in which many of the ESL courses, as well as other programs, are held. The walls throughout the building are decorated with posters, paintings, and plaques, nearly all of which commemorate different aspects of Hispanic cultures as well as education in general. For example, a poster on one of the walls in the reading room portrays a middle-aged man reading a book and reads *Leer Es Poder* (reading is power). In the reception area are four plaques that honor contributors to the HispanoFest program. A variety of works by Hispanic artists hang on the first floor walls including the following: Jose Clemente Orozco's *Las Soldaderas,* Rufino Tamayo's *Man Contemplating the Moon,* and a third entitled *Vestido Con El Sol* (dressed with the sun). One painting depicts some children scrambling for candy as a larger boy, wearing a blindfold and wielding a stick, breaks open a piñata. A Nuevos Horizontes staff person commented on the decor, "We want people who come here to see what other Hispanics have accomplished. That we have culture too."

On the wall of one of the offices is a framed poem written by a Nuevos Horizontes student, who wished to express her gratitude to a center staff member named Lilia. It reads as follows:

> *When I was growing up*
> *I never had a chance to go to school*
> *When I was married*
> *I never had a chance to go to school*
> *When Horacio was born*
> *I never had the time to go to school*

> *When Julio was born*
> *I never thought about my school*
> *When Adrian was born*
> *I was ashame I never went to school*
> *When my children were all grown*
> *I was ashame and afraid to go to school*
> *When I had a terrible accident*
> *I saw a New Horizontes in my life*
> *When I met Lilia I went out on a limb*
> *But, I had the time and desire to go*
> *When I see myself today*
> *I am proud, happy, and say look at me*
> *I can do anything to day*

Lilia helped the author of the poem through a rough period in her life. Lilia expressed great satisfaction in being able to help her after she was badly injured in an auto accident. In discussing the poem and the author's history with Lilia, it was hard to tell whose life was more affected by the other.

The woman whom Lilia helped is one example of Nuevos Horizontes' influence on the lives of Montego Park residents. There are other examples as well. In what follows, we highlight the lives of three students for whom Nuevos Horizontes has been influential.

Carlita Gonzalez is a nineteen-year-old second-year student at Outreach who recently received an award from the Clinton administration for her service to the local community. She was instrumental in organizing a group of youths to build a playground in Montego Park. Maria Vasquez nominated her for the award. Carlita, who came to the U.S. from Mexico with her family when she was five, had nothing but good things to say about Nuevos Horizontes: "It is very useful, very beneficial. Many people come here to take citizenship classes. Nuevos Horizontes plans great activities."

Carlita visits Nuevos Horizontes on a regular basis and often passes the time talking with Maria, whom Carlita sees as a role model. "I like coming here. I come here when I have problems. I get a lot of help and support." Carlita is a full-time student and talks to Maria about her problems with school and her hopes for the future. After she obtains her associate's degree, Carlita's plan is to transfer to a four-year college and get a bachelor's degree in sociology. Her ultimate goal is to work in social services so that she can serve her community: "I want to get a job someday so that I can help young people make something better of their lives. I want to do good for my community just like Maria does."

Romano Suarez, who appears to be in his thirties, came to the U.S. from Mexico about six years ago. He had studied chemistry at a university in Mexico City, but language problems prevented him from pursuing his studies when he came to the States. "When I came here, I wanted to go to school, but I couldn't speak English. When I found out about Nuevos Horizontes, I found out I could do a lot of things." Romano took ESL courses through Nuevos Horizontes and eventually enrolled in classes at Outreach. He also found other programs at Nuevos Horizontes helpful: "I went to all kinds of programs at Nuevos Horizontes: a program on how to manage a checking account. Even programs on drugs and crime. I've learned a lot of things here about the U.S. and how to get along in this country. The center has been invaluable to me." Not long after completing two levels of ESL, Romano was hired by a local bank. Now, he takes classes in the evening at Outreach, where he hopes to get a degree in business administration or computer science. Like Carlita, Romano wants to give back to his community, so he volunteers at the Center by helping people with their income tax forms.

Corrine Bolanos, whom we introduced in chapter 2, gave up on school when she was sixteen. She struggled with her English, and it seemed to her she would never graduate. Several years after leaving school, she stopped by Nuevos Horizontes with her mother and found out about a special bilingual high school completion program. For the first time in years, Corrine gave some thought to returning to school and possibly graduating. She enrolled and eight months later received her high school diploma. Upon graduating, Corrine applied for and later received one of the HispanoFest college scholarships organized by Nuevos Horizontes. Corrine is now in her second semester at Outreach, where she majors in hotel management. "Nuevos Horizontes helps me all the time. Whenever I have a problem at Outreach, I come here and they help me. The center has given me a second chance in life and I hope to make the most of it."

Discussion

Evaluating the success of a college program or unit typically is not an easy task. Unlike the business world where the bottom line—financial profit—is a fairly quick and easy gauge of success, educational programs do not always have clear bottom lines. Community colleges have great difficulty in evaluating the effectiveness of educational programs. One reason for this is the variable completion rates of students, who come from a variety of backgrounds and attend community college for a variety of different reasons (Adelman, 1992). To gauge community college effectiveness by graduation rates is difficult because a large percentage of students enter community college with little to no intent of obtaining a degree (Grubb, 1991). Obviously, students attend community colleges to achieve some educational benefit, but determining the benefit is not always easy.

Despite the complexity of evaluating community college programs, some criteria must be used to gauge whether what we do is, in fact, worth doing. In terms of Nuevos Horizontes, what measures exist that provide indicators of its success or failure?

A member of the board of trustees at Outreach commented on how she evaluates the center: "I evaluate the program by looking at the people involved in it—by looking at the scores of people who line up in front of the building to register for classes." The board member added, "I also look at the quality of programs and the innovative ideas. I look at the exposure: Does the community buy into it? Everybody knows about Nuevos Horizontes."

As the comments from the preceding board member highlight, one indicator of success is the number of people served by the program. For example, in 1993 over 8,000 local residents used the services of Nuevos Horizontes. Obviously, not all of these 8,000 residents enrolled in formalized instruction and became Outreach students, but they nonetheless reaped educational benefits from the Center. Eight thousand is a remarkable figure considering the size of full-time staff (two), and the small facility (two floors, four rooms). Of the more than 8,000 people served, over 2,600 enrolled in Adult Basic Education (ABE) programs or ESL classes.

Another indicator of success relates to the quality of various programs, workshops, or activities. Clearly, HispanoFest has been a huge success. But other programs also stand out. For example, the HIV/

AIDS Education and Prevention Program offered by Nuevos Horizontes received the National 1992 Secretary's Community Health Promotion Award from the U.S. Secretary of Health and Human Development Services. Another program that received much publicity was a naturalization ceremony. In July of 1993, Outreach Community College hosted its first-ever "Citizenship Swearing-In Ceremony," presided over and organized by Nuevos Horizontes staff. Moreover, the citizens were all prepared through programs at the Center. The program was organized in conjunction with the Immigration and Naturalization Service (INS). Sworn in as citizens were sixty-six people originating from Mexico, fourteen from Cuba, six from Guatemala, two from El Salvador, two from Italy, and one person each from Poland, Iraq, and Honduras. Immediately after the ceremony, a reception was held to honor the new citizens, many of whom bypassed the snack table in order to register to vote at another table. The voter registration was organized by Maria Vasquez. The INS District Director commented on why approval was given to hold the ceremony at the college: "The preparation for citizenship should not be a government process. All the community has an interest in this."

An additional indicator of the success of Nuevos Horizontes has been its ability to generate community support. Recently, Nuevos Horizontes cosponsored the first community education conference entitled "Celebrating Partnerships." The conference provided opportunities for local citizens, agencies, and businesses to become actively involved in the area's education and community concerns. The conference was so successful that plans have been made for the conference to become a yearly event.

The success stories of students are perhaps the ultimate indicators of the effectiveness of Nuevos Horizontes. The stories of Carlita, Romano, and Corrine provide rich qualitative data about the center's effectiveness. Carlita seeks guidance about school problems and plans to work in social services—much like Maria Vasquez, a role model for her. Romano polished his English skills at the Center and now has a professional position with a local bank. And Corrine obtained her high school diploma, won a scholarship, and is now a full-time student at Outreach.

What can we learn about Nuevos Horizontes based on the preceding data, programmatic analyses, and student narratives? What are the keys to its success? We discuss seven aspects of Nuevos that we believe contribute to its effectiveness: an emphasis on Hispanic cultures, employing bilingual staff, a commitment to holistic education, physical proximity to the Hispanic community, community and business partnerships that have been developed, individual initiatives on the part of the director, and institutional support from Outreach.

Emphasis on Hispanic Cultures Clearly, Nuevos Horizontes demonstrates a commitment to Hispanic cultures. HispanoFest is the most obvious example. The goal at the Center is to help students become more proficient in English and more knowledgeable about U.S. customs and practices; yet, at the same time, Nuevos Horizontes stresses the importance of celebrating one's own culture. The art work, literature, and posters that appear throughout Nuevos Horizontes send a clear message that Latin American cultures and diverse Hispanic groups are welcomed at the center. A member of the Nuevos Horizontes advisory board commented, "One of the secrets to its success is that Hispanics in the community feel at home there. They walk in the door and the whole place reminds them of their cultural heritage." A staff member at Outreach added, "The word has gotten out to the Hispanic community that Nuevos Horizontes is culturally friendly. They know that when they go there, they don't have to be ashamed of who they are. The whole attitude at Nuevos Horizontes has carried over to our main campus. More and more Hispanics in the area see Outreach as an option for them."

Bilingual Staff Related to its commitment to Hispanic cultures is the fact that staff at the center speak both English and Spanish. Obviously, this is an absolute necessity when serving students and local residents with limited English proficiency. Corrine Bolanos had pretty much given up on her education because of her limited English-speaking abilities. However, when she went to Nuevos Horizontes, she found out from bilingual staff that there were other options for her to complete her degree. Another student was an undocumented immigrant and was fearful of being discovered. He worked for several years, all the while fearing deportation. He wanted to learn more about how to become a resident and then possibly a citizen; but asking questions, especially when his English was poor, was dangerous. At Nuevos Horizontes he found staff who could not only relate to his dilemma, but who could speak with him in his native language.

Commitment to Holistic Education   Another reason for the center's success is its commitment to the whole person—not just the academic or intellectual part. As a staff member at Nuevos Horizontes commented, "Our theory is that education is more than the academic. We operate under the idea of community education. Community education is not only the academics, but also you need to educate yourself about all the other aspects of life and society." At Nuevos Horizontes, an emphasis on holistic education means providing information and resources about a variety of opportunities available to local residents and students. Maria noted, "For example, if we have a student who comes here to register for classes but they're sick, how are they going to go to class? So part of our role is to educate the students about different community services available to them. Show them the ropes and the different services for them."

Staff at Nuevos Horizontes also recognize the importance the family plays in the education process: "We adopt a holistic view of education that includes the family. We have a parents' education program that helps to educate parents about schooling so that they can relate to their children and help them to succeed in school."

Physical Proximity   Physical proximity to the Hispanic community is another source of strength for the center. As one volunteer noted, "I think of Nuevos Horizontes as a second home within the community. We are part of the community. We work hard to find out what the needs of the community are before we come up with programs." Another staff member pointed out how the needs of the community change and how important it is to be closely connected to the local residents. She pointed out how 10 years ago Nuevos Horizontes had to deal with a specific educational concern: "We had to set up programs that satisfy the requirements of the amnesty program." Now, many residents want to become citizens, and the emphasis has shifted to citizenship training: "Now we have a lot of leadership and citizenship classes. We also have attorneys who come here and advise people about citizenship so they don't jeopardize their residency status." Several staff at both Nuevos Horizontes and Outreach pointed out how fearful the whole idea of higher education is to some Hispanic immigrants, many of whom have never even considered a college education. One Outreach staff member noted that "Having a college community center right in the middle of the Hispanic community says something. It makes the idea of college more of a likelihood."

Community Partnerships Central to the success of Nuevos Horizontes is its effectiveness in gaining community support, not just in terms of local residents who use its services, but in terms of local businesses and agencies who collaborate with the center. A member of the local township governing body commented, "A key to Nuevos Horizontes is involving everybody in the community. That's what the community education day was all about—to let people see how collaborations and partnerships have made a difference in terms of sharing resources and accessing services." An example of the success of Nuevos Horizontes in building partnerships is the fact that many of its classes are not taught at the center, where the facilities are limited, but are scheduled throughout the surrounding communities in schools and churches.

HispanoFest is perhaps the largest project coordinated by Nuevos Horizontes that depends on collaboration. Without the help and contributions of local businesses, the celebration most likely would not have achieved the success it has. A local business leader, who was instrumental in the development of HispanoFest, commented, "We tried to get other businesses around the area to generate financial support. They tended to respond positively because they know me and they know I'm a business person too." The comments from this person highlight another key factor in the success of Nuevos Horizontes—individual initiative.

Individual Initiative Nearly every person with whom we spoke, from students to the president of Outreach, offered a similar reason for the success of Nuevos Horizontes—the talent and energy of the current director Maria Vasquez. A high-ranking official at Outreach noted, "The success of innovative programs like Nuevos Horizontes are somewhat dependent on finding an idea champion. We found one of those people in Maria Vasquez." Another Outreach staff person offered a similar appraisal: "The current director is the key. If you want to create innovation, then find more Marias." An ESL teacher also highlighted the role the director plays in the success of Nuevos Horizontes: "Individuals such as Maria are very important. She gives it her all. I can call at any point in time and ask for help with a student. There's a philosophy of service."

Institutional Support   One key to the success of Nuevos Horizontes may be its location within the overall structure of Outreach Community College. Most of the classes offered by the Center fall under the domain of Adult Basic Education (ABE). At one time, ABE classes were the domain of Continuing Education at Outreach. Recently, however, the ABE program was placed within the College of Arts and Sciences. Several faculty and staff felt this was an important shift that signified the relevance of the ABE program. A faculty member pointed out that the change made it easier to transition students from ABE courses to credit-hour courses: "We made the ABE program more academic as opposed to conversation and grammar-oriented. There is more reading and writing." This faculty member felt that the change benefited Nuevos Horizontes in particular and immigrant education at Outreach in general: "Nuevos Horizontes is the institution that welcomes the immigrant students to Outreach. It's the entry point, the doorway. It provides a comfort level for immigrant entry."

Although Nuevos Horizontes derives benefits from its structural location within the overall organizational scheme, it nonetheless seems to exist budgetarily on the margins of the organization. Some concerns were expressed that the center does not receive a level of support that reflects its success. A few years ago, there was both a director and an assistant director, but the assistant director position was cut from Outreach's budget. As a result, many of the responsibilities have fallen on the director, and some services have been affected. For example, Nuevos Horizontes no longer translates documents such as high school diplomas or college transcripts for students.

Despite all the positives that Nuevos Horizontes offers to Outreach and the surrounding communities, especially Montego Park, a significant concern exists nonetheless. By creating a center designed primarily to serve the needs of Hispanic students, Outreach runs the risk of compartmentalizing these students and their concerns. In other words, it could develop that all Hispanic students might be referred to Nuevos Horizontes instead of being dealt with as other students might be. This is the same problem academic programs such as African-American studies and women's studies have had to confront in relation to curricula matters: How does an institution encourage all faculty across all departments to rethink the contributions of women and African Americans? By creating specific centers or departments, there is a tendency for some faculty and staff to see the concerns of women or minorities to be the province of specialized departments or service-oriented student offices, such as Nuevos Horizontes. The challenge is to create specialized areas that focus primarily on issues relating to previously excluded voices, but at the same time encourage institution-wide responses to organizational silencing. Clearly, multicultural transformation must occur across entire institutions. However, this does not mean that centers should not exist. Strategies to enact multicultural communities may be best served when efforts are both centered and dispersed. At Outreach, Nuevos Horizontes centers the struggle to create a multicultural campus, specifically dealing with issues faced by Spanish-speaking immigrants and students. What is also clear, as evidenced by weak faculty recruitment practices for Outreach, is the lack of dispersion of multicultural efforts.

Multicultural Implications

In terms of multiculturalism, what can we learn from Nuevos Horizontes and from the Hispanic students who participate in its programs? First and foremost, Nuevos Horizontes calls attention to the idea that multicultural education involves much more than merely including diverse peoples in educational settings. A commitment to multiculturalism demands that we include in how the organization operates the understandings and ways of experiencing the world that diverse peoples bring to an organization. Multicultural education embraces the border knowledge diverse students bring to the educational setting by creating structures that enable multiple expressions. HispanoFest and the general organizational ethos of Nuevos

Horizontes highlight such a notion. We refer to this general process of embracing the diversity members bring to an organization as celebratory socialization. Celebratory socialization encourages the development of heterogeneous communities or communities of difference. Such communities, as William Tierney (1993) discusses in his work, are characterized not by commonality or sameness, but by difference. For Tierney, organizational cohesion ought to be developed through a commitment to understanding one another's differences.

Latino/a students attending Nuevos Horizontes and Outreach Community College bring their own understandings of the world—their own border knowledge—to the classes they attend and the campus settings in which they interact. As Hugh Mehan, Lea Hubbard, and Irene Villanueva (1994) point out, "Latinos have a different folk model of schooling that encourages different patterns of behavior. . . . [Latinos] tend to equate schooling with assimilation into the dominant group, a course of action that they actively resist" (p. 95). A similar point is made in Teresa McKenna's (1988) analysis of Jimmy Santiago Baca's *Immigrants in Our Own Land*:

Baca's title indicates the underlying irony that infuses the Mexican experience in the United States, and it points beyond the oft-quoted retort: "We were here before you came." In the United States, the immigrant is not a person but an "alien," a being less than human belonging not to this land and perhaps, the term implies, not to the human race either. Consequently, Mexicans feel not only like immigrants in their own land but like aliens to the society as well. The psychological and cultural response to this position ranges from acquiescence to rebellion. (p. 30)

Baca and other Mexican and Mexican-American authors highlight the historical, political, and cultural significance of the Mexican-American war as well as the Treaty of Guadalupe–Hidalgo. Philip Ortego (1973) explains that this treaty "identified those who came with the conquered lands of the southwest as a defeated people. And those who came afterwards in the great migrations of the early 1900s have been equally victimized by stereotypes engendered by the Mexican-American war" (p. xxi). Negative stereotypes and hostile attitudes have persisted especially with more recent waves of immigration. The students at Nuevos Horizontes proclaim their Latina or Latino identities as an act of pride; they desire to refute the negative images conveyed by others and at the same time call attention to the unique cultural and political struggles of their peoples. While the historical conflicts faced by Nicaraguans, Guatemalans, and Mexicans vary significantly, they have a common bond in the fact that such struggles are situated within the globalized colonialism of first-world powers.

Memories such as those stirred by the conquest of Mexican territory by the U.S., symbolized by the Treaty of Guadalupe–Hidalgo, are seen by some to stir emotions and encourage resentment. But others, such as Sharon Welch (1990), see such memories as fundamental to the cultural struggles of marginalized members of a society. She refers to these memories as "dangerous memories": "Dangerous memories are stories of defeat and of victory, a casting of the past in terms of a present of joy, hope, and struggle. Memories of oppression and defeat become dangerous when they are used as the foundation for a critique of existing institutions and ideologies that blur the recognition and denunciation of injustice" (p. 155). The present-day struggle of African Americans in the U.S. cannot be situated outside of a history of oppression and resistance: slavery, Jim Crow laws, lynchings, and, of course, resistance epitomized by the civil rights movement of the 1960s are all dangerous memories. The struggle for equality on the part of lesbian, gay, and bisexual people must be connected to the historical conditions that have reinforced the closet as well as those efforts to dismantle this form of social imprisonment. The persecution of "homosexuals" by Nazi Germany (where the pink triangle was born as a symbol of oppression and, later, solidarity) must be recognized as part of the historical roots of oppression that have contributed to forms of resistance such as the Stonewall Riots in Greenwich Village in 1969; the lesbian, gay, and bisexual march on Washington, D.C. in 1993; as well as the gay liberation movement in general. Likewise, the suffering and oppression of women has significant historical roots that must be connected to present-day liberatory struggle. The battle over women's suffrage, reproductive control, and economic equality, as well as the feminist movement in general must be seen as part of the struggle to transform a society and culture deeply rooted in patriarchy. Educational institutions committed to multiculturalism enact celebratory socialization processes that create opportunities for marginalized members of a society to develop their memories as a means to social transformation.

Critical multicultural education seeks not to erase dangerous memories, but instead struggles to create dialogue around the historical, cultural, and political forces that have contributed to inequality and injustice. Such a commitment must be reflected not only in the classroom and in how pedagogy gets structured but also in terms of institutional practices. When staff at Nuevos Horizontes build a library around books that recall the political and social struggles of Latin and Central American countries or develop educational programs and activities that celebrate the unique cultural traditions of the many Hispanic cultures represented in the area, they stir the kind of memory needed to advance social justice and equality.

A goal of multiculturalism is to create educational institutions that affirm cultural identities and border knowledge and, at the same time, build educational opportunities for culturally diverse students to develop the knowledge and skills necessary to succeed in mainstream society. To focus only on developing students' skills and understandings for the sake of improving their economic opportunities reflects little understanding of the importance of culture and identity. Just as problematic is a focus on cultural issues at the expense of career-enhancing experiences, be they vocational or transfer education. Clearly, to be effective institutions of higher learning, community colleges must meet both of these challenges.

From a multicultural perspective, community college faculty and administrators must ask themselves what they might learn from the lives and perspectives of people such as Corrine Bolanos, Romano Suarez, Carlita Gonzalez, and Maria Vasquez. How can their stories change the way we see our world and the way we conduct ourselves in an ever-changing society?

In *Barrio Boy*, Ernesto Galarza (1971) tells the story of his family's migration from the mountain village of Jalcocotan in western Mexico to a Mexican *barrio* in Sacramento. He describes the general plight of *Chicanos*—"the name by which we called an unskilled worker born in Mexico and just arrived in the United States" (p. 200):

As poor refugees, their first concern was to find a place to sleep, then to eat and find work. In the barrio they were most likely to find all three, for not knowing English, they needed something that was even more urgent than a room, a meal, or a job, and that was information in a language they could understand. (p. 201)

Invariably, however, newcomers to a strange land must learn something of the language, the customs, the culture, in order to negotiate their way. The problem often faced is the sense of loss involved in moving from one world to another, from a previous culture to a new one.

Moving from one country to another can be a time of great excitement, but change also may bring about remorse. In *Hunger of Memory,* Richard Rodriguez (1982) details his increasing socialization into mainstream U.S. culture, his growing dependence on the English language, and the increasing sense of distance separating himself from his parents and from his native language: "After English became my primary language, I no longer knew what words to use in addressing my parents. The old Spanish words (those tender accents of sound) I had used earlier—*mamá* and *papá*—I couldn't use anymore. They would have been too painful reminders of how much had changed in my life" (pp. 23–24). For Rodriguez, education in U.S. schools meant leaving behind the ways of his parents: "Rodriguez. The name on the door. The name on my passport. The name I carry from my parents—who are no longer my parents, in a cultural sense" (p. 4).

For those who are familiar with the life of Richard Rodriguez, it may seem ironic that we cite from his autobiography. After all, this is the same Richard Rodriguez who made something of a name for himself as an opponent of bilingual education and affirmative action. For Rodriguez, succeeding in U.S. public life has meant adopting the language and the ways of life of mainstream U.S. society. He refers to this process as "Americanization": "Only when I was able to think of myself as an American, no longer an alien in *gringo* society, could I seek the rights and opportunities necessary for full public individuality" (p. 27).

We highlight the life of Richard Rodriguez as an example of the negative effects of a one-directional form of socialization carried out

by educational structures that tend to enact assimilationist strategies. This kind of socialization, which may be described as "coercive
socialization," involves a remaking of the individual so that he or
she "conforms to an image agents carry of what is organizationally
desirable and proper. . . . Agent concern is directed toward the passage of traditional skills, values, practices within an organization and
seeks, therefore, to reduce dramatically whatever diversity exists
among recruits at entrance" (Van Maanen, 1983, p. 211–212). Coercive socialization seeks assimilation in that culturally diverse people
are forced more or less to leave behind their own cultural heritage in
order to succeed in their new surroundings.

What Rodriguez fails to recognize is that culture is not a static
phenomena. As Clifford Geertz (1973) points out in his work, people
are not only shaped by culture, but they also continually reshape
culture through their lives and their social interactions. Certainly,
immigrants to a new land ought to become acquainted with the
customs, practices, and even the language of their new surroundings. But, because culture is continually reshaped, the new culture
that immigrants are confronted with must also adjust to them: As
newcomers are socialized to the ways of the new culture, the culture
is also reshaped by them. This means that institutions in general,
and schools in particular, must do more than help immigrants to
learn about the U.S.; these organizations must change as well.

In terms of multiculturalism and the community college, our
case study of an immigrant education program and the idea of
celebratory socialization can be extended to other culturally diverse
groups. In other words, students do not have to come from foreign
soil to bring diverse cultural experiences to community college settings. Lesbian, gay, and bisexual students bring experiences far removed from many people who work and study on community college campuses. And, of course, the same is true of African-American,
Asian-American, and other students from underrepresented groups.
The experiences of diverse students have pedagogical and transformative power if we develop structures that enable and welcome such
diversity.

In Nuevos Horizontes, we witness an organizational structure
that has enabled and welcomed culturally diverse peoples. Programs
and activities have been created that not only teach Hispanic immi-

grants about mainstream U.S. social life, but programs also have been put in place that provide opportunities for the diverse experiences of Hispanic immigrants to be shared and embraced.

We live in a heterogeneous society. Multicultural education is about celebrating heterogeneity. Such a process necessarily involves coming together to learn from one another, to care about one another. Steven Mittelstet (1994) envisions community colleges organized around an ethic of care. In drawing upon the work of Carol Gilligan (1982), he suggests that community colleges ought to be structured more in terms of caring relationships (webs of connection) rather than the more common hierarchical patterns. "Seeing relationship as web [webs of connection] rather than hierarchy provides an image of community that is more affiliative, cooperative, and creative" (p. 558). An ethic of care, as promoted by Mittelstet, is consistent with feminist interpretations of education and organizational life, and is a central concern of an educational process grounded in critical multiculturalism (Larrabee, 1993; Noddings, 1984). Caring, of course, necessarily implies embracing the cultural differences of others as forms of celebratory socialization prevail.

Summary

The Nuevos Horizontes program vividly highlights how immigration from Mexico, and other parts of Central and South America, is a major force in shaping the cultural mosaic of U.S. society. Today's immigrants are perhaps much more diverse in terms of career backgrounds than what was portrayed in Ernesto Galarza's pre–World War I autobiography. Nonetheless, even for those immigrants possessing advanced skills, such as those of Romano Suarez, who studied chemistry in Mexico, language and cultural differences still limit opportunities for Spanish-speaking immigrants. Programs such as Nuevos Horizontes are needed to assist immigrants in their acquisition of the understandings needed to excel in U.S. society.

At the same time, immigrant socialization into mainstream U.S. culture should not be a one-way pedagogical encounter. Indeed, the vision of multiculturalism offered here is one where institutions also learn from the diverse constituents who participate in our contemporary organizations. Educational institutions must create classroom and out-of-class opportunities that encourage the development of dangerous memory as a way to contribute to social transformation. Nuevos Horizontes highlights some of the qualities and programs that colleges and universities might follow as they struggle to create more diverse campus environments as well as reshape the very nature of their organizational cultures.

Nuevos Horizontes also highlights a potential barrier to the building of diverse academic communities—the tendency to compartmentalize multicultural efforts. In creating a specific branch of the organization to serve the needs and interests of Hispanic immigrants and students, Outreach Community College has, in effect, excused other faculty and staff around the campus from the responsibility of educating themselves about diverse students' needs. Thus, this case study calls attention to the need to have both broad and specific organizational commitments to multicultural education.

The concept of celebratory socialization highlights how multicultural organizations must develop inclusionary practices which embrace cultural difference. Such organizational practices must include opportunities for members to shape the organizational culture. This is the bidirectional view of socialization and cultural change suggested in this chapter. The fact that underrepresented students continue to have the highest attrition rates among postsecondary institutions is a sign that fundamental structural and cultural change is needed. Until academic organizations can enact more celebratory socialization strategies, such cultural change is unlikely to occur.

Notes

1.   Our use of the term "Hispanic," as opposed to "Latino/a," reflects the language of Outreach Community College.

Chapter Five
Organizational Restructuring and Leadership
A Case Study of Community Responsiveness

This chapter examines the creation of a high school within an urban community college setting. The high school is a joint effort between Divided Community College (Divided) and the local school district; the college provides the facilities, and the district supplies the teachers. The vast majority of students who attend the high school are African American and the collaboration between the community college and the school district serves as an example of how multicultural educational innovation may involve challenges to traditional organizational boundaries. The collaborative effort has the full support of the state Board of Regents, the governing body for the state system of higher education in Divided's home state.

Divided is situated in a major U.S. city in the south central region of the country. The program that we examine is called Middle College High School (MCHS) and borrows from the original community college and high school collaborative implemented in 1974 at LaGuardia Community College in New York City. As Janet Lieberman (1985), founder of the LaGuardia program, explains, "Developed to solve some of the academic problems that the City University of New York faced in dealing with its underprepared students, the Middle College is a new substructure emphasizing the 'seamless web of education'" (p. 48). The notion of a seamless web derives from Ernest Boyer's (1983) analysis of education in which he discusses the need to create "communication between the sectors" (p. 265).

Middle college high school as an educational structure has caught on elsewhere as well. In 1988, the California legislature authorized the creation of two middle college high schools within community college settings: Los Angeles Southwest College and Contra Costa

College. Analyses have shown that the programs reduce the high school dropout rate, contribute positively to the educational participation of underrepresented minority students, and increase high school graduation and college attendance rates (Board of Governors, 1993).

We have two goals in this chapter. First, we examine how Middle College High School has contributed to enhancing the learning experiences of local high school students. We include in our discussion various issues Divided has had to deal with in implementing and sustaining the program. Our second goal is to relate the developments at Divided to the larger issues of multiculturalism and organizational innovation. More specifically, we examine how organizational boundaries may be reconceived as a means to better serve local communities and culturally diverse students. We also focus on the role leadership plays in creating multicultural innovation.

We use two concepts derived from organizational theory to highlight issues related to the adoption of MCHS and multicultural innovation in general. The first is the idea of organizational culture, defined as the values, beliefs, attitudes, and norms that shape the social life of an institution (Tierney, 1988; Rhoads & Tierney, 1992). Although organizational culture guides members' action, it also is reshaped by organizational members through their social interactions. In this light, organizational culture is seen as an ever-changing by-product of and framework for behavior within colleges and universities.

The second organizational concept we use is that of boundary spanning—a term used to describe organizational efforts to increase resources through greater interdependence with the organization's environment or with other organizations. Richard Scott (1987) writes how boundary spanning activities may help two or more organizations pool their resources and thereby increase their ability to serve clients. Scott describes one type of boundary spanning activity as a "joint venture": "A joint venture occurs when two or more firms create a new organization to pursue some common purpose. . . . They entail only a limited pooling of resources by the participating organizations" (p. 189). Middle College High School, thus, may be analyzed as a joint venture between Divided Community College and the city school district and represents an effort on the part of both (through the pooling of resources) to improve their services for minority high school students. For the school district, such an activity is part of its role as a provider of K–12 public education. For the community college, this boundary spanning activity is seen as part of its responsibility to the local community and its role in community education. The actions of Divided highlight how (especially in times of financial exigency) enacting multicultural structural change may involve bridging organizational boundaries and forming joint ventures. Before we discuss Middle College High School and the theoretical implications of the program, we provide some background information about Divided Community College and its surrounding urban community.

Organizational Background

Divided Community College is accredited by the Commission on Colleges of the Southern Association of Colleges and Schools to award the Associate of Arts and Associate of Science degrees. The institutional motto—"students are number one"—speaks to the importance Divided places on students; as with most community colleges, teaching is primary and research is virtually nonexistent.

Divided opened in 1972 as one of ten community colleges governed by its home state's Board of Regents. The mission of Divided centers on providing educational opportunities to area citizens that will "enrich their lives intellectually, culturally, and economically." The college takes its responsibility to the local citizenry seriously, and, in many ways, Middle College High School epitomizes that commitment. Divided has developed three learning centers throughout the city to better serve the needs of residents. The centers offer courses in both degree and nondegree programs.

Total student enrollment at the college in 1993 was seven thousand. In terms of student composition, Divided has a large enrollment of African-American students constituting approximately fifty-nine percent of the student body. White students make up roughly thirty-nine percent, and the remainder of the students derive from Latino/a or Asian backgrounds. Although African-American students make up the greatest portion of students, the faculty are predominantly white: sixty-four percent of the faculty are white, and thirty-one percent are African American. Ninety percent of the faculty possess at least a master's degree, and roughly thirteen percent hold a doctorate.

The president of Divided is relatively new to the institution, having arrived in 1990. He is an educator who expresses a commitment to achieving social and economic equality through education. Recently, the president gave a speech at a state legislative retreat. The following is extracted from that speech:

Education must become a right for all able-minded citizens. We must make education the single overriding objective and make all other considerations bend to that. . . . We must retrain those in the work force who have obsolete skills. We must mandate that all high school students complete high school. They can become productive members of society. . . . Knowledge is both power and confidence. When citizens identify their educational goals and work toward them, life is better. Life is a joy. We must commit, commit, and recommit ourselves. We must redouble our efforts, redetermine our destiny and be resolved to make our families and our communities strong and positive through education.

The president of Divided calls attention to the fact that educational and economic problems faced by local communities have been a major force in shaping the direction of the college. The development and ongoing support of Middle College High School reflects such a commitment. A Divided staff member with mixed feelings about having a high school program on a college campus nonetheless opined, "Middle College High School really does save the students from ending up on the streets."

The Local Community

Divided Community College is about ten blocks away from the downtown section of the urban community it serves. The city is known for its "blues and barbecue," and its economy revolves around the manufacturing of cotton and hardwood products, wholesale markets, mixed feed production, and extensive medical and educational facilities. The area is also known for its agricultural production especially involving livestock and poultry, cotton, soybeans, vegetables, and forest products.

The geographic setting in which Divided is situated is a contrast of urban renewal and inner-city disintegration marked by high crime rates. Gentrified urban townhouses with BMWs and Jeep Grand Cherokees parked in front stand adjacent to dilapidated and boarded-up apartment buildings and warehouses. Green and yellow polished cable cars wind their way along brick-paved streets complete with newly remodeled shops, boutiques, restaurants, and nightclubs. The rejuvenated downtown is a sharp contrast to the many homeless citizens, who panhandle on those same brick-paved streets.

In terms of the larger geographic scene, the county served by Divided has experienced high unemployment and serious economic problems, particularly within many of the area's African-American communities. Of the 116,000 African-American families within the county, approximately 29,000 receive welfare. Thirty thousand African-American adults in the county have less than a ninth grade education, and 50,000 have not graduated from high school. Eighty percent of the students who attend the city's schools are African American, and the overall high school attrition rate is 40 percent. Educational and economic warning signs such as these have helped to shape Divided's commitment to the local city and county. The development and ongoing support of Middle College High School reflects the college's responsiveness to its community.

Findings

The notion behind a middle college high school is to incorporate within a college (typically a community college) a high school that serves a specific population of students (Greenberg, 1991; Lieberman, 1985, 1989; Moed & Greenberg, 1982). Divided's official stance on the high school program is summed up best in the college's handbook: "By placing a high school in a college environment and providing personalized support for academic and career preparation, this school enables capable students to complete their high school education and meet the challenges of the 21st century."

Undergirding the philosophy of MCHS at Divided is what Lieberman and Anne Callagy (1990) delineate as the "three pillars" of the middle college–high school concept: high school-college collaboration, experiential learning in terms of student internships, and intensive guidance counseling. Thus, students at Divided's Middle

College High School not only get the benefit of a collegiate environment for their high school studies, they also have opportunities to participate in internship programs, some of which pay quite well, and to attend a school with reduced student-teacher and student-counselor ratios. For example, the ratio of faculty to students is 1:15 at Middle College High School compared to 1:25 throughout the surrounding school district. The ratio of counselors to students is 1:150 compared to 1:450 throughout the school district.

Most faculty and staff at Divided and MCHS believe that the success of the middle college high–school idea is that it puts students in a new environment, a more adult-like, collegiate environment. A staff member at MCHS, who is actively involved in educational reform, discussed the problems of traditional school settings and the advantages of treating high school students in a more collegiate manner:

We need to do something with students who are not performing in the traditional school. We've got to break down the barriers that keep them from succeeding. One of the barriers is the way we treat students. We need to treat students, adolescents, more like adults, rather than corralling them into rooms with bells where they go from this room to that. I just don't think that you can warehouse kids or that you can legislate them to do the right thing. You have to show them a better way.

A Middle College High School teacher echoed this view: "When you look at the population of a school, not everyone fits into the rubber-stamp mold. There's a lot of need for students to go to a school where they will feel accepted and wanted. Where they will have a different learning environment."

The learning environment promoted by the middle college–high school idea is one that encourages "school membership and academic engagement" (Cullen, 1991, p. 83). A sense of school membership is accomplished by allowing students to make more choices: They can leave the school during lunch, walk the halls without a pass, and, in general, make choices that are part of being an adult. Academic engagement is promoted through lower student-teacher ratios and an emphasis upon collaborative and cooperative learning, pedagogical styles that often are more difficult to enact in large classes.

The population served by Middle College High School is described by faculty and staff as "at-risk" students who also have demonstrated some potential for academic success. "At-risk" is defined as students who have failed at least one grade or fallen behind their age cohort. A staff member at Divided commented on the types of students MCHS recruits: "The kids that come here are supposed to be those with real academic problems—like they were held back at least one year in school. The very obvious potential dropouts." However, falling a year or two behind in school is not enough to gain admittance to MCHS. "Also, they must have academic potential. These are not supposed to be disciplinary problems. They are students who you can just feel could do something if given the right situation."

MCHS students are typically a year or two older than other students in their same grade. They are nontraditional in other ways as well: "Some are teen parents. Some live in group homes." Being in a college environment offers these students a chance to blend in with a more diverse group of older students. As one MCHS staff member pointed out, "If you are already behind, you feel bad about yourself. Age is real important to a high school student. But once you go to college, it's not. You might have a grandmother or grandfather in class."

A fundamental premise behind the middle college–high school idea is to remove the social stigma that often accompanies repeating a grade or two, having a child, living in a group home, or being in a rehabilitation program. Middle College High School provides students with opportunities to begin anew, without social stigma. Building self-esteem is critical to the success of middle college–high school programs, and situating students on a college campus helps. A staff member at Divided commented that, "Students feel good about themselves here. Probably better than they've ever felt. They tell their boyfriend or girlfriend that they're going to college. They walk around with college paraphernalia rather than high school stuff. I mean they really have a different demeanor."

Several students confirm what the preceding staff member noted. Alton, an African-American male and a junior at MCHS, offered the following: "This is the first year I passed all of my exams. I feel more like an adult here, instead of being treated like a baby. I feel more self-confident. I get more respect." For the first time in his life, Alton sees obtaining a college degree as a distinct possibility.

Charlene, an African-American female and a senior, struggled in her previous school. She resented what she perceived as "condescending attitudes" on the part of teachers toward her and other students. Things have changed for Charlene since coming to Middle College High School; she enjoys the close interaction with her teachers, who she feels treat her as an equal. Her motivation and interest in school has increased dramatically: "I like having teachers who will work with me. I was going to be a cosmetologist; but since I came here, I have done well in science, and now I want to be a mechanical engineer."

Denise, also a female African-American senior, enjoys the smaller classes and plans to attend college when she graduates. While she attended her previous school, her prevailing concern was how to finish high school, put education behind her, and figure out what kind of work she might be able to find. Now, she envisions going on for more schooling after she completes high school: "When I came here I didn't really have my mind set on what I wanted to do. Now, I know exactly what I want to do when I graduate. I am going to college. Algebra is my favorite, and I'm going to go as far as I can."

Alton, Charlene, and Denise plan to attend college upon graduating from MCHS. Exposure to a college environment has been a new experience for them. None of their parents attended college, nor did their parents do well in high school. As a consequence, schooling and the prospect of going to college seemed remote and somewhat meaningless to these students. Like many high school students around the country, when college is not within one's reach, excelling in academic classes in high school seems to make little sense. For the most part, academic courses prepare students for college. If students are not planning to attend college, then such courses seem quite removed from their lives, their futures. But once Alton, Charlene, and Denise started at MCHS, college was no longer foreign or distant. College became part of their everyday experience and part of their hope for a better tomorrow. Students whose family background is removed from the college-going experience seem most suited for educational experiments like MCHS.

Middle College High School started in 1987 by recruiting a tenth grade class of one hundred students and then added an additional grade each year. By 1989, MCHS reached its capacity with three hundred students enrolled in grades ten to twelve. During the academic year 1992–1993, MCHS enrolled 301 students in grades ten to twelve. Of the total students enrolled for that same year, ninety-five percent were African American and five percent were white. In terms of gender, the students were fairly evenly divided: fifty-one percent were male and forty-nine percent were female.

To enroll in MCHS, students must submit an application and copies of their high school transcripts, and they must participate in an interview with an MCHS guidance counselor. The interview serves three purposes: (1) it helps the counselor to determine if the student is well-suited for MCHS, (2) it provides an opportunity for the student to learn more about MCHS, and (3) the interview establishes a relationship between the student and the counselor that can be built upon in the future.

One of the biggest problems that Middle College High School has had to face is the fact that the decision to implement the program at Divided was more or less mandated by the former president and senior members of his staff. As a result, faculty and staff have felt slighted by their exclusion. The president at that time had much experience with high school programs on college campuses and was a firm believer in their potential to assist at-risk students. A staff member noted that, "Middle College High School only happened because of the vision of key leaders. It only happened because the dean, president, and superintendent, all three, saw MCHS as something special. Something that would be valuable."

From the perspective of many of the faculty and staff at Divided, the initiative to create Middle College High School was top-down and to some "heavy handed." Such a view was reflected by a high-ranking administrator who commented, "There is no doubt that anybody who knows anything about administration knows that you have to have people buy into something before you command that it is done. This was a decision that was made, and people were brought on board after the fact." Another administrator added, "This was a 'thou shalt' decision. Middle College High School was a given. . . . This has never been a matter of popular choice. It was an administrative decision by the president." And a faculty member pointed out, "We were told one day that there was going to be a high school and all of a sudden there it was. We had no input. They took our space with no input from us."

But other significant internal factors were also at work back in 1986 when early plans were being made by the president of Divided and the superintendent of schools. Most significantly, Divided was in the midst of a serious enrollment decline. "Our college enrollment had been going down about fifteen percent per year, and the result was that we had a lot of empty classrooms." The college was faced either with filling those classrooms with college students or having them deleted from their books by leasing them to another agency. Thus, Middle College High School not only was an opportunity to better serve the local community and contribute to improving educational equity; it also was a response to financial exigency. An administrator reflected on the situation back in 1986: "By committing about a dozen classrooms to Middle College High School, we were able to delete them from our college inventory. This took some of the financial pressure off our college."

In addition to internal forces at work in implementing MCHS, external forces also played a key role. The declining enrollment at Divided in the mid-1980s was, perhaps, as much a reflection of its faltering image within the community as it was the result of changes in student demographics. Building a bridge with local schools was seen not only as a way to assist high school students; it was also a way to increase attendance at the college. A Divided staff member commented, "At least we're not an unknown anymore in the city school system. Everyone knows about us. They may think of us as a high school, which is a problem. But at least we've developed a lot of contacts because of our initial efforts. There have been good payoffs." A staff person from MCHS added that, "I try to view these young people as future community college students." Along these lines, MCHS and Divided have established a dual enrollment program so MCHS students can get college credit for some advanced courses they take. The idea is to give them a step-up on their college education and hopefully encourage them to pursue advanced study at Divided or at other two- or four-year institutions.

Another external factor involved was the overall problems of the local city school system, in particular the high dropout rate (forty percent). There was a sense that Divided, as a community college committed to serving its local citizens, had an obligation to address this serious problem. Pressure for colleges to play a more proactive role in the problems of K–12 was also coming from the state. State reforms called for schools to prepare *all students* for postsecondary study, either for college or technical study. Reform writers addressing national concerns also called for increased linkages between public and postsecondary schooling (Boyer, 1983; Hodgkinson, 1985). The push for a seamless educational system was certainly on.

An additional factor involved in this cooperative project between Divided and the city schools was the concern and eventual financial support of local businesses, particularly a local bank. A bank executive commented on their concerns, "There was a perception that companies would not relocate here because of the schools. We wanted to make an ongoing contribution to a project that students could get some benefit from." Executives from the bank met with Divided officials and endorsed Middle College High School. They offered a one-time grant of $50,000 and pledged ongoing staff support and internship opportunities. The internship program has helped students to gain valuable work experience and an income. Internship positions with the bank are highly valued among Middle College High School students. A staff member at Divided commented on the internship program sponsored by the bank:

If students choose to work at the bank, in the data processing part, they start as helpers and some end up becoming highly skilled data entry operators. For many, it's the first time they have ever experienced the discipline of work. Plus they get paid for it. Remember that these kids have all failed at least one grade. They're older than the average high school student and many have families. So this is a real service program that provides them a transition into being successful as an employee.

This staff member questioned how successful Middle College High School would be without the financial and staff support provided by the bank: "I don't know if MCHS would have done as well as it has without the support from the business community, and, in particular, the financial and personnel support from the bank."

The circumstances that led to the creation of Middle College High School are a combination of several internal and external factors—many of which have interactional effects. For example, separating the college's image problem in the 1980s from its declining enrollment is difficult: Did one cause the other? Or is there another factor responsible for both the college's image problem and its declining enrollment? Also, separating the actions by administrative leaders from historical, cultural, and social concerns of the day is next to impossible. For example, the ongoing struggle of African Americans to achieve educational equity is not only a concern Divided has for its enrolled students, it also is a concern voiced by the president in speaking of responsiveness to the local community.

Discussion

As with most examples of organizational change and innovation, multiple perspectives exist as to the degree of success or failure of a specific program. At Divided there are strong supporters as well as vehement critics of Middle College High School. Some see MCHS as an inconvenience in their lives as college faculty and staff. Others see the program as an opportunity to contribute to improving the local educational system and the educational opportunities for African-American students. In what follows, we attempt to sort out some of the strengths and weaknesses of MCHS in terms of benefits for Divided Community College and the local community.

Strengths of Middle College High School In terms of strengths, two issues stand out: (1) the educational effectiveness of MCHS, and (2) the role that MCHS has played in creating a positive image of Divided within the local community. In what follows, we expand upon the positives that have come from MCHS.

Clearly, the strength of Middle College High School is its success with students who have struggled with traditional high school structures. The statistics are revealing. During its first semester of operation, the school had a retention rate that was 10 percent higher than the LaGuardia model and nearly thirty percent higher than the average high school within Divided's home state. From its first graduating class of sixty-eight students in the spring of 1990, nearly half had already earned college credit through dual enrollment at Divided. Half of the class also indicated plans to attend college. This is indeed significant in that these graduates were once labeled "at-risk" because of the likelihood that they would drop out of school altogether.

More recent statistics are just as telling. During the 1992–1993 academic year, the attrition rate at MCHS was twelve percent, compared to the local district's rate of thirty-five percent. During the same year, fifty students earned college credit in the dual enrollment program. Upon graduation, fifty percent attended a postsecondary institution with thirty-three percent receiving scholarships, the majority of whom planned to attend Divided.

From the standpoint of serving its local community, Middle College High School has helped Divided polish its once tarnished image. Divided as well as MCHS have reaped the benefits of local and national publicity. For example, in 1990 when MCHS was threatened to be closed by the city school district because of budgetary constraints, extensive media coverage may have helped to save the school. Support from local business leaders helped as well. A representative of a major company located in the area attended an important city Board of Education meeting and noted his company's support for both Divided and the school district's efforts. He stated that failure "to give MCHS the right to survive is nothing short of telling this community you don't care whether the people in it or the businesses which locate here, stay or go." Outpourings such as the preceding helped to cement MCHS as a city school enterprise and to reinforce its importance in the minds of many at Divided and throughout the city.

Various articles have appeared in the city newspaper that have focused on some of the student success stories. One story highlighted a student who had been labeled as "at-risk" and who had participated in MCHS. This student went from a C average prior to MCHS to a 4.0, and acceptance at one of the nation's most prestigious college preparatory programs. The preceding example is one of many, although not all of the local media coverage has been positive: One article noted the ill feelings generated among some of the college's faculty after MCHS was implemented.

Problems Related to Middle College High School Despite the success of MCHS and the accolades Divided has received for its contribution to the city's (and state's) overall educational mission, many problems exist and there have been frequent complaints. In terms of problems, four issues arise: (1) noise and disruption supposedly caused by high school students, (2) damage to the college's image because it may be perceived by some as a high school, (3) loss of space that could be used for Divided students, and (4) problems related to having multiple governing bodies and reporting channels because of the coexistence of two educational structures—a high school and a college.

During a debate in 1990 about whether or not to close MCHS, a number of faculty at Divided were highlighted in a local newspaper article in which they voiced their disdain for the program. A faculty member was quoted as saying: "There was great joy, dancing in the hallways." Another added that, "We were so happy. It felt so good to finally be rid of it." The reactions of these faculty are part of a larger group who see MCHS as contributing negatively to the campus environment as well as to the image of Divided as a high school and not a college. Another faculty member noted in the same newspaper article, "These kids go down the halls making noise, kicking holes in the wall, making faces in the windows. They're very disruptive."

Because MCHS students are generally older, they blend in with Divided students. After all, this is one of the supposed advantages to providing high school students with a collegiate environment. But while they may resemble college students, they are not; and many reflect the maturity of other high school students around their age. As one MCHS staff member mentioned, "Adolescent behavior is adolescent behavior. When there is a fight, it takes us almost six months to heal. Faculty at Divided say, 'Look at those kids. They're so disruptive.' But I say they're fighting at some of the most gifted schools in the city. . . . And, there are some community college kids that fight too."

There is much disagreement about the extent of noise and disruption that Middle College High School students cause. Many at MCHS and Divided believe faculty may be overreacting, and that a tendency exists to blame any disruptions on MCHS students. Others point to an increase in the number of fire alarms as evidence of MCHS students' disruptive behavior, while still others note that college students pull fire alarms too. The opinion of faculty and staff is divided, and it appears as though one's degree of initial commitment to MCHS affects that opinion.

Complaints about noise and disruption relate to a general concern that several faculty and staff expressed: their fear that Divided may be perceived as "the alternative high school." As one faculty member noted, "I chose to work in a college as opposed to the public schools, and now some people think we are an at-risk high school." Another faculty member highlighted his frustration: "MCHS has destroyed the college atmosphere. I mean, we have teachers walking up and down the halls with walkie talkies. If you're going to put a high school on a college campus, put them in their own building."

On top of the controversy over perceptions of Divided as a high school, the college now has severe space shortages. Not long after adopting the MCHS program, in part to fill space, enrollment at the college began to increase. Now, nearly seven years later, the college needs to build more classroom buildings or have the classrooms occupied by MCHS returned to Divided's facilities plan. A faculty member discussed the problem: "We've had a severe space problem. We have essentially lost all our space. . . . I have two classes to use for my department. MCHS has seven [it's actually closer to twelve]. They might only have six to eight students in a class. . . . While MCHS has a lot of potential, it has kept us from growing."

The loss of space is clearly a problem for the college. As faculty have pointed out, some programs have been limited space-wise, effectively ending any chance for growth. For those fields in high demand, loss of space has proven counterproductive to serving Divided's students and local residents. Recently, steps have been taken to add buildings as part of Divided's long-range plan. In the meantime, cooperation must prevail.

A fourth and final problem relates to the organizational complexities of joining two organizations that have different governing bodies. For example, MCHS students not only have to observe campus rules associated with Divided, they also have specific school district rules that apply only to them as high school students. One example is that Divided students are allowed to smoke on campus, but MCHS students cannot because of a school district rule against students smoking. Another issue relates to the fact that some teachers at MCHS have larger salaries than the college faculty. Again, this is the result of two different governing bodies—the school district and the college.

Clearly, MCHS has had its share of success, although it certainly has its detractors. As a community college program, MCHS extends Divided's commitment to the community in a far-reaching manner. By helping to retain a greater percentage of African-American high school students, Divided contributes to the future prospects and well-being of individual students, and these students may, in turn, contribute in significant ways to the community at large. Although some may question the role of colleges in K–12 education, few can take issue with the positive contribution that MCHS makes to the local community.

Multicultural Implications

At the outset of this chapter, we delineate two goals that we intend to accomplish in this chapter. The first is to highlight the middle college–high school program implemented at Divided, including a discussion of its strengths and weaknesses. This is our focus up to this point. Now, we turn to some of the multicultural implications that such an organizational arrangement has. We focus on two issues: organizational restructuring and leadership.

Organizational Restructuring Meeting the needs of diverse students within an educational system struggling with changing demographics, financial burdens, and social problems is a complex task that demands multiple strategies. Not every college or university is able to implement a college high school. Nor will every student find educational advantages and opportunities at such a school. Middle college high school as an idea is not a panacea for the woes of American high schools. It is only one innovation designed to meet specific types of problems.

As we have already noted, the general philosophy behind a middle college high school reflects a larger movement often described as seamless education. The "seamless web," as Juan Lara and Ruth Mitchell note, evolves from the criticism that "education as a field has no consciousness of what it could be. Schooling follows models that were developed in the nineteenth century for a society with a very different set of values and morals" (1986, p. 25). The problem is that we are trying to force today's students into a mold that is not relevant to their experience nor relevant to the task that Lara and Mitchell argue is at hand—"to enable all citizens to read, write, think creatively and critically, appreciate art and culture, and understand science and technology" (p. 25).

Seen in this light, the emergence of middle college high school as an educational innovation is an attempt to move beyond nineteenth century modernist structures emphasizing a separation between K–12 and postsecondary education. As college attendance rates verify (Almanac, 1994), this separation has been especially taxing for students from diverse cultural backgrounds. Middle College High School represents one effort to remove obstacles that limit postsecondary participation on the part of high school students served by Divided Community College. It is significant to note once again that ninety-five percent of the students served by MCHS are African American.

In terms of organizational theory, the adoption of the middle college–high school program at Divided may be seen as an example of boundary spanning explained by open systems theory (Scott, 1987). From an open systems perspective, organizations exist in a continuous state of interaction with their environments. Some theorists discuss such organizations as "cybernetic systems" in that they continually monitor their environment through a series of "feedback loops" (Birnbaum, 1988; Morgan, 1986). As a result of ongoing interaction, a state of interdependence evolves in which the environment shapes the organization and the organization, in turn, shapes its environment.

Oftentimes, an organization can maximize its opportunities by spanning boundaries that separate the organization from other external social collectivities. Through boundary spanning activities, an organization may increase its resource input and thereby ensure greater control over its environment, enhancing its organizational niche. "Faced with environmental uncertainty, the adaptive organization, operating under norms of bounded rationality, establishes boundary spanning roles as the vehicles for searching and learning in the environment" (Middaugh, 1984, p. 9). Bounded rationality refers to the idea that "a series of actions is organized in such a way as to lead to predetermined goals with maximum efficiency. . . . Rationality refers not to the selection of goals but to their implementation" (Scott, 1987, p. 31).

In terms of Divided Community College, building connections with the local school district may be seen as a boundary spanning activity in that the traditional dividing line between K–12 and postsecondary education is erased. As one MCHS staff member noted, "We're all in this together. Education really has no boundaries." The organization, Divided, expands its own boundaries by encompassing some of the functions of organizations existing within its environment. In effect, the organization and parts of its environment merge as one and a new organization and environment form.

As we note in chapter 2, the community education role of the community college is central to achieving a democratic vision in which all students have opportunities to fully participate in economic, political, and social life. Meeting the community education role involves responding to the needs of the local community or surrounding communities. Community colleges ought to reflect the needs and concerns of the community through the types of programs enacted. In the case of Divided, perhaps the most significant need of its local community relates to the high attrition of local high school students, a vast majority of whom are African American. Middle College High School may be seen as a community education response that has involved collaboration between Divided and the local school district. Collaborative, boundary spanning activities may be necessary in times of financial exigency and have demonstrated their positive impact for students from disadvantaged backgrounds. The LaGuardia Middle College High School as well as the recent University of Southern Colorado and Pueblo School District 60 Alliance are two collaborative, boundary spanning efforts that come to mind (Schwartz, 1992; Lieberman, 1985, 1989).

As a result of its boundary spanning activities, Divided has created a new organization composed not only of a community college, but also a high school. As various faculty and staff have indicated, many are not pleased with the nature of this new organization and some have not completely bought into the idea. In effect, the fabric that holds Divided together as an organization and as a community has been stretched by its organizational restructuring.

The term fabric is, of course, metaphorical and relates more or less to the organizational culture, which for Divided has changed with the inclusion of MCHS. Divided provides an example of how boundary spanning activities, which are often required to meet the needs of the local community, pose a challenge to the organizational culture and sense of community. Thus, not only do community colleges face organizational identity problems in seeking to fill the multiple roles of transfer, vocational, and community education; community responsiveness itself leads to a variety of pulls and confused organizational boundaries. How are community colleges to resolve the identity issues caused in part by boundary spanning? Possible solutions lie in better understanding organizational identity and ideas related to academic community.

A traditional view of academic community tends to stress the idea of a group of like-minded individuals who meet on occasion to decide institutional matters (Birnbaum, 1988). This idea is often referred to as the "collegial model." However, college campuses are no longer composed of homogeneous cultural groups. Furthermore, the purposes served by postsecondary institutions are far more complex than in previous eras. Colleges and universities have not simply become more culturally diverse; programmatic diversity has also become a reality.

What is suggested throughout this book is an organizational identity defined by multiplicity. William Tierney (1993) captures part of this idea in his discussion of academic communities of difference. In this discussion, he focuses on diverse students, faculty, and staff and the perspectives that colleges and universities need to embrace if they are to truly enact democratic ideals. Although Tierney speaks of difference primarily in terms of diverse racial, ethnic, gender, and sexual identity groups, the idea of organizational multiplicity expands the notion of difference to also include diverse roles, relationships, identities, and processes encompassed by today's complex organizational settings. The challenge facing today's community colleges is learning to deal with organizational and environmental uncertainty and complexity by thinking of organizational life and identity more in terms of multiplicity. Organizational multiplicity represents a move from modernist conceptions of organizational life to a postmodern perspective. We expand upon this idea in chapter 7 as we focus on one community colleges's efforts to balance multiple roles and serve multiple constituencies.

The conflict and disagreement at Divided over the inclusion of Middle College High School is one example of the kind of multiplicity with which today's community colleges must come to terms. The challenge is to escape modernist goals of harmony, and instead learn from diverse perspectives that continually challenge organizational members to rethink their positions and the organization's multifaceted identity. Organizational boundary spanning offers one strategic device for meeting some of the challenges of a postmodern organizational environment.

In spanning organizational boundaries, new individuals, resources, and problems are brought to an organization. We see in the case of MCHS that new students suddenly appeared on campus—African-American high school students for the most part. With these students, new resources emerged—financial savings from classrooms being dropped from the facilities plan as well as an ongoing supply of current and future students. Along with the new organizational members and new resources came problems—noise, disruption, changes in organizational image, confusion about organizational structure. Clearly, boundary spanning efforts pose a challenge to the organizational identity of any institution.

A concern for critical multicultural education challenges community colleges to think about ways in which they might better serve their diverse communities. Middle College High School is one example of how boundary spanning strategies might be used to improve an organization's ability to develop multicultural programs and thus better serve an increasingly diverse student population.

From the perspective of critical multiculturalism, issues of community responsiveness ought to be guided by concerns for justice, equality, and freedom. Boundary spanning strategies may be a vehicle to improve an organization's ability to better meet these concerns. Such a perspective suggests that one way to evaluate community responsiveness is to ask questions framed by critical multiculturalism: How does the proposed community initiative relate to issues of equality? Does the initiative create a more just academic community? Are culturally diverse students offered opportunities that once were not present? Do students and residents have a voice in the creation of the program?

If we apply the preceding questions to the middle college–high school program at Divided, several issues arise. Clearly, Middle College High School has helped with student retention and college participation. The program also stresses career opportunities for underrepresented students through its extensive internship program. But have the relationships between students and teachers been altered? More specifically, has MCHS moved toward more democratic classrooms where the knowledge that students bring to the classroom is relevant?

In moving the high school to the community college, teachers and staff have effectively created a new organizational ethos in which students are seen in a more adult manner. Additionally, in providing a smaller teacher-to-student ratio, the school has enabled and encouraged more collaborative and cooperative classrooms to emerge. Because of the smaller classrooms and an emphasis on collaborative learning, the students have greater voice in the classrooms at MCHS than students attending the surrounding city schools. Nonetheless, the curriculum is still grounded in traditional assumptions of knowledge; and, despite more collaborative learning opportunities, teachers are still envisioned as the keepers of knowledge. What is left for MCHS to achieve then is not merely a reduction in class size; now, efforts need to be taken to integrate the multiple forms of knowledge and ways of knowing its students bring to the classroom into the pedagogical process.

About ninety-five percent of the students attending Middle College High School are African American, yet the curriculum differs in only minor ways from the surrounding city and county schools (which are half White and half African American). Part of the problem reflects the bureaucracy of the school district and the responsibility of Middle College High School to fit its curriculum into the basic scheme of the district. Yet, there is always room for resistance and teachers and administrators at MCHS have a great opportunity to create a more empowering curriculum designed to help students understand the social, historical, and political forces that contribute to their experiences as African Americans in this country.

A few teachers have attempted critical forms of pedagogy, but only on a limited basis. For example, one instructor of an honors class has asked students to write about a significant event in the history of black struggle and then relate these historical events to the students' present-day lives. The instructor's goal is to encourage students to see the role they might play in the writing of their own histories and the history of African Americans. This type of activity helps students to connect history to their lived experience and is to be encouraged. Unfortunately, few other teachers at Middle College High School seem to recognize the importance or the need to encourage dangerous memory as part of individual and social transformation.

Although ad hoc efforts are commendable, pedagogies committed to naming and then transforming social life must be far-reaching and cut across the entire curriculum. Our point here is that race matters; MCHS has an opportunity to challenge students to come to terms with how various forces (including educational institutions) have helped to frame the experiences of African Americans in anti-democratic ways and at the same time contributed to regressive cultural images. Raising racial issues in the classroom is central to democratic views of education. Cornell West (1993b) reminds us, "A candid examination of *race* matters takes us to the core of the crisis of American democracy. And the degree to which race *matters* in the plight and predicament of fellow citizens is a crucial measure of whether we can keep alive the best of this democratic experiment we call America" (p. 156).

A critical multicultural analysis of Divided's venture into K–12 raises other important issues. Concerns about how the program was developed and how it was implemented must be addressed. More specifically, the lack of collaboration on the part of the president has created resentment and bitterness among many faculty and staff at Divided. Critical multiculturalism challenges those organizational members in official positions of authority to measure their actions wisely and invest in democratic and collaborative processes wherever possible. In what follows, we examine issues of leadership and discuss how a critical multicultural view might inform organizational change efforts.

Leadership How is leadership to be conceptualized when democracy provides the underlying framework to administrative action? From a critical multicultural perspective in which democracy is the central organizing concept, academic environments ought to encourage open discussion and debate about important issues. The early planning and implementation of MCHS did not involve the campus community; only individuals at the top of Divided's organizational hierarchy advanced the development of Middle College High School. As a result of the top-down decision making, there has been much fallout and lack of support largely because of resentment on the part of those faculty and staff left out of the process. From a critical multicultural perspective, organizations exist first and foremost as democracies. This is the cornerstone of our argument throughout this book: Community colleges are not only to be democratizing agents in terms of their contributions to social mobility; but, just as importantly, they must be democratic educational centers.

The authoritarian manner in which the previous Divided president went about developing and implementing Middle College High School reflects a view of the president as a heroic leader capable of transforming an institution by himself. Writings about community college presidents tend to perpetuate this "great man" theory of leadership. For example, in discussing the early "founding presidents," George Vaughan (1989) offers the following passage: "A founding president moved into an area, constructed buildings, employed faculty, developed curricula, recruited students, placed the teaching and learning process in motion, and spread the mission of the college to anyone who would listen" (p. 7). God did less in *Genesis*. Even in community college works that argue for a more "shared vision," the significance of one individual—the president—is still apparent. John Roueche, George Baker, and Robert Rose (1989) write about the importance of developing working teams committed to a shared vision, but they discuss such teams as primarily the by-product of presidential influence, as if others within a community college are incapable of generating a unifying vision. Their following passage about organizational change highlights our point: "Transformation—or change—is accomplished, in part, through the development of a leadership team—a cohesive group of people working and moving together in the same direction. The cohesion of these teams is due to the *acceptance of the CEO's influence* [our emphasis]" (p. 11).

Traditional views that stress presidents or CEOs as leaders miss two fundamental points of leadership: that many organizational members have leadership abilities and that leadership is often situational. Community college leaders do not simply reside in the president's office and the opportunities in which leadership may be enacted are variable and complex. An academic community committed to democracy establishes conditions whereby a variety of organizational members (including students) have multiple opportunities to exercise leadership. Furthermore, the idea of leadership is not a static notion in which specific traits can be delineated as those that leaders must have. Instead, leadership is seen to be contextual in that different settings and circumstances call forth a variety of personal and group qualities necessary for effective democratic action.

Let us return to the idea of the organization as a culture. When we think of organizations as cultures—as systems of shared meanings—it is easier to understand why the great man view of leadership is more myth than reality, and why organizations are better suited to collaborative and democratic processes. Although high-ranking officials may be able to impose structural changes—such as the creation of Middle College High School—altering shared understandings takes more than an executive fiat. Instead, for change to take root, organizational members must envision the organization, their role within the organization, and the roles of others in a new and perhaps innovative way. If this change in sense-making strategies does not occur, then change is unlikely to take root. Such is the case at Middle College High School where every day a new challenge to the program's existence springs forth from among the faculty.

Because a fundamental change in the way members make sense of organizational life is needed, involving them in the early stages of any change effort is essential to success. Change efforts need to be based on inclusionary practices involving a wide range of organizational members and tapping the leadership abilities of diverse campus constituents. From this perspective, good leaders also know how to be good followers and encourage other organizational members to utilize their abilities.

In democratic organizations, leadership is not so much about commanding followers or subordinates as it is about contributing to how others make sense of the organizational reality. As Linda Smircich and Gareth Morgan (1982) contend, "Leadership is realized in the process whereby one or more individuals succeeds in attempting to frame and define the reality of others" (p. 258). For organizations committed to democratic principles, sense-making strategies ought to revolve around issues of justice and equality. This is the kind of leadership James MacGregor Burns (1978) writes about when he discusses intellectual leadership. For Burns, intellectual leaders are "concerned critically with values, purposes, ends that transcend immediate practical needs. . . . Intellectual leaders are not detached from their social milieus; typically they seek to change it" (pp. 141–142).

Critical multiculturalism is guided by democratic principles that ought to shape an organization's commitment to students, faculty, and staff. We are not suggesting that the decision-making capability of community college presidents and other administrative leaders be shackled. What we are suggesting, however, is that, over the long haul, innovation needs to be deeply rooted within the culture of the organization; this means involving faculty, staff, students, and local residents in a more democratic process.

Leadership from a critical multicultural perspective is not merely situated with one's location within the formal organizational structure. Critical multiculturalism stresses the multiple ways of knowing and forms of knowledge a wide range of people bring to organizations. Community colleges committed to building empowering and democratic communities create conditions whereby diverse voices have leadership opportunities. In such organizations, all members have responsibilities as democratic participants to take up positions. However, presidents and senior officials have unique opportunities and a view of the organization that others may not have. Such a position should be used to contribute to a wider organizational vision founded on democratic principles. If a president of a community college desires to create a more egalitarian organization committed to equal opportunity and social justice, embracing a hierarchical management style is antithetical and counterproductive to such educational ideals.

Summary

Middle College High School represents an educational innovation designed to assist "at-risk" students, the vast majority of whom are African American, through high school and possibly into college. MCHS has achieved significant success based on the low attrition rates and increased college attendance. Students in general have responded well to being treated more as adults and to lower student-to-teacher and student-to-counselor ratios. Students also have found being on a college campus to be beneficial. One result has been that many have, for the first time, given serious thought to pursuing a college degree.

We argue in chapter 1 that education fundamentally relates to student identity. And, of course, identity involves how students envision their futures and what they believe they are capable of accomplishing in their lives. In the stories of Alton, Charlene, and Denise, we see how their self-definitions have changed, and how these changes have led to different aspirations for the future. They see themselves in a more confident light and have altered their educational and career plans accordingly.

However, while Middle College High School has helped individual students to rethink their career aspirations, the school has done very little to help students deal with the many social forces that have situated African Americans on the margins of society. A critical multicultural curriculum that fosters a critique of cultural identities and the historical and contemporary inequalities prevalent throughout our society is needed.

Despite its success, MCHS has had its share of opponents within Divided Community College. Numerous faculty and staff, still angry over their exclusion from the decision-making process, complain about the noise and disruptions caused by high school students as well as the potential damage to Divided's image as a collegiate institution. They also are angry about the loss of classroom space and they are confused by the dual governing boards that now have influence over organizational life at Divided.

The problems raised by faculty and staff at Divided highlight the complexities of organizational restructuring related to boundary spanning activities. Boundary spanning is a way to restructure an organization and potentially increase resources: In essence, a new organizational identity emerges through partnerships created with one or more other organizations. In the case of Divided, partnerships involve the local school district as well as local businesses.

The restructuring at Divided may be understood through a critical multicultural lens in that the effort itself is designed primarily to improve the educational opportunities of underrepresented minority students. Critical multiculturalism requires institutions to consider the impacts of organizational decisions in terms of democratic principles such as equality, justice, and freedom. Middle College High School may be interpreted as a multicultural organizational innovation in that it provides educational opportunities for African-American high school students who may likely leave the educational pipeline.

Although the MCHS program represents Divided's commitment to the community and to the educational needs of underrepresented students, enactment of the program did not follow the ideals of democratic governance. By most accounts, the program was thrust upon faculty and staff at Divided through authoritarian decision making that has undermined the sense of college-wide participation. As a result, much resentment has developed among faculty and staff, whose input largely was excluded in the development and implementation of Middle College High School. The emergence of the program highlights the importance of involving a wide range of faculty, staff, and community residents in organizational restructuring if change is to take deep root. Consequently, MCHS is on tenuous turf and must continually guard against its extermination.

Chapter Six
Cultural Capital and Border Knowledge
A Case Study of Developmental Education

This chapter describes how Remedial Community College has struggled to develop effective remediation for less academically prepared students through its developmental studies program. Because some students are underprepared for college-level work, their low academic achievement and high dropout rates have been problematic for community colleges. This is true at Remedial where faculty and staff at the college have enacted a developmental education component as a means to rectify problems faced by less-prepared students. The developmental program provides a battery of services for underprepared college students including testing and advisement, remediation courses, tutoring, and career counseling.

Part of the problem at Remedial Community College reflects the general difficulty educational institutions have in addressing the needs of culturally diverse students and the wide range of knowledge and experience students bring to the teaching and learning process. What tends to occur is that the experience and knowledge of middle- and upper-class students get legitimated and those of other students get situated on the margins. This is especially true for developmental education at Remedial where the vast majority of students are from minority or lower- and working-class backgrounds. Throughout this chapter, we use the concepts of cultural capital and border knowledge to highlight some of the problems with how Remedial views and evaluates the knowledge, skills, and cultural attributes of students enrolled in developmental courses that, in part, contribute to their low achievement.

The centerpiece of our discussion hinges on Pierre Bourdieu's (1986) notion of cultural capital. As we note in chapter 1, cultural capital is the idea that certain forms of knowledge are elevated over others, and thus are more readily exchangeable in social settings. The concept of cultural capital is central to understanding Bourdieu's theory of cultural reproduction. Bourdieu argues that different sets of linguistic and cultural competencies are learned by individuals and relate to the social location of their families. Those individuals and families most connected to mainstream social institutions have a greater opportunity to assert their linguistic and cultural competencies as norms. Those individuals and families removed from mainstream institutions and sources of social power are more likely to have linguistic and cultural forms defined for them as norms.

As Michel Foucault (1978, 1980) notes throughout much of his work, the power of the norm to regulate social behavior is significant. Regulation occurs not only through the power of norms to limit or constrain behavior—a kind of negative force; norms must also be seen as having a positive force—as a shaper of knowledge and of identity. Norms define what knowledge is significant and whose identities have relevance in particular social contexts. Thus, the power of the norm is not only to contain, it also plays a defining role. This is clearly evident in the way the knowledge and identities of lower- and working-class and minority peoples, as well as women, are treated as inferior and irrelevant.

Let us return to the educational context. Through the power of linguistic and cultural norms, Bourdieu calls attention to the fact that children incorporate a set of meanings, qualities of style, modes of thinking, and behaviors that are assigned a certain social value and status. Jean Anyon (1981), Hugh Mehan (1978), and Ray Rist (1977) demonstrate that White middle-class children display linguistic forms, modes of style, and values that are acknowledged as a privileged form of cultural production. This cultural capital is honored by those dominant groups in society that define and legitimate the meaning of success in education (Giroux, 1983). In contrast, culturally diverse students, who often exhibit behaviors outside the mainstream norms of society (such as different speech patterns and modes of dress), or reject academic knowledge based on cultural perspectives of teachers and faculty, are at a decided educational disadvantage when compared to middle-class white students (Aronowitz & Giroux, 1991). Lower- and working-class students enter territory where their own cultural resources and values are not celebrated or even recognized, and their forms of knowledge—border knowledge—remain subordinate to the preferred cultural capital of the white middle and upper class (Hanson, 1994).

Educational institutions play a particularly important role in legitimating and reproducing the dominant culture (Apple, 1988; Giroux, 1983, 1992). The cultural capital of upper socioeconomic groups is legitimized through the assignation of privileged status to middle- and upper-class values and gets reinforced through an educational institution's preference for and selection of particular textbooks, teaching styles, curricula, and classroom discourse. The culture transmitted by educational institutions confirms and sustains the culture of dominant groups while marginalizing and silencing the culture of subordinate groups (Cherryholmes, 1988). These institutional preferences and practices define what counts as knowledge and authorize those who may speak about it. Conversely, by authorizing those who may speak, it silences those whose cultural experiences have become peripheral to mainstream educational processes. Minorities, women, and lower- and working-class students in particular have found that their views and perspectives have not been heard with equal authority in education (Apple, 1988; Fine, 1991; Giroux, 1992).

The challenge for community colleges is to develop programs, courses, and pedagogical practices that offer diverse students opportunities to learn new ideas, concepts, and ways of seeing the world without rejecting the cultural forms these students bring with them. Hence, institutions must develop educational strategies that embrace the border knowledge culturally diverse students bring to the college setting. All students should have the opportunity to participate in discussions about how various forces have situated their lives in relation to others. This means critically examining issues of culture and identity. Henry Giroux (1992) elaborates on this point in his discussion of border pedagogy: "Critical educators need to provide the conditions for students to speak differently so that their narratives can be affirmed and engaged critically along with the consistencies and contradictions that characterize such experiences" (p. 32). This seems especially pertinent to community colleges because of the diversity of the student population. Our goal in this chapter is to view the developmental studies program at Remedial Community College through a critical multicultural lens, which stresses the importance of border knowledge and the relevance of critical pedagogy. But first, we provide some background about Remedial and its surrounding community.

Organizational Background

Remedial Community College is situated in the southern region of the United States and was established in 1967. In the 1960s, community colleges grew more rapidly than any segment of American higher education had ever grown (Brint & Karabel, 1989). The expansion of community colleges brought postsecondary education to millions of Americans who might not have previously considered higher education (Cohen & Brawer, 1989), and Remedial was a part of this expansion. Many of the new students entering community colleges were less prepared for higher learning than their predecessors and posed a new challenge to community college education. These problems persist nearly thirty years later, and Remedial Community College provides a case study of an institution struggling to serve less-prepared students.

Remedial serves about one thousand students in a variety of one-year vocational, two-year technical, and college transfer programs. An additional fourteen hundred students participate in the college's continuing education programs. Of the one thousand students in vocational, technical, and college transfer programs, seventy-one percent are white, twenty-six percent are African American, and the remaining three percent are Native American or Latino/a. Sixty-two percent of the students are women.

Faculty at Remedial Community College are predominantly White (eighty-seven percent). Eleven percent of the faculty are African American, and two percent are of other racial backgrounds. Thirty percent of the faculty have as their highest degree the bachelor's, forty-nine percent have a master's as their highest degree, and eleven percent have doctorates. Nearly all the full-time faculty (eighty-two percent) received their terminal degree from institutions within the state. As far as administrators are concerned, four of the six senior administrators (deans, vice presidents, president) are white and two are African American. One of the senior administrators is an African-American woman and another is a white woman.

Remedial is a small campus with a friendly and intimate feel to it. Members of the college frequently spoke of the campus as "one big family." As we watched students move from building to building, we could not help but notice the number of students who acknowledged one another as they passed by heading in opposite directions. The same was true of the faculty and staff, whom we found to be both friendly and helpful. The college president, Ross Grayson, exemplifies "southern hospitality" through his openness and charm toward the staff and students. President Grayson grew up in the area and is a well-known and respected individual on campus and in the community. He exhibits a bit of homespun personality as he walks about with an unlit cigar in his mouth, displaying a jocular, unassuming quality. Little emphasis is placed on formality. During our interview, for example, Grayson paused every few minutes to answer his phone as he talked to students in a fatherly manner.

Because of the small size of the college and the community, faculty and staff often come in contact with each other in social settings outside of the college. Many participate in community or church-related activities or have children who attend the same schools or play on the same soccer teams. Along with the president, many of the faculty and staff grew up in this county or in adjoining counties. There is a close, almost family feel to the institution. The metaphor of the family, in fact, is one that was mentioned by several faculty and students when they described the institution.

The Local Community

Remedial is located in a rural county where agriculture and manufacturing provide most of the jobs. In fact, manufacturing accounts for thirty-seven percent of the jobs. Most of these jobs tend to be low-skilled, low-paying jobs in textile mills, food processing plants, or other factories. In the past, agriculture was dominant in the local economy. However, agriculture has experienced a precipitous decline in recent years, with thirty-seven percent fewer farms in the county in 1990 than in 1980.

Despite the growth of population and the relative health of the economy in urban areas of Remedial's home state, the county has not shared in the bonanza. Remedial's county has shown moderate growth (five percent), but it pales in comparison with the state's urban growth rate (seventeen percent). The median household income in the county ($25,800) lags behind the statewide household median income ($26,647). There is also large disparity in the median household income between Whites ($29,500) and African Americans ($17,500). Educational attainment also is lower in the county when compared with the state at large. The statewide proportion of students twenty-five years of age and older with high school diplomas is seventy percent (Bureau of the Census, 1990), whereas the county lags behind with sixty-three percent of Whites and fifty-four percent of African Americans in the same age group having high school degrees (Bureau of the Census, 1990).

The contrast between Remedial's local community and its home state is somewhat paradoxical. Remedial is situated in close proximity to more populous and prosperous urban and suburban counties. But Remedial and its surrounding residents do not, for the most part, share in the economic prosperity of their neighboring counties. As a result, Remedial exists as a rural community college struggling to provide education and job training to a largely undereducated population of students whose hopes for a prosperous economic future may lie outside their county of residence. In what follows we examine the struggle within the institution to educate its citizenry for a more prosperous future. We describe the problems faced by Remedial in its efforts to guide less-prepared students toward achieving their goals.

Findings

We discuss our findings in terms of significant organizational practices that Remedial has enacted as a means for making decisions about students and appropriate curricular options. We organize the findings into three parts. In the first part, we discuss the types of knowledge valued by the institution and how Remedial uses such judgments to make decisions about students. In the second part, we consider the way in which Remedial uses placement tests to direct students. We conclude the presentation of findings by focusing on the crucial role advisement plays in shaping the experiences of students at Remedial.

School Knowledge   Besides skills needed to succeed in the classroom, faculty and administrators expect students at Remedial to master the skills associated with being a successful student. Many of these skills are essential for academic success, such as note-taking and study skills, but others are associated with the cultural competencies expected of college students. As an example, faculty expect students to use certain styles of communication associated with academic discourse. Many Remedial faculty believe that students should have learned these skills in high school and had them reinforced by parents, counselors, and peers. A number of Remedial students, however, do not exhibit such competencies. The result is that some students lack essential knowledge for achieving success in the classroom. Students who lack this essential knowledge—cultural capital—are channeled to the developmental studies program where they take specific courses designed to raise their level of understanding in specific knowledge areas. A faculty member discussed his experience and frustration with less-prepared students:

Some of these students don't even know how to take notes. I tell them that if I write it on the board, they should be writing it in their notes because there's a good chance that this information will be on the test. These are skills they should have picked up in high school. The skills that they need compared to what they have is really shocking. Somewhere along the line, they didn't get it. And it goes beyond not knowing math or English, but just the responsibilities that a student should take for their education. Time management, turning in their assignments, coming to class. I really give them a lot of slack if they have responsibilities to take care of. Frankly, though, they let things get in their way. The problems seem insurmountable. There are so many things. It's like one little thing will interfere. Like car trouble, and they won't come to class.

This instructor contrasted the developmental students with other students he teaches who "come to class prepared" and "know what they have to do to pass the course." He noted that the nondevelopmental students have "more stable home lives" and "fewer distractions."

Many students lacked basic skills because of poor advice or the generally inferior quality of schooling they received during their previous educational experiences. As an example, of the sixty-six developmental studies students interviewed at Remedial, thirty-seven had never taken high school algebra. Some of these students were advised not to take high school algebra, while others simply skipped algebra because it seemed irrelevant. It was not unusual for developmental studies students to have selected high school courses without sufficient knowledge about the implications of their choices for their academic future. Sixty of the sixty-six students interviewed did not have parents who attended college, and few of their peers had college experience. Students indicated that high school counselors, when available, did not always give students accurate information about the courses needed to prepare for college. The following are comments from Sheila, an eighteen-year-old white student:

I was working in a doctor's office. Filing, waiting on patients, typing. It was not the kind of thing I wanted to do forever. I was going to school part-time, but I quit because it was just too much. I wasn't prepared for college. I didn't take much math in high school, and I never took algebra. A teacher talked to me in the ninth grade and asked if I was going to college, and at that time I didn't think I was, so he said I should take consumer math instead of algebra. I wish I had known then what I know now. All those years in high school seem like such a waste. There was no one else who could give me help. My parents are divorced, and my mother never went to college, so she really couldn't tell me much; and I don't think she ever thought about me going to college. It was just something that never came up. I suppose she thought it was something that was out of reach.

College was not part of the expectations that Sheila had while in high school. But how many sixteen-year olds have a good idea of what their future might hold? The advice that Sheila received from her high school guidance counselor resulted in certain doors being closed to her. And her mother, through no fault of her own, was unable to offer any helpful advice about college and educational choices. Clearly, Sheila's lack of cultural capital served as a limiting force in her own economic and educational aspirations.

Charles, an eighteen-year-old African-American student, explained that he never took algebra because, after he took a math placement test, he was advised to take a lower-level math course in high school: "I think I was in the ninth grade. I took a test and they placed me in something else. In special education courses." Although Charles did not understand the importance at the time, he now has grave regrets about not having had algebra in high school. While Sheila had to make an important decision about her education without a great deal of knowledge about its long-term impact, Charles had a similar decision taken out of his hands and now suffers for its consequences. The impact of these early decisions has been significant for both students. Students such as Sheila and Charles find it difficult to enter a math-based college curriculum because of their inadequate high school preparation. The result is that their career choices become limited because of the types of college curricula they are prepared to handle. These students are not necessarily less intelligent than their peers, but their knowledge in specific areas is limited. They are left with few alternatives except to take developmental courses to bring their level of knowledge up to par with other students.

The experiences of the preceding students is symptomatic of many lower- and working-class students whose families oftentimes have insufficient knowledge of higher education and of educational choices in general. Despite their shortcomings, students in developmental studies courses possess a wealth of knowledge. Unfortunately, their knowledge is a form of border knowledge that faculty have failed to recognize and incorporate into classroom pedagogical practice. In brief, faculty at Remedial have done a poor job of tapping what students *do know*. Thus students are not able to use their existing knowledge in ways that enable them to learn what they *need to know* in order to succeed academically (and perhaps professionally). By failing to include the experiences and forms of knowledge of these students into the pedagogical process, teachers have contributed to their already low sense of academic ability.

In many cases, the students' own storehouse of knowledge, along with their values and cultural perspectives, conflicted with the expectations of faculty members. Faculty pointed frequently to the students' linguistic styles as an area of concern. One faculty member commented, "It's fine for them to talk like that with their friends, but it's not appropriate in certain situations." Faculty expected students to master a particular way of speaking and also emphasized that students should appear and act in specific ways. Another faculty member said, "It is important that the students learn now that certain forms of behavior or appearance will cause problems for them when they are on interviews." Although there is obviously a degree of truth in the notion that many employers have certain expectations about appearance and behaviors, there was little effort on the part of Remedial faculty to understand the diverse linguistic and dress styles of students. And there was virtually no recognition that such preferences reflect aspects of culture and therefore are political and negotiable.

Some faculty at Remedial regarded themselves as the standard-bearers for the values and traditions of the college, and they tended to be unwavering in their demands that students conform to the academic standards of the institution. One teacher was firm in her belief that faculty have to maintain standards: "I won't lower mine. Students need to learn that when they get out into the world of work, they are not going to be spoon-fed." Others suggested that developmental studies programs should be eliminated and that students needing remedial help should get it elsewhere. "Some people are just not college material" was the attitude often conveyed by the standard-bearers.

Pierre Bourdieu (1977) proposed that the policies and practices of education, and the expectations of teachers concerning the cultural and social competencies of students, favor individuals from middle- and upper-income families. At Remedial, not only did the lack of school knowledge work against lower-income students, but the cultural codes they exhibited, such as their manner of speaking and dressing, also were seen as deficient. Some students, however, recognized the inequality in the stance of Remedial faculty and staff, and challenged existing conditions. These students offered a form of resistance to the cultural reproduction taking place at Remedial. For example, students complained about the organization of the developmental courses. One student felt overly confined by his status as a developmental studies student: "We should be more on our own. If I want to just read the book and skip class, I should be able to do it." Another student complained to the administration about the lack of quality instruction in some of his development studies courses. A third felt that more money ought to be allocated so that smaller teacher-student ratios could be achieved in developmental studies courses: "There's really no time to talk to the teacher. We sit at our desks and do problems, and if we have a question, we have to wait in line to talk to the teacher. Sometimes I just say forget it."

The knowledge that faculty at Remedial expect students to possess is not only reflected in classroom practices; it is also evident in the way placement tests are used to make decisions about students. In what follows, we examine another significant cultural practice of the institution, that of the placement exam.

Placement Exams Placement tests are an example of an institutional practice used by nearly all community colleges to assess student skills in mathematics, language, and reading in order to assign students to appropriate curricular levels. Use of the exams is taken for granted by most institutions and is viewed as an essential part of student advisement. Despite the good intentions behind using placement exams, the tests have the inadvertent effect of creating barriers to students' achieving their educational and occupational goals. The placement exams serve to sort students into those prepared for college and those the institution deems to be in need of developmental education. Unfortunately, those channeled to developmental education experience the highest dropout rates at the college; and those who do survive rarely emerge fully prepared for college-level work.

A couple of staff at Remedial commented on the placement tests and expressed the prevailing attitude of the college. "It's for their own good," noted one staff member, while another added, "It wouldn't be fair to the students to put them in a course they couldn't handle." The institution places a great deal of significance on these exams, and faculty and administrators maintain that the exams provide a fair measure of students' abilities. An administrator in the developmental studies program commented on the impact of the placement exam on admissions to the various college programs:

We are an open-door institution. We don't leave anybody out. As long as students can pass the placement test, they are allowed into the college transfer courses. The curriculum is not limited. We have many students who begin as college transfer, but first they have to take the placement test; or they can take the SAT and get a minimum of 400 on both tests.

If they don't pass the placement test, then they need to enroll in the developmental courses. After they take the developmental courses, they can retake the placement test and if they get the score they need, they can enroll in transfer courses. That makes us open door.

The community college advertises itself as open-door, but all students are not free to enroll in any course they choose. This becomes most apparent as one walks through the corridors of the nursing department. Photographs of past nursing graduates adorn the walls along the corridors. Perhaps what is most striking is that the graduates are predominantly white women, with only one or two African Americans among the graduating classes of approximately twenty-five students. Nursing was among the most popular programs at the college, with long waiting lists, but the process for entering the program eliminated many students. If students fail the placement exam, they can take developmental courses to prove their competence in reading, math, and language through successful completion of the courses. After they complete the courses, the students have to retake the placement exams and achieve the cutoff score before they are admitted to the nursing program.

Though Remedial places a great deal of importance on the placement exam, all students do not seem to understand the significance of the test. Just as Charles had found his educational career sidetracked earlier by a high school math placement test, he faced a similar situation at Remedial. Once again, the extent of the implications were vague to him:

I took the placement test that everybody takes. It was timed and I didn't have enough time to finish. I was too rushed. Then I got something in the mail about the courses I should register for. No one talked to me about the results from the placement test except for my math teacher, who said I need to take two other courses before algebra. I know algebra is one of the courses I'm supposed to take, because I want to transfer in two years.

Charles accepted the idea that the exam assessed his educational skills and that he would need to take a series of courses before he could enroll in college transfer courses. When asked whether he knew if developmental courses could be transferred to a four-year institution, Charles did not know, but he thought they could. And, of course, they do not count as credit toward transfer. When asked if he still believed he could transfer to a four-year college in two years even if he had to take one year of developmental courses in math and English, he replied that he thought he could. And, of course, he will not be able to transfer after two years at Remedial, because approximately one of those years will be spent in developmental courses that carry no academic weight. Charles' case is not unusual. He highlights the lack of understanding that some lower- and working-class and minority students have about the nuances of college life. Things such as the impact of institutional practices like placement testing, or even the types of questions college students need to ask about their futures, often are foreign to these students. The fact that many of their parents do not have college experience (and therefore may be of little help in advising their sons and daughters) makes the problem even more difficult. For example, the placement exam had an enormous impact on Charles' life: His first year in college consisted of taking developmental courses, none of which could be used toward graduation, and none of which will be accepted by an accredited four-year college or university.

Not all minority and lower- and working-class students were uninformed about the importance of the placement test or were passive about accepting the results. One student challenged the validity of the test and successfully argued that she should be allowed to retake the test. She retook the test, passed it, and was placed in college transfer courses. Other students who did not question or challenge the results of the test went through the developmental studies program and, depending on their test scores, spent a year or more taking these courses. One student explained: "I feel like I'm in high school again, it's not like I'm in a real college. Even though I'm in these courses, I know I shouldn't be in them."

Many of the students who took the placement exam and later were channeled to developmental studies did not believe that the test was a true indicator of their abilities. Some students expressed surprise at their low scores. Most blamed the pressure of the setting associated with the exam. Others talked about the years they had been away from formal education and the "rustiness" of their skills.

For example, one student explained that he could do the math at one time, but it had been so long that he forgot some of the mathematical rules. He felt that with a brief refresher, he could have done much better. And, of course, if this student would have had the money to hire someone to prepare him for the test, as middle- and upper-class students often do in preparation for their SAT's, he no doubt would have done much better.

Placement tests and faculty understanding about the knowledge students need to have are integral to the academic advisement process at Remedial and at many other community colleges. In what follows, we highlight some of the interactions between students and college personnel regarding students' academic and career decisions. We point out how faculty attitudes about students in the developmental studies programs contribute to their inability to succeed at Remedial.

Academic and Career Advisement In general, the sentiment of faculty toward students at Remedial Community College was quite positive. One faculty member boasted, "We have a lot of good students here." A nursing instructor was particularly pleased about "the high quality and industriousness of the nursing students." Faculty spoke glowingly of the hard work students put into their courses and how the vast majority came to class well prepared. However, students in the developmental studies program were characterized in a much different manner. These students were described as "unrealistic about their career aspirations." As one faculty member noted, "The trouble is they want to come here and be in college transfer programs." And another stated, "Some of these students are not going to be brain surgeons, and unfortunately they have not been told."

Clearly, there was a widespread impression among the faculty and staff that developmental studies students, because of poor high school preparation or their "disadvantaged backgrounds," were long shots for academic success. As another faculty member noted, "If we can train them for a job, get them to become contributing members of society, then we have been successful."

In chapter 2, we introduced Bill Jenson, a white male student from a working-class background. Bill typifies many developmental

studies students. He is twenty-nine years old, a high school dropout, and recently lost his construction job because of a disabling
injury. He is married with three children, and recently decided that
he wanted to return to school. Bill's story is not unusual because
there are many other returning students who lost their jobs or who
are stuck in low-skilled, low-paying occupations. Such students enter Remedial believing they "will get retrained" for jobs that promise
better pay and a chance for social mobility. Bill and other students
like him, who have never planned or given much thought to higher
education, find themselves in situations where they have limited
educational experience; yet, they are expected to make critical academic decisions. Bill was determined to go to college, but he found
that he had to depend on faculty and staff at Remedial to give him
good advice, or at least helpful information. And, for the most part,
he was quite pleased with the advisement he received:

*I leave a lot up to my advisor. He helps me get the classes I need. I
decided on a curriculum, architectural technology, and he tells me what
I need to take. He is careful not to overload me. I knew it was going to be
tough in the beginning. When I got here, I didn't even know how to
divide. I've been doing well though, and everyone in my family is surprised.*

Because of their limited experience with higher education, first-
generation college students such as Bill may not even know the right
questions to ask and frequently suffer the consequences of an ill-
informed decision. Another student in the physical therapy program
wanted to transfer to a four-year program at a nearby state university. She became disappointed and disenchanted when she later found
out that her courses would not be accepted by the university.

First-generation college students from lower- and working-class
families are at a disadvantage to other students who call upon parents, relatives, or peers with experience in higher education as a source
of information for making academic decisions. Students such as Bill
Jenson have significant understandings about life, and sometimes
the world of work, but their knowledge of college oftentimes is deficient. Such students lack the cultural capital of many middle- and
upper-class students. For this reason, Bill had to rely on his advisor

to guide him through some of the educational process. But Bill also pointed out that his advisor took the time to get to know him, to understand his background and what he knew about and wanted from life. In fact, his faculty advisor had much in common with Bill; this, in part, enabled them to connect on a personal level. Not only was his advisor a White male, but also he had made a mid-life career change and had been a first-generation college student himself. The border knowledge that Bill brought to Remedial was embraced by his advisor, who wanted to learn more about Bill before he gave him important career and educational guidance. Unfortunately, Bill's relationship with his advisor was more the exception than the rule at Remedial.

Most faculty at Remedial recognize that student advisement, especially for developmental studies students, is an area that needs improvement. As one faculty member said, "Students' goals are undefined, and they know very little about what college is about." Teaching responsibilities and heavy advising loads limit the time that faculty can spend with students. An instructor commented, "There's only so much that we can do," and "So many students fall through the cracks." Another faculty member complained, "There are only two full-time counselors in student services to provide students with career counseling and information on college transfer."

Faculty talked about the "frustration levels" associated with losing developmental studies students because they could not spend enough time with them. One faculty member pointed out, "If we only had the time or resources to work with them. They need encouragement. So many of them have the desire to complete college, but they get lost in the shuffle. If I had the time to make a phone call to the students, find out why they didn't re-register, it might make a difference."

Evident throughout this section is the importance that academic and career advising play in assisting underprepared college students to succeed. Lower-and working-class students, as well as minority students, are more likely to be first-generation college-goers and may lack some of the vital cultural capital needed to make sound educational choices. Our discussion of academic and career advisement highlights some of the key issues. Most important from our perspective is the example of Bill Jenson and how he was able to connect with his advisor and obtain helpful insights about his education and career opportunities. We return to Bill Jenson later in this chapter as we examine some of the implications our findings have for multicultural education.

To this point, we have discussed three significant components of the institution's view of knowledge and how it envisions developmental studies. Our discussion has revolved around school knowledge, placement exams, and academic and career advisement. We now discuss how the assumptions faculty and staff at Remedial make about knowledge and developmental coursework pose significant problems for culturally diverse students. We then use our case study of Remedial to inform multicultural educational practice.

Discussion

Developmental studies students entered Remedial Community College with aspirations for finding good jobs and improving their social positions. Many of these students viewed Remedial as a place where they could transform their lives. Most faculty and administrators agreed that the community college ought to provide opportunity to students, particularly those who ordinarily would not attend college. However, the faculty and staff expressed their ideas differently about how they wanted to help students achieve their goals. Most supported the career and educational goals to which students in the transfer program aspired, but most also raised doubts that developmental studies students could achieve their ambitions. As one faculty member explained: "Everyone thinks they are four-year college material. Their goals are unrealistic."

Faculty believed that developmental studies students were not prepared for college-level work and were unlikely to ever attain those standards. Although the developmental studies program was designed to remediate students and raise them to standards acceptable to the social and cultural norms of the institution, the dropout and failure rate for developmental students remained high. Faculty consistently expressed an attitude that developmental students had little probability of attaining the standards needed for advanced college study and would achieve a measure of success if they could be trained for jobs.

Part of the problem at Remedial is that staff have not recognized the cultural differences between faculty and students relating to social class. Faculty, for the most part, do not understand differences in linguistic style and modes of dress as well as other cultural matters, such as the importance a car may have to a low-income student who may have family responsibilities. It is ignorance at a minimum and insensitivity at best for a faculty member to complain about a student missing class because of car problems.

Developmental students at Remedial were driven primarily by economic need and measured their success by the type of job they could get. The students, however, did not always understand fully the consequences of their academic decisions. Developmental studies students did not always have access to the necessary information to help them make such decisions. At Remedial, middle-class students had access to information that produced a greater economic and educational return than that which was available to lower- and working-class students. In particular, middle-class culture provided the students with experience and practice in the discourse and behaviors associated with a college education, and their transition to higher education was eased. Middle-class students at Remedial drew upon these experiences and relied on their social networks to help them with educational decisions. For example, one student at Remedial, whose parents had attended college, highlighted how helpful his father had been in filling out financial aid forms. Another pointed out that she had a good idea of what to expect at college because her sister had graduated from the state university. Obviously, when students have access to knowledge through family or peers who have experience with higher education, it is to their benefit. Such students have available to them a form of cultural capital that lower- and working-class students do not typically have. It is more than coincidence that first-generation college students were more likely to be assigned to developmental studies curricula than other students. As this case study indicates, many lower- and working-class students made their own decisions (often uninformed) or relied on the services provided by the institution to guide them through the educational process. The scarcity of resources, however, often meant that these students had limited access to help with career and academic concerns.

The findings of this study agree with assertions made by other researchers that social class position and class culture become a form of cultural capital in higher education (Bourdieu, 1977, 1986; Bourdieu & Passeron, 1990; Lareau, 1987). Clearly, developmental students bring different social and cultural skills to the college, and educators interpret these skills in a variety of ways. Students' social positions influence the kinds of understandings they have about life as well as the manner in which that knowledge is displayed. Educators interpret the knowledge exhibited by students and make judgments about students based on their assessments. Few faculty at Remedial make any effort to understand the cultural nuances of culturally diverse students, whether that diversity is rooted in class, race, or gender. It is hardly surprising that the one positive example of outstanding advisement revealed through our research was Bill Jenson and his advisor. Bill is a white male from a working-class family, and his advisor has a similar background. We are not suggesting that only white males can advise or understand other white males. What we are suggesting though is that significant cultural differences based on race, class, and gender exist, and that every effort needs to be made by faculty and staff to understand cultural differences. A helpful step community colleges such as Remedial can take is to recruit a number of diverse faculty and staff who can serve both as mentors for students as well as educators for colleagues.

The findings of this case study of Remedial Community College offer evidence that institutional practices of the community college (such as assessment, advisement, and placement) are not structured to take advantage of the skills and knowledge of lower- and working-class students, but instead work to the benefit of the middle class. This supports previous theory and research of Bourdieu and his position on the role of cultural capital in the reproduction of society (Bourdieu, 1977, 1986; Bourdieu & Passeron, 1990).

Our point is not that assessment and placement tests are bad, or that advising is not important, or that remedial courses are not sometimes needed. What we suggest is that the fundamental purpose and usefulness of such institutional strategies need to be more closely examined and thought about in terms of their implications. For example, should placement tests be used to create an entire category of students who by nature of the academic label assigned them—"developmental studies students"—become second-class citizens?

To understand more fully the role the institution plays in influencing the decisions and aspirations of students, we must, as Hugh Mehan (1992) suggests, examine the social construction of these arrangements. Unless we analyze the interactions among the institutional actors (students, faculty, and staff) involved, we are left with a highly structured account of the relationship between social origins, schooling, and subsequent achievement. Coming to terms with such interactions has been a central concern of this chapter and book. The experiences of students such as Charles, Sheila, and Bill are helpful in making sense of larger cultural concerns, which ultimately relate to issues of equal opportunity.

Even if we acknowledge that many lower- and working-class students tend to opt for working-class jobs regardless of the efforts of community colleges, we are still left with the vexing problem of the stratified nature of community colleges. Alan Kerkhoff (1992) noted that it may be unreasonable to expect educational institutions to prepare an undifferentiated group of students because students have different abilities, levels of motivation, and aspirations. What is not unreasonable, however, is to expect community colleges to reduce the inequality of opportunity that exists for their developmental students by reducing the barriers for their achievement. Reducing inequality requires that we examine the structures and arrangements that influence achievement, and also those arrangements that affect students' academic and career decisions.

In order to understand and then improve the problems faced by students who most often get assigned to developmental tracks, community colleges must recognize the role cultural capital plays in limiting the educational opportunities such students face. Community colleges confront a dual challenge then: to help educationally disadvantaged students develop the understandings they need to succeed academically, and at the same time to recognize that various structures within the college itself must be rethought because of the cultural bias they reflect. In theoretical terms, community colleges must find ways to embrace the border knowledge of culturally diverse students and at the same time provide learning opportunities for them to acquire necessary cultural capital. Such a process requires re-evaluating the institution's conception of knowledge in order to determine which forms of cultural understanding are relevant to all students regardless of their cultural background. Community colleges must also challenge faculty and staff to become more learned about cultural differences and the various forms of cultural knowledge diverse students possess. In our concluding chapter, we provide some practical suggestions for how such goals might be accomplished. For now, our concern centers on what this case study of Remedial Community College offers to our understanding of multiculturalism.

Implications for Multiculturalism

In our analysis of Remedial Community College, we found it useful to return to the recurring metaphor of the family that was used by several faculty and students to describe the institution. It is true that the friendliness and apparent openness of the institution seemed to provide a caring climate for students. The small size, the intimacy, and the informality of the president helped to place a human face on the institution. There is a certain irony, however, in ascribing the term *family* to the institution. Comparing the institution to a family implies that the members are fairly similar in terms of their personal qualities, backgrounds, and language. The evidence presented in the study indicates otherwise. Students expressed different linguistic styles, patterns of dress, attitudes, and behaviors that violated many of the expectations of faculty and staff. If these students were embraced in a family-like manner, it was in the form of paternalistic attitudes and remarks made to and about the students. This attitude was reflected in the personality of the president, who casts himself in a father-like role.

Faculty and staff generally believed that they knew what was best for their students' educational and occupational careers. Little effort was made by faculty and staff to meet and interact with developmental students at their cultural locations. Instead, the differences between faculty, staff, and the educationally advantaged students were seen in terms of a superior/inferior dichotomy in which the developmental students needed to have their shortcomings remedied through a kind of parental, supervisory influence.

Paternalism suggests unequal relations in which one party has a degree of authority and control over the other party. Such a view also suggests that the college conceptualizes the pedagogical process in a one-directional manner, in which the students do the learning and faculty do the teaching. The unfortunate by-product is that any hope of achieving a multicultural vision must involve a significant change in the way faculty and staff view the cultural ways and forms of knowledge brought to the institution by diverse students.

Remedial Community College faces an enormous challenge in providing academic help to its underprepared students. These students, after all, have never been particularly successful in school and are returning to school with insufficiently developed reading, language, and mathematics skills. The problem is not whether or not Remedial ought to provide academic assistance, because clearly these students need some type of institutional assistance. The problem is the medical model used by Remedial, which situates underprepared students as marginal members of the academic community, as if their underdeveloped skills are some sort of learning pathology. This model precludes the idea that these students enter the institution with strengths and forms of knowledge that ought to be included in various ways throughout both the curriculum and educational practice. We have not seen this at Remedial. Instead, we see interventions that have unintended consequences that are injurious to the participants. More specifically, students participating in the developmental studies program are labeled as deficient and often are treated in that manner by faculty. Labeling students in this way seemed somehow to absolve the institution of any responsibility to provide a sound education for students with underdeveloped skills. The developmental label singled out students as incapable of college-level work and in need of a treatment program that would get them on the right track. And, of course, for most faculty, the right track was a vocational track, as expecting any more from developmental students was unreasonable. As a developmental studies administrator commented, "The students are branded . . . but it's for their own good." We are left to ponder: Where is the good in such a strategy?

The administrator's comments raise two important issues. First, the developmental students are categorized, and the category denotes that, in the minds of the institutional actors, these students are failures and must be remediated before they are allowed entry into the "real college" courses. The fact that students refer to these courses as "dumbbell English" or "baby math" provides insight into how these courses are regarded. The second point raises an issue about the institution's structural arrangements and how decisions are made regarding student placement. Implicit in the comments throughout our interviews was the message that the institution knows what is best for students and has the authority to track students into appropriate categories. The voices and ways of knowing that the students bring to Remedial rarely are considered in these decisions because the institution takes the position that it is acting on behalf of developmental students, even if this arrangement means that the students have to spend far more time, money, and effort to get to the same place as nondevelopmental students. As the program is presently structured, developmental studies at Remedial promote an authoritarian view of knowledge and culture in which faculty set standards and judge students accordingly. There is little room for student participation in these arrangements as democracy is effectively silenced.

Critical multiculturalism calls attention to the need for educational institutions to forge opportunities that provide access for everyone. The developmental program at Remedial does not provide equal access for lower- and working-class students. Instead, Remedial creates additional barriers for underprepared students by tracking them into developmental programs where they are expected to take a significant number of credits before they can even enroll in a college course. The result is that these students drop out and return home with few skills with which to alter their social standing. In the end, Remedial does an outstanding job of reproducing social class by graduating its share of middle-class students and filtering out the lower and working classes.

Obviously, some type of educational program must exist to assist underprepared college students. But such programs should not be full of disincentives. Instead, programs designed to help underprepared students must contain incentives for them to continue their education and pursue degrees or certificates. The challenge is to raise the level of understanding of students without requiring so many additional courses that an extra year or more is added to degree completion. This may be accomplished by increasing expectations of underprepared students and offering additional assistance to them as they work through regular college-credit classes. As Jaime Escalante has clearly demonstrated in his innovative teaching methods, students rise to the teacher's level of expectation. If they are expected to perform as developmentally weak students, then they will.

We have suggested throughout this book that community college classrooms need to be structured in a more democratic and collaborative manner. If such a change occurs, the diverse experiences underprepared students bring to the classroom will have a chance to inform the teaching and learning process. Moreover, through increased collaboration, these students will have the opportunity to learn from other students.

Although it is fundamentally necessary to offer academic assistance to less-prepared students, it is equally important to offer students the opportunity to express the abilities and forms of knowledge they already possess. It is also important that they come to understand how their lives have been shaped by their interactions with the schooling process. In a democratic conception of developmental education, underprepared students learn essential skills and at the same time are able to inquire about the nature of educational institutions that have at times failed them. In such a setting, they are more likely to seek answers to questions regarding their social standing, as well as to pursue issues related to the limited educational choices they have been offered. The result is a questioning and critical student who is beginning to understand her or his own role in the learning process. Such a student understands the role that power plays in situating knowledge—some of which is seen as cultural capital and some as border knowledge.

Recognition of the relevance of border knowledge can be a vehicle for student learning and development, but only when cultural diversity is embraced within the institution and within the classroom. This means that issues of culture and identity must be tied to the content of the courses in one way or another, and staff must be cognizant of race, class, and gender differences. It is evident in the remarks made by faculty and staff that these issues are outside the mission of the institution and hence are ignored by the curriculum and the classroom pedagogy.

Critical multiculturalism contributes to an environment that invites and celebrates difference and provides the setting for students to display their knowledge. For the most part, the knowledge of marginalized groups has not been given a place in the community college's curricular organization. As we mention in chapter 1, the canon, as defined and promulgated by the dominant groups in higher education, becomes a form of privileged knowledge. The knowledge, values, and ways of knowing of marginalized groups are not acknowledged and reside at the borders of education. Critical multiculturalism invites culturally diverse students to become full participants in the educational process. Critical multiculturalism does not situate students as stigmatized outsiders because their forms of knowledge are not part of the canon. Instead, we must develop ways to incorporate border knowledge into the classroom and thus provide a vehicle for culturally diverse students to be confident about the things they know and experience in life. We offer more concrete suggestions for achieving such a goal in chapter 8.

Summary

Our case study of Remedial Community College paints a portrait of how cultural capital contributes to the reproduction of class inequality in the United States. Social class gets reproduced through institutions that reward certain forms of knowledge and culture while regarding others as inferior. This happens to underprepared students at Remedial whose knowledge and culture are considered irrelevant. Concomitantly, the culture and knowledge of the middle class forms the basis for education and for administering the college.

In general, lower- and working-class students, minorities, and other marginalized groups do not possess the cultural capital deemed necessary for academic success. Their cultural and linguistic norms become denigrated as middle-class norms are thrust upon them. Additionally, because educational structures and processes at community colleges reflect the cultural capital of the middle class, marginalized groups find it difficult to access this privileged form of culture and knowledge despite their forced compliance. The lack of access to privileged knowledge serves as a barrier to marginalized students in their struggle to improve their economic and social conditions.

A critical multicultural pedagogy that focuses on more democratic and collaborative classrooms offers opportunities for culturally diverse students to contribute to the teaching and learning process. Increased collaboration encourages students to link their own success to the success of other students and thus encourages a more caring and cooperative learning environment. In such settings, all students become teachers, and in many instances, teachers become learners themselves. This goes against traditional views of the teacher as knowledge broker and the student as the unknowledgeable neophyte. Traditional pedagogy encourages passivity on the part of students whereas a critical multicultural pedagogy encourages active participation and learning. Such strategies establish conditions whereby all students have the opportunity and encouragement to contribute to the educational process.

This chapter suggests that students typically marginalized in community college settings need to be brought to the center of pedagogy and administrative practice. Developmental and remedial education programs that situate underprepared students as stigmatized members of the academic community are inconsistent with a critical multicultural education stressing inclusiveness. Community colleges such as Remedial need to do a better job of recognizing the influence of cultural differences by developing strategies to include a wide range of cultural knowledge within their pedagogical and administrative practices.

Chapter Seven
Organizational Multiplicity
A Case Study of Community College Identity

In chapter 2, we introduced Alicia Fernandez. Recall that Alicia works full-time at a restaurant and attends college part-time. Her goal is to transfer to a four-year college once she completes her associate's degree at Perplexity Community College, an urban college situated in the western region of the United States. Alicia's experience at Perplexity has not been completely satisfying. For example, Alicia gets frustrated at times by the lack of intellectual challenge presented in courses and by her teachers. She turns in a paper she believes to be average and is surprised and a bit disappointed when it comes back with an A+ marked on it. She knows her writing and mastery of English will not improve if her teachers do not have higher expectations. Alicia hopes to attend a top college such as Stanford or Harvard but worries about her academic preparation.

While Alicia pushes herself despite the lack of challenge posed by her classes, Carlos Vargas struggles to get through his coursework. Carlos lacks the academic preparation that students like Alicia bring to Perplexity. He dropped out of high school when he was 16 and never envisioned himself as college material—at least not until three or four years later when he met a Perplexity faculty member involved in a drug education program. Carlos was a participant in the program as a result of some legal matters related to a drug problem. The faculty member was a source of encouragement for Carlos, who for the first time in his life began to see education as an opportunity and not as "a waste of time." Carlos went on to obtain his GED and then enroll in courses at Perplexity. Although college certainly has been a challenge, Carlos is determined to obtain certification as a social service technician. He wants to use what he has learned through his difficult childhood and young adult life as a tool to help youth in the area.

The experiences of Alicia and Carlos at Perplexity Community College highlight a fundamental challenge community colleges face: in order to meet the diverse needs of students, community colleges must enact a wide range of programs. As a result, community colleges are pulled in a variety of directions and often lack a clear sense of organizational identity. Community college faculty and staff are challenged to develop the college's curriculum without any clear sense of what the college's vision is or ought to be. Issues about the relevance of transfer, vocational, or community education are left to be pondered by faculty, oftentimes in isolation from one another.

In this chapter we explore Perplexity in terms of its efforts to balance the multiple missions of the community college while serving a diverse clientele. Multiple missions and multiple clients produce an organization where members often have an unclear sense of what the organization represents. This is what we mean by organizational multiplicity. As a result of multiplicity, organizational members naturally seek some guiding vision by which to direct their energy, their behavior, and their decisions. At Perplexity, the guiding vision that has emerged is grounded in *careerism*—a belief that the central purpose of education is to prepare students as prospective employees. We offer a critique of careerism and expand upon our earlier discussion of education as the preparation of democratic citizens. Central to our discussion is the role critical education (critical pedagogy) might play in creating a democratically oriented community college.

Perplexity was selected in part because of its high minority student enrollment and a sense that innovative programs are in place in all three areas—transfer, vocational, and community education. Our sense that innovative practices were in fact in place came from community college practitioners who recommended Perplexity. Our case study of the college attempts to pull together many of the complex and confusing roles that community colleges face as we discuss the idea of an organizational identity founded on multiplicity. This case study also presents the possibilities that a critical multicultural perspective offers for forging a connective vision despite organizational multiplicity.

Organizational Background

For anyone driving past Perplexity Community College, one of the prominent images is that of the large Olympic mural painted on the side of the gymnasium. A closer look at the mural reveals the multicultural character of the Olympics: the faces and clothing of the athletes portray a wide range of countries and nationalities. The mural may also be interpreted as a symbol of the diversity of Perplexity's campus—a source of pride for many students, faculty, and staff. Indeed, with most of the student body coming from Chicano or Asian backgrounds, "underrepresented" takes on an entirely different meaning at Perplexity.

Perplexity was founded just after the end of World War II as part of the local school district in conjunction with the state's community college system. Originally situated at a local high school, the college later moved to its current location. Perplexity serves 16 bordering communities and is one of nine community colleges serving the larger metropolitan area. The mission of Perplexity is the same as the other community colleges in the district:

To provide comprehensive lower-division general education, occupational education, transfer education, transitional education, counseling and guidance, community services, and continuing education programs which are appropriate to the communities served and which meet the changing needs of students for academic and occupational preparation, citizenship, and cultural understanding.

The college has approximately 16,000 students, and the vast majority are Hispanic (seventy percent), most of whom identify as Chicano. Another twenty-two percent are Asian American. The remainder of the student body is composed primarily of whites (four percent) and African Americans (three percent). Of the nine community colleges in the district, Perplexity has the highest percentage of Hispanic student enrollment and the second-highest percentage of Asian-American students. Perplexity's African-American student enrollment is the lowest, and its enrollment of white students is the second lowest.

In the fall of 1992, thirty-five percent of the student body was enrolled in at least twelve hours (full-time), another thirty-five percent was enrolled for 6 to 11.5 hours (for some students this unit load is considered part-time, and for others, such as international students, it is full-time), and the remaining thirty percent was enrolled for less than 6 units (part-time). Eighteen percent of the students are under twenty years of age, thirty-seven percent are between twenty and twenty-four, twenty-eight percent are between twenty-five and thirty-four, and seventeen percent are over thirty-five.

In terms of faculty and staff, the college is composed predominantly of whites, who occupy roughly half of the professional positions. Nearly thirty percent of faculty and staff are Hispanic and the remainder derive from Asian-American or African-American backgrounds. Overall, Perplexity employs close to one thousand full- and part-time faculty and staff with approximately a 60/40 ratio of men to women.

The Local Community

Perplexity Community College (PCC) is situated in a suburb of a major western city. PCC, along with the other eight community colleges in the district, serves what might be the most culturally diverse area of the United States. The diversity of the city is highlighted by the racial breakdown of all students attending the city's community colleges: thirty-five percent Hispanic, twenty-eight percent white, eighteen percent African American, seventeen percent Asian American. The city's economy is dominated by the banking industry, insurance companies, steel plants, research and development facilities, oil refineries, and manufacturing plants specializing in aerospace equipment, electronics, glass, rubber, and cement.

Perplexity's campus is situated within the community of Stanton Heights, one of sixteen communities within the larger metropolitan area served by Perplexity. Stanton Heights is primarily a mixture of Hispanic (mostly Chicano) and Asian American residents (Chinese, Japanese, Korean, and Vietnamese). Many of Stanton Heights' street signs are written in both Spanish and Chinese. The other fifteen communities are also predominantly Hispanic and Asian-American.

Racial tension within the surrounding communities sometimes is a concern of students, faculty, and staff at Perplexity. A few years back, racial tension peaked and outbreaks of violence occurred in several of the college's service communities. The college was closed for a few days, not because of problems in Stanton Heights, which by most standards is a quiet and peaceful area of the city, but because the administration feared for students and staff traveling through other parts of the city.

The racial diversity of Perplexity's sixteen surrounding communities provides a backdrop for the organizational identity that has emerged at the college. In general, faculty and staff are committed to creating greater educational and career opportunities for the diverse students who attend the college.

Findings

Alicia Fernandez attends classes in the afternoon and evening, where the class composition is mostly nontraditional students, a characteristic she enjoys: "Adults tend to be people who want to get ahead and are serious about schooling. They have been a good influence on me, particularly on my study habits." For the most part, Alicia has positive things to say about the faculty at Perplexity: "We really do have good teachers here. They try to be your role models. They believe in you. They encourage us to believe that we have what it takes to get ahead. They try to get us involved and they get involved with us. One of my teachers came over to my house and met with my family."

Despite a generally positive attitude toward Perplexity, Alicia sees two weaknesses with the college. First, as we have already noted, the courses she has taken have not been challenging enough for her: "If the classes were really difficult for me, it would take much more of my time. I have not found the curriculum challenging at all." A second concern of Alicia's relates to transfer programs: "One of the problems here is that everyone who goes on to four-year schools goes to State [the local state university]. That's partly because of the close family ties that Latino families have. We need transfer programs that challenge students to think beyond the local area. Transferring is basically left up to a student's initiative." Alicia complained about lack of transfer information as well as limited number of counselors available for advising students about transfer: "I feel lost. There's no one here to ask about other schools. There's just not enough advisors for that. Students end up applying to whatever schools send us materials."

Although Alicia Fernandez has always excelled in school and envisions a career as a lawyer, Carlos Vargas has quite a different story to tell. As a child, his life was one of continuous disruption: His mother moved the family ten times before Carlos turned eighteen, primarily because his older brother "was always getting into trouble." On one occasion, they had to move because Carlos "hurt some guy pretty bad in a fight." Another time, the family was evicted for loud noise coming from one of his mother's parties.

At the age of ten, Carlos started drinking and soon thereafter joined a local gang. The gang offered him a sense of belonging, something that he did not get at home. However, it did not take Carlos long to realize that gang life was not for him, but escape was difficult.

I got into weed, but I didn't like it too much—it made me feel like I was dumb, stupid. Then I got into rock-cocaine for about a month. I didn't like that stuff either. I wanted to change but I didn't know how. I knew that that wasn't really me—I was another person. I went to a rehab home at the age of 16 and began to turn my life around. I've given my life to the Lord. I want to use my life as a testimony of what God can do.

Today, Carlos is interested in social service work. After he finishes his certificate, he wants to work with gang members and drug addicts by helping them to see other possibilities in life. Carlos was first exposed to Perplexity Community College through an outreach program in which he was involved. Presently, he works for this same program and is pleased with the doors that have opened up for him: "I have learned a lot so far." Carlos is not only getting academic training for a career; through his work at the outreach program he is sharpening the social service skills he will need once he completes his coursework.

Alicia and Carlos are unique students whose *ganas* (desire to learn) in many ways transcends the institutional limitations of Perplexity Community College. Although their stories are unique, they nonetheless tell us a great deal about the role not only of this college, but of the community college in general. In Alicia's case, transfer issues are central. In the case of Carlos, his education at Perplexity is an opportunity to pursue a career in social services. Carlos also highlights the role community colleges play in reaching out to the local community. He was a direct beneficiary of one such community education program.

Although Alicia and Carlos have provided the *ganas*, Perplexity has created an opportunity for them to succeed. The stories of Alicia and Carlos highlight the three essential roles of the community college: transfer, vocational, and community education. In what follows, we highlight efforts that Perplexity has undertaken to establish successful educational programs in all three areas. We discuss how the multiple missions enacted by the college have created confusion among faculty and staff about the central purpose of the institution. In our discussion, we focus on the idea of organizational multiplicity and how such a view of the community college might help us to better meet the complex and diverse needs of today's students.

That much is demanded of the community college is clearly the case. Four-year colleges and universities have great expectations as well, but often have many times the funding to meet those objectives. Despite the numerous challenges faced by the community college, Perplexity has found ways to cope. In what follows, we highlight the various programs the college has enacted as a means to meet its multiple roles. We explore how faculty and staff have found a way to deal with organizational multiplicity before we offer a critical multicultural interpretation.

Transfer Education Within Perplexity's home state, the number of transfer students significantly declined from 1978 until the late 1980s. Since then, the transfer rates have gradually increased, although the rate is still not as high as it was in 1978. Several indicators point to the fact that Perplexity's commitment to student transfer has improved over recent years. For example, the college ranks fifth in the district in terms of FTE (Full-Time Equivalency), yet ranks third in the number of transfers to public and private institutions within the state (figures are unavailable for out-of-state transfers). Although the overall transfer rate remains quite low (roughly three percent), for the academic years 1989–1990 and 1990–1991 the number (not the overall percentage) of student transfers increased each year at

Perplexity by fourteen percent and then twelve percent: from 331 students in 1988–1989, to 378 in 1989–1990, and then to 424 in 1991. This increase at Perplexity occurred while the numerical increase within the overall district rose annually only two percent and five percent, respectively.

Several factors help to explain the relative recent success of Perplexity. First, the college has implemented a number of programs designed to encourage student transfer. Like other community colleges within the state, Perplexity has developed an office that coordinates student transfer and transfer information. Counselors in the transfer office work closely with four-year institutions to ensure that academic expectations at the college meet course requirements at other schools. Unfortunately, the transfer office is greatly understaffed (one counselor for every sixteen hundred students), which in part explains the frustration Alicia voiced earlier: "There's not enough good advisers for [transfer information]."

Although counselors play an important part in advising students and communicating with other institutions, faculty involvement in the transfer process is imperative, especially in creating articulation agreements (Berger & Ruiz, 1988). Judith Eaton (1992) affirms this view when she notes the "centrality of meaningful faculty dialogue about transfer in order to bring about institutional change" (p. 7). Faculty and department chairs have to stay in continuous contact with peers at four-year institutions. One faculty member at Perplexity noted that he periodically meets with representatives of other institutions, speaking with faculty in similar departments. "I look at possibilities of student transfer. What's required. What's expected of students. How to better prepare our students. It's also a way of letting them know what kind of program we have. It's a way of educating them about our students." This faculty member supports Caroline Sotello and Viernes Turner's (1992) claim that informal interactions play a major role in building transfer programs.

In addition to the transfer office, another program that has helped the transfer of students from Perplexity derives from a grant obtained by a local state university. The minority engineering program offers financial assistance to minority students majoring in engineering. The program enables students to take courses at Perplexity and then transfer automatically to the state university. Here we must clarify "minority." Asian-American students, because of their high representation within the field of engineering, do not qualify for this program. As a result of the policy, the great majority of the eighty students in the minority engineering program are Hispanic.

Another transfer program gives priority consideration to Perplexity students for admission at colleges and universities within the metropolitan area and throughout the state. Related to this program is a personal development course that focuses on improving student skills needed to pursue more advanced academic work (such as study skills, reading comprehension, and so forth). The course covers information related to transfer and includes tours of local colleges and universities.

The college has developed another project designed for working adults who cannot attend regular classes. The working adult program is team-taught and interdisciplinary. The program is also *lock-step*, meaning that students are grouped in cohorts and take the same sequence of courses. An academic administrator spoke of one of the advantages to the lock-step approach: "The lock-step component allows students to develop a cohort cohesiveness. They all have to deal with the same problems." Perplexity has established an articulation agreement with a nearby college where an upper division of the working adult program is available.

The Puente Project is another transfer program at the college that has achieved some success. The program is a statewide initiative designed to increase the retention of Mexican-American and Latino/a community college students and to increase the number who transfer to four-year colleges and universities. The program focuses on the development of reading and writing abilities by bringing English teachers and counselors together as part of a collaborative effort. Part of the program's success is believed to be the integration of culturally based academic counseling:

The Mexican-American counselors selected for Puente share the cultural background of the students, and that of their parents and Puente mentors. This familiarity with the culture allows counselors to help students recognize their personal and academic strengths, thus encouraging student retention and accelerating their preparation for transfer. (Meznek, McGrath, & Garcia, 1989, p. 11).

Students gave the Puente Project glowing reviews. One student stated that the instructors involved in the Puente Project helped him with his self-confidence. Another felt that the program had been crucial to her academic success. Both students planned to transfer at the end of the academic year and pursue the baccalaureate. Additionally, statistics kept at the state level indicate that the program has made a positive contribution to increasing student transfer. For example, the rate of transfer to state universities of students in the Puente Project throughout the state is 13.5 percent compared with about nine percent for non-Puente students.

Vocational Education An important vocational program at Perplexity is the Tech-Prep program, short for Technician Preparation. The Tech-Prep program prepares students to operate a variety of technical equipment as assistants in fields such as surveying, medical laboratory work, and drafting. The money for this program comes from the federal government and is passed on to the state. The college qualified for about $35,000 in 1992 and $50,000 in 1993. Some of the money goes toward articulating with local high schools so that Tech-Prep builds upon the high school experience. As one faculty member noted, "We continue what students might have begun at the high school level." Tech-Prep is not designed for transfer to four-year institutions. The expectation is that eventually the program will be institutionalized and the external funding discontinued. A Perplexity faculty member explained, "Supposedly these programs are self-sustaining. Once you get your program in place with soft money, eventually it should be able to run itself. I've put that together in my own mind, but I'm not sure how it's going to work."

Another important vocational component to Perplexity's curriculum is the Allied Health Program, which prepares students for careers in areas such as health services management, medical record technology, medical assisting, electron microscopy, and emergency department assistance, to name just a few. Participation in the Allied Health Program has led to a number of employment opportunities for Perplexity graduates. Financial assistance in terms of student scholarships has been obtained through a local HMO, which provides as many as thirty scholarships per year. Despite the scholarship funds, the Allied Health Program has lost about ten specialty areas over recent years—the result of funding cuts. Perhaps the most creative component of the program is the final-year experience in which students actually work at a local hospital.

The college provides other less technical vocational opportunities. One program focuses on preparing AFDC (Aid For Dependent Children) recipients, unemployed persons, disabled persons, and social security recipients for careers in either Child Development or Office Administration. This program operates in conjunction with the Job Training Partnership Act (JTPA), a federally funded program to help train and re-train unemployed people. A related project helps students develop the necessary skills to conduct a job search and focus on a vocation. One administrator discussed this option: "The whole goal of the program is to get somebody a job. So if their skills are too low, the goal is first to get their skill level up and then to get them in a vocational track." The program is *open entry*, meaning that students can enter the program at any time. It does not follow Perplexity's regular semester schedule. "We work in modules so that you can come in any time so that once the next module begins, you won't be lost."

A variety of other vocational tracks exist at the college. For example, construction is under way to build an advanced auto technical building that will have equipment to construct an entire automobile from scratch. The money invested in this project reflects a relatively recent budgetary move on the part of the community college district. A high-ranking official at the college offered the following appraisal: "We've been neglected for years in terms of monies and projects. It's been the failure of the district leadership to do anything about it." Despite the limited funds, this same official felt good about what Perplexity has been able to accomplish: "We're performing well for the amount of money we're given. But we're not doing well in the sense of finances."

Community Education A number of programs designed to meet the needs of the local community exist at Perplexity. Many of the programs derive from federal or state revenues, although a few represent individual efforts to acquire funding and create new opportunities. One example in which individual initiative has played a key role is an educational program designed to improve the skills of local elementary, junior high, and senior high students. The project has been modeled around the teaching methods of Jaime Escalante, made famous in the movie *Stand and Deliver*, and is relevant for two reasons. First, the Escalante Educational Program has had great success in helping underrepresented students improve a variety of classroom skills; and second, the program raises fundamental questions about the purpose of the community college as we once again are forced to consider the idea of seamless education.

The Escalante Educational Program (EEP) began in 1989 as part of a grant from the National Science Foundation (thirty-seven percent), along with the ARCO Foundation (fifteen percent) and Ford Motor Company (twelve percent). The college contributed the remainder of the funding. EEP provides five hundred elementary, middle school, and high school students with additional educational instruction in preparation for the Advanced Placement Test in calculus, computer science, chemistry, English, and physics. Students participate in the program after school, on Saturdays, and during the summer. The overwhelming majority of student participants are Hispanic (ninety-two percent). Perhaps the most important feature of the program is that the teachers have all been trained in the teaching methods of Escalante.

The central educational tenet of the Escalante teaching method is to restructure students' thinking so that students develop an "I can do it" attitude. Cognitive restructuring involves teachers placing expectations upon the students—expectations that they will succeed. Research on EEP students has demonstrated students' perceptions of high teacher expectations. Additionally, if cognitive restructuring occurs, then the expectation is that students will attribute their own effort and ability to any successes, further instilling self-confidence and self-esteem. Again, research on EEP students has demonstrated this to be the case—eighty-four percent of the students in one study attributed their success to internal factors such as talent and desire (Kester, 1993).

By most accounts the program has been highly successful. Students who participate in the program score consistently higher on the Advanced Placement Tests than other students from similar cultural and socioeconomic backgrounds. Yet, questions about EEP's relevance to the mission of PCC exist. A faculty member sarcastically recalled the complaints of a colleague: "Oh, these kids aren't going to come here to our institution. They're going to go to Stanford, Harvard, or Yale. The four-year colleges. They are going to by-pass the two-year schools." Although this statement may be true, at least one faculty member had a response to such criticism: "Well I say more power to those students. They are only going to benefit the community where they grew up. This institution should be proud that they have enabled these students to go to a four-year college and by-pass this college."

Another community education program at Perplexity is the Amnesty Program, which offers ESL, life skills, and social skills courses for undocumented immigrants who arrived in the U.S. prior to 1982. If the students take a forty-hour English and civics class, they can obtain residency status; and after five years they can become citizens. The program is the by-product of the Emigration Reform Control Act (ERCA). Ultimately, the Amnesty Program is designed to matriculate participants into vocational degree or certification programs.

A variety of other community-oriented programs and services are offered including the following: foster care education, GED courses, Adult Basic Education (ABE), ESL courses, a campus child development center, and recreational and cultural events. The college has a Community Services Office that coordinates specific educational programs geared to meet community concerns and needs.

Community education programs, such as the Escalante Education Program and the Amnesty Program, along with the many vocational programs as well as the transfer track, highlight the multiple roles and endeavors Perplexity has had to enact to serve its surrounding communities. As a result of being pulled in so many different directions, the college suffers from a lack of organizational identity. As one faculty member opined, "I'm not sure what we are trying to accomplish here. Every time I think I have it figured out the district or the president changes something and it's back to square one." And another faculty member offered the following in response to questions about the college's mission: "Mission? What mission? I'm not clear on what our mission is. I used to think it was to train students for jobs, but over the past few years I've become more confused about that." In what follows, we discuss some of the identity problems to which the preceding faculty refer.

Discussion

Many faculty and staff at Perplexity believe that the transfer function is central to the college's institutional mission. Faculty and staff alike have initiated a variety of programs to aid the transfer of students to four-year institutions. The impetus for these programs derives largely from federal or state pressure, or funding, or both. Nonetheless, these programs have demanded a great deal of individual commitment and creativity. Faculty and staff have worked hard to create educational opportunities for their students. They have established a number of transfer options enabling students to pursue bachelor's degrees. Numerous articulation agreements have been worked out and appropriate courses have been developed that prepare students for upper-division coursework. And faculty have developed transfer programs for students with special needs, such as working adults. Many faculty and staff are devoted to overcoming educational barriers that might limit student transfer.

But only about three percent of the students enrolled at Perplexity at any one time tend to transfer; some faculty and staff believe too much time and energy is spent on transfer-related activities, and too much money is directed to academically oriented curricula. Some faculty and administrators envision vocational education as the future for community colleges in general and Perplexity in particular. Along these lines, faculty and staff have developed vocational tracks that offer a variety of career avenues. As is the case with transfer programs, the ultimate goal is economic benefit for students and the opportunity for social mobility. Staff have fostered professional relationships with local and regional industries and businesses with the hope of placing their students in such settings. Faculty have also helped to clear obstacles that prevent culturally diverse students from developing the skills necessary to begin vocational training by providing ESL instruction and other skill-development courses.

The faculty who believe transfer education to be central to Perplexity's mission complain that vocational education lures many students away from academic programs with shaky promises of a better future and immediate economic return. Many of the students in vocational programs are highly qualified students whom transfer-oriented faculty believe could do well in academic programs. For many of the students in vocational tracks, money is a major concern and going to college for four or five years to get a bachelor's degree seems inconceivable. One student in the Allied Health Program, who once dreamed of becoming a doctor, has given up his dream because the cost is so prohibitive. Economic concerns were central to most of the students with whom we spoke, some of whom work full-time and help to support their parents and siblings, as Alicia Fernandez does.

Only a few faculty at Perplexity felt that efforts ought to be increased in the area of community education. Nonetheless, a significant cadre of faculty and staff are devoted to providing ongoing services for local communities and their constituents. Through programs that serve immigrants; returning adults; elementary, middle, and high school students; AFDC recipients; and others, the college has enhanced the educational and career opportunities of local residents. These activities clearly represent a significant commitment of Perplexity to community education.

Most of the faculty and staff have their own views on which form of community college education ought to take precedence—transfer, vocational, or community education—and the great majority are involved one way or another in all three roles. As a result, faculty and staff must portion their time and energy accordingly and thereby make choices about institutional priorities. Because the mission of the college is vague, faculty are left to their own individual interests and judgments about what is important and what is not.

Although there is much confusion about what programs ought to be emphasized and which ones ought to be eliminated or curtailed, there is a common thread that has emerged in the culture of Perplexity. Despite the fact that the many roles that the college serves have produced confusion, an overarching concern for improving the employment opportunities of underrepresented students provides a common basis for action. Nearly every project or educational program at Perplexity reflects a commitment to enhancing the economic well-being of underrepresented students. Thus, within an organizational structure designed to serve three basic and at times conflicting roles, a common understanding has emerged and has enabled people to make sense of a multiplicitous organizational life. This is what some might term a symbolic interpretation of Perplexity's organizational identity, in that we focus on how the organizational members have created a common understanding of their roles.

The central thread that connects students, faculty, and staff at Perplexity Community College is a commitment to preparing students for employment and for careers. Even in transfer programs, careerism is central. That careerism has become so vital to how faculty and staff see themselves and their roles at the college is understandable given that the student population predominantly derives from low-income backgrounds. Career concerns are quite obviously paramount to Perplexity's students.

The college has developed its own way of dealing with the complexities of organizational multiplicity. An organizational ethos characterized by careerism has become the connective thread joining Perplexity's diverse roles and constituencies. Arguably, careerism constitutes the college's organizational identity. In what follows, we relate our discussion of how Perplexity has dealt with organizational multiplicity to critical multiculturalism. How can a critical multicultural view of Perplexity help us to understand organizational multiplicity and issues of organizational identity?

Multicultural Implications

Multiplicity is a concept that describes the complexities of identity in a postmodern world. Typically, we use this term in discussing issues of individual identity, but the term may also be applied to organizations as well as to other social groups. Throughout this text we suggest that organizational multiplicity best describes today's community colleges. Not only do community colleges face multiple roles, they also must serve multiple constituents and, in some cases, multiple communities. To help us understand the concept of multiplicity, it is helpful to review modernist and postmodernist views of organizational life.

Modern and Postmodern Views of Organizational Life The concept of multiplicity can help us to reconceptualize organizational life in that it rejects many modernist assumptions about how organizations operate. For example, the following characteristics are often associated with modernist views of organizations: instrumentalism, hierarchy, autonomy, and commonality. Organizations are instrumental in that they may be thought of as machines designed to serve specific functions. Even the subcomponents of an organization are seen as precision instruments in the performance of specified tasks. This is what Gareth Morgan (1986) refers to as the machine metaphor. To carry out precise functions, organizations are organized in a hierarchical fashion so that clear rules and regulations guide the actions of subordinates. In this manner, organizational leaders or managers are better able to control organizational members' behaviors. From a modernist perspective, organizations are seen to exist separate from their environment, their surroundings. They are seen as autonomous organisms that take in resources from the environment and reshape them to produce a product. Modernist views of organizations also stress commonality—a sense of sameness must exist in order for an organization to be held together. Difference and diversity thus pose threats to the machine-like functioning of the modernist organization.

Organizational multiplicity is informed by feminist and postmodern views of organizational life. Postmodernists, for example, take issue with organizational theories derived from scientific management that stress prediction and control—often described as instrumentalism. Postmodernists reject the idea that organizations are social machines with clearly defined identities in which organizational members guide their actions as a means to achieve certain predetermined ends (Parker, 1992). Instead, many recent organizational theorists see organizations as social constructions: "Organizations are essentially arbitrary definitions of reality woven in symbols and expressed in language" (Greenfield, 1980, p. 44). By using the term *socially constructed*, postmodern organizational theorists stress the role people play in shaping how organizations get defined and redefined. Organizations are first and foremost the by-products of culture (Smircich, 1983). A cultural or symbolic view of organizations does not reject the idea that organizations exist to perform tasks or serve specific responsibilities. Such a view does, however, question the preeminence of organizational identities grounded in functional analyses. In other words, understanding organizational life is more than merely examining the tasks people perform and what gets accomplished. From a postmodern perspective, organizational identity is rooted in the meaning people create as a way of making sense of organizational life (Smircich & Morgan, 1982).

Feminist theorists provide the most sustained critique of organizations as hierarchies. For example, Kathleen Iannello (1992) describes organizational hierarchy "as a vertical and horizontal system of domination with varying degrees of centralized communication" (p. 17). Iannello suggests a "consensual" model of organizational decision making in which group participation is vital and the process itself is central to the organization's identity. Likewise, Kathy Ferguson (1984) maintains that feminism opposes all forms of institutionalized dominance and subordination, because the deployment of such tactics has led to women being situated on the margins of organizational life. She suggests instead a commitment to equality and active participation in organizational life: "Active, participatory citizenship is a process through which individuals create themselves with others through the shared processes of speaking, deliberating, and judging, ordering their collective lives through institutions they have designed and in a language they have made their own" (p. 174).

Postmodern and feminist organizational theorists also challenge the idea that organizations are autonomous. Organizations are seen as intimately interwoven with their environments—so much so that separating the organization from the environment is next to impossible: "As organizations join with their surrounding cultures for purposes of mutual empowerment, and the circle of interdependence is ever widened, we may become aware of the world as a total system" (Gergen, 1992, p. 224). In building upon the work of Carol Gilligan (1982), Linda Smircich (1985) suggests that differences in male and female systems of thought influence how we construct organizational life. Specifically, male systems of thought tend to emphasize autonomy and control, whereas female systems tend to emphasize connection and relatedness. Thus, from a feminist perspective, organizations should be seen as intimately connected to their external environments.

And finally, both postmodernists and feminists criticize essentializing views of organizations and social life that seek to render differences invisible. Most recently, William Tierney (1993) offers an organizational analysis of higher education institutions from a critical postmodern perspective. Tierney argues that modernist conceptions of organizations based on similarity and harmony limit

the possibility   . He
suggests that   :wed
as communiti   erely
something tc   basis
for people c   e another. Dialo   : cultural diversi   rbules
and Suzanne Rice (1991) highlight such a notion.

*There is no reason to assume that dialogue across differences involves
either eliminating those differences or imposing one group's views on
others; dialogue that leads to understanding, cooperation, and accommodation can sustain differences within a broader compact of toleration
and respect. Thus what we need is not an antimodern denial of community, but a postmodern grounding of community on more flexible and
less homogeneous assumptions. (p. 402)*

From a postmodern perspective, organizational multiplicity thus
is not something to be overcome, but instead creates a challenge of a
different sort. The challenge is not to simplify organizational life by
limiting the roles, services, partnerships, or clientele served. The
challenge is to create a connective vision that brings people into
communication despite diverse and complex roles. Dialogue across
differences is needed. Here we return to Perplexity Community College and the organizational identity that has emerged as a response
to organizational multiplicity.

Organizational Mission and Identity The curriculum and mission
of Perplexity is envisioned as the development of programs and activities enabling students to advance career interests. This overarching
vision has helped faculty and staff to work through some of the tensions resulting from their work at Perplexity. An organizational identity grounded in careerism has helped them to resolve some of the
confusion resulting from organizational multiplicity. As a result, even
community education programs relate, for the most part, to helping
students progress toward vocational careers. As we note in chapter
3, education grounded on careerism is limiting and fails to deal with
students as citizens. We draw from Brint and Karabel (1989):

The task is not simply to help them [community college students] ac-
quire a marketable skill, though that is desirable; it is also to assist them
in developing the capacities that will prepare them for life as citizens in
a democratic society, where the gap between leaders and the general popu-
lation may be growing ever more profound. According to the precepts of
classical democratic theory, the citizenry of a democratic society must be
able not only to participate in the governance of its own affairs, but to
do so in a thoughtful and informed fashion. (p. 231)

We need to be clear here. We are not suggesting that helping students prepare for careers is not important. Indeed, students from low-income backgrounds need to develop the skills necessary to gain meaningful employment if the idea of social mobility is to be less myth and more reality. Our criticism of the organizational ethos that has emerged at Perplexity (and at many other community colleges around the country) relates more to what is lacking—a critical discourse about education and its role in the development of democratic citizens. Perplexity, like many other two- and four-year colleges and universities, suffers from a lack of vision of underrepresented students as full participants in the democratic process. Careerism frames nearly all the decision making at Perplexity, and any notion of preparing thoughtful and critical citizens is a distant echo.

How can we criticize the college's lack of commitment to developing students as democratic citizens when they have enacted a variety of citizenship-related programs? For example, Perplexity has taken on the challenge of educating undocumented immigrants who have been living in the U.S. since 1982. The basic goal is to help these individuals improve their English and then channel them into vocational training. In this example of citizenship education, *good citizens* get defined as English-speaking and occupationally skilled. Herein lies part of the problem. When the principal function of education, especially a community college education, is to provide trained individuals who are able to enter the labor force, are we not failing to educate our students as whole persons? What of their role in the social and political concerns of their communities? The problem we have with Perplexity's notion of education is the definition of citizenship that gets enacted.

Let us return to the mission statement of Perplexity Community College. The mission discusses providing programs "which are appropriate to the communities served and which meet the changing needs of students for academic and occupational preparation, citizenship, and cultural understanding." Clearly the emphasis at the college is on academic (with a career orientation) and occupational preparation. Some programs exist that are designed to meet the changing needs of citizenship, but essentially these programs are ESL courses or other skill-related offerings. As far as advancing cultural understanding, the vision seems to be founded on the idea that culture is somewhere *out there* to be discovered and understood. This is evident throughout the curriculum where the consistent message is that undocumented immigrants, Hispanic students, and Asian-American students must acquire certain forms of knowledge to more clearly fit into mainstream U.S. culture, and thus obtain the proper cultural capital (Bourdieu, 1986). One cannot help but wonder how education might be enacted at Perplexity if the faculty and staff more closely reflected the makeup of the student body. Would there be as much emphasis on teaching students mainstream cultural values and forms of knowledge?

For underrepresented peoples, acquiring the proper cultural capital is, in many ways, the reality of existence within U.S. society. We are not suggesting here that Perplexity should stop educating students to speak better English, or that the college curtail its efforts to help students vocationally. What we are suggesting is that there are other issues that also need to be addressed. Fundamental to these issues is the way culture, and necessarily education, gets conceptualized at Perplexity.

The view of culture at Perplexity stands in sharp contrast to the idea of culture as continually constituted and reconstituted by people engaged in interaction (Geertz, 1973). Paulo Freire (1970) discusses differing conceptions of culture and of reality in terms of the banking concept versus a problem-solving view of education: "In problem-solving education, people develop their power to perceive critically *the way they exist* in the world *with which* and *in which* they find themselves; they come to see the world not as a static reality, but as a reality in process, in transformation" (p. 70–71). The goal then of education should be not only to prepare people for jobs, but, just as importantly, students ought to be encouraged to develop the critical thinking necessary to participate in shaping reality, shaping society. They need to understand their potential as democratic citizens to contribute to the social and political concerns of society.

Educating students for democratic citizenship is not another phrase to tack onto the organization's mission statement. In many ways, achieving democratic citizenship is not a goal at all. Instead, it reflects a way of doing—"education as the practice of freedom" (Freire, 1970, p. 69). Or, in our words, education as the practice of democracy. In this way, education as the practice of democracy becomes the social and philosophical thread weaving connections across the multiple identities inherent in today's community colleges.

To a degree, the emphasis on careerism at Perplexity and at many community colleges is understandable. Lower SES students are more likely to attend community colleges and less prestigious four-year institutions. For these students, many of whom have experienced the strains of poverty, finding a job, a vocation, oftentimes is crucial. But the assumption that seems to get played out, not only at this college, but at other two-year institutions, is that a community college cannot simultaneously enact a curriculum that is career-oriented and also challenging in others areas.

Often during our visit to Perplexity staff spoke of the calmness and cooperative nature of the students. They talked about how easy their students were to work with because they rarely complained or created problems. The following are some exemplary comments:

- The kids here are so polite. Everything is "Thank you. God bless you." It's very rewarding as a staff person.
- Our students are not demanding at all.
- Students here are very compliant. Easy to work with. They do what you ask of them.
- Even during the riots in the city, there were no problems here. Our students are not like that.
- The students here are hungry to get jobs and are willing to do what we ask of them.

Inherent in much of the discourse at Perplexity is the idea, the belief, that docility is a quality of good citizenship. One administrator voiced his observations about Perplexity's students, whom he feels are not willing, for the most part, to speak up for their rights:

The unique thing about our campus first is the high percentage of Hispanics and Asians, and many of those folks are immigrants from Taiwan and Hong Kong. So we have very few if any Anglos and Blacks, and within this group you have a different attitude toward seeking assistance or help. They tend to be very humble and not seek out things they have a right to. Their culture does not encourage reaching out or being assertive about what they have coming to them. The nature of both these groups, and I'm generalizing, is that they are not aggressive.

Obviously, generalizations about cultural differences run the risk of essentializing racial and ethnic identities. Although the preceding staff member suggests some essential cultural differences, such as "humility," perhaps a better interpretation is that some students may not have the cultural understanding to know how to act assertively on a college campus. With the general hostility toward immigrants— which often gets enacted against any non–English speaking, non-European, as evidenced by the fallout from Proposition 187 in California—it is certainly no stretch of the imagination to understand why Mexican Americans and Asian Americans may not want to seem too assertive. Becoming actively engaged in educational decision making and in constructing their own educational histories may be seen by some students as a threat to their very existence in the U.S.— especially for immigrants. And, of course, the dilemma is that a certain degree of assertiveness is needed to master all the bureaucratic nuances of both college and public life.

Toward a Critical Multicultural Pedagogy Nonetheless, some students are aware of the power of student engagement. Take for example comments made by Carlos about the courses he enjoys the most: "One thing I've learned is that teachers teach differently. One teacher doesn't give you a chance. He doesn't really let students interact and make class exciting. I find the classes that are the most fun, the most interactive, are also the most helpful." In his allusion to active student participation in classroom dialogue, Carlos highlights a central quality of what a critical multicultural education might resemble.

However, a critical multicultural education involves much more than encouraging students to interact in class. A critical multicultural pedagogy seeks to engage students in the historical, political, and cultural circumstances that frame their lives. At the same time, it conveys the role individuals and groups might play in reshaping social life (Giroux, 1983). A critical multicultural pedagogy embraces the cultural understanding, the border knowledge, students bring to the classroom as a means to reconstruct student understanding of their lives and the society in which they live. From such a view, culture is not a static phenomenon but is something that is continually transformed by members of a society or organization engaged in interaction. Students have the opportunity to reshape their own cultural experiences and contribute to broader understandings of social life.

Enacting a critical multicultural education involves the development of an environment, an attitude, that embraces cultural differences. The development of a critical multicultural pedagogy involves engaging in dialogue about institutional goals and objectives with students, faculty, and staff. Students need to have opportunities whereby they can shape what the organization is to become, what society is to become. Such discussions are often conflict-riddled. There are no quick-fix solutions. A critical pedagogy "points educators toward a mode of analysis that stresses the breaks, discontinuities, and tensions in history . . . that highlight the centrality of human agency and struggle while simultaneously revealing the gap between society as it presently exists and society as it might be" (Giroux, 1983, p. 36).

How can students become more active participants in their educational process and, in effect, learn to write their own cultural histories? In other words, how can a community college create an organization-wide attitude that embraces the full participation of all organizational members? What we are talking about here relates to organizational identity. We suggest that community colleges must move from a modernist understanding of organizational life founded in functionalism to a more postmodern, multiplicitous view of education founded in process. Of course, the process we suggest is a view of community college identity in which education is seen as the practice of democracy.

Conclusion

Faculty and staff at Perplexity have focused on building bridges: bridges to the four-year colleges and universities, bridges to the community, and bridges to local and regional industries, businesses, and professional organizations. But despite the hard work and efforts of dedicated faculty and staff, the student experience at Perplexity lacks a critical dimension. Careerism has firmly taken root. Of consequence is that students do not engage actively in challenging the political and cultural forces that have shaped their very existence. The result is that students may not develop the critical awareness of their own mitigating role in human oppression or the power of self-discovery, self-representation, and self-organization in the process of cultural struggle.

Preparing critical citizens ought to play a role in any curricular and structural changes enacted at community colleges. Accomplishing such a goal involves invoking a discourse framed by the principles of critical multiculturalism. The task is not simple. There are no prescriptions. There are no recipes. But little financial burden comes with the struggle to engage in a critical dialogue. Without such a dialogue, the expense is great, and what appear as bridges to equality may become only illusory dreams grounded in short-term benefit.

It may seem as though we are suggesting an improbable mixture of transfer, vocational, and community education framed by an overarching concern for students as prospective employees and as democratic citizens. Unlike other critics of the community college who often debate the relevance of one form of education over another, such as transfer education over vocational or community education, we see all three as vital to serving the democratizing role of the community college. To elevate one over the other is to limit student options and possibilities. To create a "collegiate" community college, as Eaton (1994a) suggests, is to marginalize those students who need remedial or ESL courses.

Instead, community colleges have little choice but to come to terms with organizational multiplicity. We suggest that a critical multicultural view, in which community college education is seen as the practice of democracy, is a way to form the connective thread needed in organizational life and, at the same time, contribute to the democratizing role of the community college. What better way to help democratize than to be a democracy in every way possible.

In our concluding chapter, we offer more specifics about community college education as the practice of democracy. We introduce Democratic Community College as an "ideal type"—in the Weberian sense—as a means to ground our discussion. We conclude our work by relating the issues raised throughout this text to earlier discussions of culture and identity and by offering some general principles that might help community colleges achieve more democratic multicultural academic communities.

Chapter Eight
Toward a Democratic Vision of the Community College

A brief summary is in order. Community colleges, in the struggle to come to terms with their multiple roles, must balance commitments to provide vocational education, college transfer, and community education for their communities and students. Because their goals are widely dispersed, community colleges strain to establish a clear sense of organizational identity. In this struggle, many colleges embrace careerism as a guiding philosophy and the organizational mission gets defined solely as preparing students for the world of work.

Students come to the community college from a wide range of backgrounds and possess diverse expectations. Some come for continuing education and seek special programs designed to meet specific needs. Others come for remedial education as they seek to improve their basic skills. Other students use the community college as a stepping-stone for entry into a four-year college and the opportunity to obtain a bachelor's degree. And, of course, many come for vocational training as they hope to acquire skills necessary for employment. The vast majority of community college programs—whether they are community-, transfer-, or vocationally-oriented—are tied in one way or another to students' career advancement and concerns for economic opportunity.

Community colleges ought to prepare students to enter the work force. Such a responsibility is important to this country's economy and is a primary concern of many of the economically disadvantaged students who enter the community college. But, community colleges must envision students in a broader and more encompassing sense. Although it is true that community colleges need to prepare students for their life's work, they also must envision students as citizens and community members who have obligations to public life as well.

In addition to the challenges posed by multiple roles and multiple expectations, community colleges also struggle to serve a diverse clientele. Never before has the diversity of the student body been so great. Students come from a variety of cultural backgrounds that influence the way they see the world and how they embrace new knowledge. Community colleges, like other educational institutions, are guilty of responding too slowly to the diverse needs of their students and the many ways students go about the learning process.

Thus, the problem we lay out in this book is twofold. First, because of the multiple responsibilities community colleges must assume, they are pulled in so many directions that they lack a clear sense of identity. When an identity does emerge, it oftentimes is overly rooted in careerism. A second concern relates to the cultural diversity of the students community colleges typically serve. This too presents a challenge to the community college and in combination with the multiple roles they must embrace, there are times when the expectations and responsibilities seem overwhelming and unreasonable.

As a possible solution to the problems faced by today's community colleges, we suggest a different way of thinking about what ought to guide action and decision making. A move away from modernist conceptions of organizational life toward a postmodern perspective is needed.

A modernist view of organizations stresses commonality rather than difference. Difference, in fact, is viewed as a sign of disharmony within organizations and measures are taken to suppress such threats to harmony. In contrast, a postmodern view of organizations, captured in what we call organizational multiplicity, welcomes difference and views conflict as a learning opportunity and a chance to engage in organizational dialogue.

Our emphasis on the multiple and sometimes conflicting roles community colleges must embrace, combined with the institution's obligation to provide services for a diverse constituency, runs counter to modernist conceptualizations of organizations. Instead of thinking about organizations as singular in mission and scope, and unitary in the makeup of members, community colleges must think in terms of difference, complexity, and process. Indeed, from a postmodern perspective grounded in multiplicity, organizational identity is more likely to be defined by the process embraced by the institution than by the various roles or functions delineating behavior. The ideals of participatory democracy discussed in the work of John Dewey and reflected more recently in critical multicultural perspectives of education is offered as a process that ought to guide community colleges.

Critical multiculturalism embraces cultural difference by emphasizing inclusionary practices that go beyond mere visibility within the organizational setting. Like views of participatory democracy, critical multiculturalism stresses that a wide range of individuals and groups must have opportunities for substantive involvement in organizational decision making. This goes beyond merely assuring that a college has a representative body of African-American, Hispanic, or Asian-American students; it means creating opportunities for their participation in key organizational processes framed by democratic principles.

Reflecting Back

In our first case study (chapter 3), we examine Vocational Community College. Our discussion of Vocational focuses on the production of working-class identities as students move through vocational programs at the college. We highlight how Vocational's definition of what counts as knowledge affects the educational experience of lower- and working-class students. Knowledge is seen to be important if it contributes to students' employment opportunities. The college's instructional philosophy highlights how the mission centers on producing students prepared to enter the work force. Instructional practice emphasizes the mastery of competencies that correspond directly to employer needs. In addition to specific competencies defined by the institution as necessary for finding employment, students are also immersed in an ideology that implicitly alters students' cultural characteristics to suit faculty perceptions of the culture of the workplace.

The knowledge transmitted by Vocational meets with varying degrees of acceptance by the students. Younger students in particular resist the knowledge that falls outside the definition of work promulgated by the institution; when students are asked to learn skills that do not appear directly related to work, they question the value and relevancy of such knowledge. Instructors find that they have to justify their academic subjects, or place them within the context of work to convince students that they need to learn these topics. Because students have accepted the institution's definition of worker education, other knowledge is interpreted as superfluous, and they resist or reject it.

We argue that education organized around the concept of "good work" provides the basis for promoting democratic practices in the classroom. Joe Kincheloe's (1995) notion of good work challenges employers to create more participatory and empowering work settings. This view also challenges educational institutions to work with prospective employers to achieve such environments.

Good work calls for a different kind of vocational education. Because good work promotes opportunities for employees to make critical decisions and participate in creative and constructive aspects of the production or service process, educational institutions need to prepare students for such a challenge. Participatory and collaborative classrooms and college governance based on the ideals of democracy need to be embraced. Such classrooms and administrative practices provide the setting in which students might acquire the creativity, communication skills, and caring to work together in democratic settings, both in the workplace and in public life.

Our second case study is a description of the Nuevos Horizontes immigrant education program situated at Outreach Community College. Nuevos Horizontes captures some of the impact of Latin-American immigration on U.S. educational institutions. The program calls attention to the idea that multicultural education involves much more than including diverse people in educational settings. A commitment to multiculturalism demands that educational institutions struggle to understand the perspectives of the diverse students who comprise today's student body. Because the knowledge and ways of knowing of many culturally diverse students exist outside the mainstream of what is considered relevant within higher education, institutions must develop structures and processes that invite students to share the knowledge they bring to campus. In our discussion of Nuevos Horizontes and Outreach Community College, we term this invitational process "celebratory socialization."

The strength of Nuevos Horizontes is that it affirms the cultural identities and border knowledge of the immigrant students it serves, while at the same time building educational opportunities for them. Nuevos Horizontes creates a learning environment in which immigrant students feel at home and safe to explore their new cultural surroundings, and, in many cases, take their first steps into the realm of higher education.

The program embodies an ethic of concern that strives to achieve connections among its participants. It achieves a caring atmosphere by honoring the strengths and differing views of the students who use its services and by giving students opportunities to discuss and value their cultural heritage.

In chapter 5, we describe another institution that expends significant energy responding to community needs. The focus of this case study is a high school program created at Divided Community College and designed primarily to serve African-American high school students. The development of the program—known as Middle College High School—was, in part, a response to the high attrition of secondary students in Divided's surrounding urban community, and subsequently, the relatively small number of high school students who pursue higher learning.

Middle College High School relates to our discussion of multiculturalism not only because the program effectively educates and retains African-American students (many of whom go on to college), but the creation of the program demonstrates how organizational restructuring may present opportunities for multicultural innovation. In this case, the boundaries between Divided Community College and the local school district have been bridged as a means to consolidate resources and provide extra support for local high school students. In effect, Middle College High School represents the idea of seamless education in that K–12 and higher education have joined efforts.

On the surface, the partnership between Divided and MCHS has been successful. Students respond well to the arrangement; they benefit from lower teacher-student ratios and a climate that encourages teachers to treat students as adults. Administrators are pleased that student attrition has declined and more students are proceeding on to college.

The downside of the program relates to the resentment among faculty and staff at Divided, which has grown since the program's inception. Few faculty and staff were involved in the process and they have felt a sense of powerlessness ever since the program began to take shape. The decision was autocratic on the part of the previous president. As a result, Middle College High School as a multicultural innovation has in many ways failed to take root within the organizational culture of Divided. The case study highlights how organizational change must involve a variety of campus constituents in a democratic process if change is to become part of the culture of the academic community.

In chapter 6, we describe Remedial Community College. We discuss how Remedial provides a range of services to its developmental students, including remediation, advisement, and career counseling. Many underprepared students come to Remedial for college-level work and need additional preparation in order to progress within the college. The success of the developmental students is defined not only by their mastery of academic subjects; students must also demonstrate knowledge and acceptance of how the institution views the college student. For example, certain patterns of speaking, acting, and style must be accepted by students. These cultural codes reflect what faculty at Remedial see as the characteristics prospective employers desire in college graduates.

Underprepared students labeled as "developmental students" by the institution have very little experience with both the formal and informal knowledge expectations placed on them by the institution's culture. In effect, these students lack much of the cultural capital needed to negotiate their way through Remedial Community College. The students, most of whom are poor and African American, are at a disadvantage because of their lack of privileged information and experience.

Despite a lack of what can be defined as a privileged form of knowledge, underprepared students bring a storehouse of knowledge and resources to the campus. The border knowledge these students have must be intentionally incorporated into the pedagogical and structural features of Remedial. As it stands now, Remedial is firmly rooted in a middle-class mentality that benefits primarily White students and situates African-American students on the margins of the organization, thus creating additional hurdles for these students to negotiate.

The fifth and final case study takes place at Perplexity Community College. Perplexity is similar to Vocational Community College in that it too is driven largely by the idea of careerism, a belief that the quintessential purpose of education is to prepare students to fill slots in the economic sector. Certainly, there is a need to emphasize the role colleges must play in preparing students for careers. However, Perplexity, Vocational, and other community colleges as well, must also recognize their obligation to challenge students to be critical and participatory citizens.

In its efforts to provide transfer, vocational, and community education to a diverse student body, Perplexity has had to deal with a confused organizational mission and a fractured organizational identity. Faculty and staff at Perplexity often feel confused about what it is they are trying to accomplish with the culturally diverse students they serve. Some believe that vocational education should take precedence as many of its students come from lower SES backgrounds. Others believe that transfer education ought to be central as students from lower- and working-class backgrounds need to achieve four-year degrees if they are to advance up the economic and social ladder. And still others see the economic problems of the local communities and envision community education as a central concern.

What has emerged at Perplexity in response to confusion and lack of understanding about the mission is a strong commitment to careerism. Again, colleges ought to be concerned with whether students are prepared for careers. But, to focus on careerism at the expense of other key concerns is an injustice to students and to a democratic society, which requires highly educated and participatory citizens.

Critical multiculturalism challenges community colleges to prepare good workers as well as good citizens. We define good citizens as individuals capable of understanding and criticizing the social, historical, and economic forces shaping social life, and who actively participate in creating a more just and democratic society. The problem with Perplexity Community College is that it fails to embrace a democratic mission and thereby fails to prepare students for important roles in society. Embracing the ideals of democracy also might enable colleges such as Perplexity to develop a common connection (instead of a connection based on careerism) that, we argue, is more in line with the broad goals of higher learning.

What we describe in these case studies are examples of organizations struggling with multiple concerns and responsibilities. We see varying degrees of success, ranging from significant improvement to little progress. We suggest throughout this book that a critical multicultural perspective embracing a democratic view of education offers solutions to the many problems of today's community colleges.

In what follows, we offer a fictional portrait of Democratic Community College (Demo) and its struggle to enact education as the practice of democracy. We stress, however, that every community college around the country is unique. Each has its own culture and a unique set of strengths and weaknesses. Thus, in presenting our example of Demo, we offer the following caveat: The types of organizational and pedagogical changes needed by community colleges to embrace a more democratic form of education vary from one institution to the next. To be overly prescriptive misses this point.

With the preceding caveat in mind, we offer some ideas about what community college faculty, staff, and students might face and think about as they struggle to enact more democratic organizations. After highlighting Democratic Community College, we go on to suggest some general principles that community colleges ought to consider as they move to build a critical multicultural community college framed by democracy.

Democratic Community College

Democratic Community College is known for inclusionary and collaborative administrative and academic processes. Over recent years, the college has attracted a great deal of publicity, both positive and negative. Some community college leaders, educators, and researchers see Demo as an example of successfully restructuring an organization around a collaborative and democratic vision. Others scoff at the president of Demo's inability to lead the organization and believe that senior officials are shackled by encumbering processes that contribute to organizational inefficiency. Many of the members of

Democratic Community College see themselves as part of an idealized vision that is always in process: They never fully achieve a democratic community, but they find the struggle gratifying because they
are offered numerous and multiple opportunities to shape the institution.

Things were not always so democratic at Demo. Over the past
ten years the organizational culture has slowly moved in a more collaborative direction. At first, it was only a few faculty who spoke
about the need to be more inclusive. Then several administrators
bought into the idea of a college based on democratic principles.
The real turning point was when some of the more collaboratively
oriented faculty guided the search for the current Vice President for
Academic Affairs and hired Dr. Josephine Shirley.

As a department chair at her previous college, Josephine Shirley
was known for her commitment to multiculturalism and democratic
leadership. Not long after being hired at Demo, she and a group of
faculty convinced the president to create a task force charged with
examining the college's commitment to multiculturalism. There was
a concern on the part of the president and others within the local
community college district that Demo was not doing enough to
serve the large number of underrepresented minorities who live in
the area. There was a general sense that Demo needed to be more
user-friendly for culturally diverse students. Dr. Shirley and the faculty group felt the college needed a significant change of direction.
They also realized that such a change would require a broad and
collaborative effort if the culture of the institution was to be modified.

In organizing the task force, Dr. Shirley made sure that a wide
range of campus as well as community constituents were included.
Although the task force was charged to examine issues related to
multiculturalism, Shirley and the faculty group believed that a more
collaborative college was needed if the institution was to create the
kind of environment that welcomes diverse students.

The task force met on many occasions before any specific recommendations actually emerged. Nonetheless, these were considered productive times as ideas about what multiculturalism means
and how it might shape an institution were discussed and debated.
Two distinct camps emerged from the task force and reflected dif-

fering opinions around the campus. One group saw multiculturalism as primarily a curricular idea and did not make theoretical or practical connections between cultural diversity and administrative or pedagogical practices. The other group, composed of Dr. Shirley and some of the faculty involved in her hiring, saw multiculturalism in a much broader sense. This group equated multiculturalism with a more democratic and collaborative college as a whole. But, Dr. Shirley and her group recognized the need to be inclusive or else the entire task force and its multicultural initiatives might fail. They knew that differing perspectives about multiculturalism would most likely involve compromises down the road.

Two general initiatives emerged from the task force and reflected the split in how the two camps envisioned multiculturalism and its impact on campus life. One initiative focused on reviewing the curriculum to examine how multiculturalism could become a more significant portion of the knowledge conveyed at Demo. This initiative reflects what we term in chapter 1 as "mainstream multiculturalism." The initiative dealt with revising the curriculum and adding some multicultural courses. In essence, this camp sought to create a more inclusive canon. Dr. Shirley and her group believed that such an initiative was problematic because of the static view of knowledge embraced by this group. But, again, they knew that collaboration and cooperation meant difficult compromises had to be made at times.

The curriculum group developed what became known as Initiative 1 and succeeded in implementing a number of multicultural courses. However, they failed to see the importance of also enacting recommendations that encouraged all faculty to incorporate diverse perspectives into their courses. Shirley's group saw a way around the other group's lack of commitment to democratic pedagogy in the form of a second initiative, which focused on process.

Initiative 2 reflected the thinking of Shirley's group and involved a more encompassing vision of multiculturalism. They pushed for an examination of the processes that guide employee and student behavior at Demo. Their hope was to restructure the college by implementing more collaborative and inclusionary practices, policies, and structures. They believed that a fundamental philosophical change was needed in how organizational members viewed themselves in relation to other employees and students. An attitude of caring and consideration needed to be encouraged if diverse students, as well as faculty, were to find Demo a great place to work and to learn.

Initiative 2 was twofold: One aspect dealt with pedagogical practices and the other focused on administrative and management activities. After several months of meetings, Shirley's group developed several recommendations. The recommendations focused on how faculty and staff might better enact more inclusive classroom and office management styles.

In terms of pedagogical issues, the following items were addressed by Initiative 2: Teachers need to see learning as more dialogical and to stress student involvement and interaction in the classroom. Students need to work more often in smaller groups to create opportunities for student collaboration and for learning from other students. Students need to become involved in writing their own educational histories and to do so they must understand the social forces they face. Relatedly, teachers need to understand and at times raise issues related to race, gender, class, and sexual orientation as forces that contribute to how students experience the educational process. And finally, students need to be encouraged to support and at times teach other students who may lack knowledge in certain areas.

In terms of administrative processes, Initiative 2 challenged officials of Democratic Community College to rethink their administrative practices, polices, and structures. The task force suggested that all staff within both academic and administrative offices hold meetings to begin the long process of restructuring around increased participation by all organizational members. Departments were challenged not only to revise internally, but collaboration was sought between departments and divisions, as well as the great divide separating academic and administrative areas.

To help faculty and staff fulfill these organizational challenges, a series of faculty and staff development activities were planned. First, an all-college retreat was held to discuss how the recommendations might be enacted. A major goal of the retreat was to get a large segment of the college community actively involved in the process of implementation. As part of the retreat, each department developed its own series of implementation strategies as a means to best achieve the recommendations. All members of departmental staffs as well as students were involved in this process. As a follow-up strategy, the multicultural task force recommended a series of campus-wide, year-long forums as a means to discuss and debate various problems and solutions related to implementation and evaluation. A formal evaluation plan was developed by each department and shared during the year-long forums.

The next two years at Demo were filled with change, turmoil, and complaints as a number of faculty, staff, and students resisted the move toward a more democratic and collaborative college community. For many, this "new way of thinking" was inefficient and time-consuming, not to mention that it generated heated debate and campus conflict. But many others were excited about the possibility of providing feedback and having a say in the operations of the college. The latter group represented the majority of Demo's academic community; many felt democratic restructuring was an idea whose time had come. Their efforts to embrace democratic processes helped Initiative 2 become a fundamental force in shaping Demo's culture.

In what follows, we describe some of the characteristics exhibited at Demo resulting from nearly a decade of struggle to achieve a more democratic community college. We deal with the following areas: administrative practice, pedagogical practice, campus climate, and concerns about multiple demands.

Administrative Practice The president and other organizational officials at Demo seek employee feedback and hold organized discussion on all matters important to the campus community. In nearly every department or office at Demo, a decision-making team has emerged with administrative officials typically chairing these decision-making bodies. Nearly everyone at Demo has come to expect that individual officers of the college will not make decisions by fiat. On the rare occasions that such decisions have been made, the community has challenged officials for an explanation. Challenges come in the form of faculty or staff seeking out the appropriate official for a proper explanation. It has become an expectation that nonparticipatory decisions will be challenged and there is little to no fear of administrative reprisal.

On some occasions, Demo officials have been seen to be justified in making nonparticipatory decisions. For example, when the state office of education called the president and asked for an immediate decision concerning Demo's request for funds established for building renovations, the president had to make a decision immediately. Some at Demo were upset that their buildings were not targeted for improvements but accepted the president's explanation about the immediacy of her decision. On another occasion, the director of the admissions office made a decision to require all office staff to inform him six weeks in advance of any vacation requests. The staff was quite upset that such a decision would be made without a meeting of the department and complained to both the director and his immediate supervisor. After several days of high tension and heated communications, the director held a meeting to discuss his decision and consider revisions of the policy. A compromise was reached and the staff in the admissions office was satisfied that their concerns had been heard.

Officials at Demo, in addition to including a wide range of voices in decision making, do not turn a deaf ear to criticism. Criticism is a major part of the process used by administrators as they focus internally to detect problems and identify important issues. This critical look inward is intended to prevent any lapses into orthodoxy or dogmatic practices that characterize traditional administrative educational practice. As a result, policies and processes are continuously assessed as part of the normal everyday operations of the college. Total Quality Management is passé at Demo as working to improve has become an essential quality of the college.

Pedagogical Practice Democratic Community College has faced difficulties in establishing the kinds of pedagogical processes deemed compatible with a democratic view of education. The primary barrier has been the dependency of the college on part-time instructors and the inability to involve these instructors in an emerging view of pedagogical practice and a changing organizational ethos. Many of the part-time faculty were employed full-time in positions outside the college and taught only one class at Demo. Vice President Shirley and other members involved in Initiative 2 made recommendations to the president and the college's governing board that Demo make every effort to develop a significant body of full-time faculty. They set as a goal that eighty percent of instructors for any semester be full-time employees. Such a goal, of course, has had financial implications but has been largely offset by involving administrators in teaching. Administrators at Demo are encouraged to teach one course per academic year. This suggestion was offered by several faculty and staff, who felt it a good step in bridging the chasm between the academic and administrative sides of campus. Implementation of administrative involvement in the classroom has increased collaboration between faculty and staff as the two groups have been forced to engage in significant and ongoing interactions. Some faculty and administrators now meet on a regular basis to discuss course content and pedagogy. Various administrators around campus are regular participants in academic departmental meetings. The opposite has occurred for faculty as they are more enmeshed in administrative processes. Moving to a more democratic decision-making style has led to much greater involvement on the part of faculty in decisions that typically were considered the domain of administrators. In fact, the Task Force has recommended that all decision-making teams include at least one faculty member. Although some faculty were reluctant at first to take on this responsibility, others welcomed the chance to interact with different colleagues around the campus.

As a result of moving to a greater percentage of full-time faculty and greater reliance on full-time administrators as teachers, a strong faculty culture at Demo has emerged. With the ongoing changes in the college have come continuous debate and discussion about the nature of teaching and how teachers ought to relate to one another and to students. Although agreement is seldom reached, the discussions generate a great deal of thinking about pedagogy—thinking that often spills into the classroom.

Out of a concern for enacting multicultural pedagogies in the classroom, faculty at Demo organize their courses to take advantage of the strengths, values, and knowledge of minority, lower-, and working-class students. All students have histories, cultures, and communication styles that are rich and expressive. Courses built to take advantage of these strengths invite students to participate and display their knowledge and experience. The importance of border knowledge has become central to how faculty think about the students and how they structure the classroom setting. Openness in the classroom has become the norm and students have multiple opportunities to share their own understandings of the world. Openness and collaboration combined with a growing commitment to an ethic of care have produced classrooms in which students and their cultural differences are validated instead of denigrated.

The validation of students is promoted through a teaching philosophy at Demo that reflects the Freirean notion that all students must be understood in terms of where they are, culturally, historically, and socially. This means that issues of race, class, gender, sexual orientation and other significant factors that contribute to shaping students' lives are not only considered, but are discussed and debated. Students are viewed not as receptacles of facts and figures in which instructors pour knowledge into empty containers as if to make a deposit of capital. Instead, faculty recognize that teaching and learning are social acts, and students and faculty must work together to construct knowledge.

At Democratic Community College, students are not seen as deficient and the term developmental education is rarely used. It is recognized that some students have more cultural capital than others and those lacking in one area are seen to have knowledge in other areas. Because faculty and staff think about and discuss students in terms of cultural capital, no student is situated as deficient or unknowledgeable. Simply put, some students are seen to lack a certain form of knowledge and should have expectations just as high as other students. Along these lines, faculty and staff at Demo set high expectations for all students.

At Demo, students who lack certain forms of knowledge are not seen to be the problem. As Dennis McGrath and Martin Spear (1991) explain, "We need to deflect the idea that students are at fault for not acquiring the knowledge transmitted by educational institutions" (p. 106). McGrath and Spear go on to cite the weak and disorganized academic culture of the community college as problematic in that it fails to engage students intellectually. They suggest that community colleges create settings that encourage students to think and talk reflectively about education, about careers, and about their lives. Because classrooms and faculty are open and students are expected to voice their experiences and understandings, Demo has accomplished much of what McGrath and Spear suggest.

This is not to say that there are no students at Demo who need extra classroom attention or help in progressing to college-level material. There are many. Demo has developed some preparatory courses that offer students a chance to achieve certain forms of knowledge. But, for the most part, Demo challenges less-prepared students to work within college-credit courses by offering them peer tutoring and close faculty monitoring and support. Because classrooms are more collaborative, less-prepared students at Demo receive a great deal of support from fellow students. The idea that students learn from one another is vital to pedagogy at Demo.

Nonetheless, students who lack cultural capital face a significant challenge, and faculty and staff at Demo push students to work harder and encourage all students to work collaboratively. Outstanding students at Demo are expected to help other students who may struggle with specific material or coursework. An attitude of caring is continuously expressed by administrators and teachers and the college has seen a similar attitude reflected in the student body. To succeed only as an individual is not held in high regard. "To succeed and to help others succeed" is the ideal at Demo and the phrase that has been emblazoned above every blackboard and even in the gymnasium above the school banner.

Campus Climate The campus climate at Demo reflects an environment that invites debate and sees conflict and struggle as a natural progression toward an empowered faculty, staff, and student body. Critical multiculturalists concern themselves with addressing various forms of organizational oppression (most evident by authoritarian decision making) in everyday life and look toward the transformation of the institution and the achievement of a more just and participatory organization. At the center of this project is a concern for inclusiveness and for overcoming barriers to equality for all. This is why issues of race, class, gender, and sexual orientation are so paramount in many of the debates at Demo. Students are continually challenged to understand and care for other students. The aim is "to create conditions in which students become border crossers in order to understand otherness in its own terms" (Giroux, 1992, pp. 23–24).

Students and their views are not relegated to the margins of the institution. Instead, their concerns and recommendations are given serious consideration in discussions and decision making at the col-

lege. As alternative voices have been given a central position in decision making, issues of power that underlie education have become
more apparent to students at Demo. Some have begun to question
the curriculum and why certain vocational tracks are offered as well
as why all courses do not count for transfer. Over recent years, the
student voice has grown stronger as students have offered numerous
critiques of how the college operates. In fact, many outsiders have
begun to refer to Demo as the Berkeley of community colleges. The
president has had to speak continually to this characterization as
some members of the governing board perceive negativity in such a
description.

Despite the voice of democracy that arises at Democratic Community College, it continues to struggle with maintaining the sense
of freedom and participation it strives to achieve. Kelly Estrada and
Peter McLaren (1993) explain that democracy is not seamless,
smooth, or always in a relative state of political and cultural equilib-
rium. Critical multiculturalists recognize that society may exist in a
state of conflict or crisis and that harmony does not always prevail.
The challenge Demo faces is to learn to adapt to its own multiplicity
and convince those in positions of power that the never-ending quest
for democracy is necessarily a confusing and challenging struggle
fraught with conflict and debate—but one, nonetheless, that ought
to be pursued.

Many of the students entering Demo have only a limited understanding of what is expected from them to achieve their goals.
Most students do not have parents or siblings who attended college
and therefore cannot depend on them as resources for addressing
vexing problems concerning college life. The college attempts to
activate the border knowledge that students bring to campus as an
effort to validate a broad array of students' experiences and backgrounds. Because the college honors and validates students' previous life experiences as legitimate forms of knowledge and learning,
students make the transition to Demo more easily than they would
at other institutions.

Student service professionals at Demo struggle to help students
come to terms with their own identities and to understand their role
in educational settings and in society. Student development professionals at the college recognize that students speak from a particular

place, out of a particular experience, and from a particular culture. Students are encouraged to express themselves with their own voice, not to expect that one voice will speak for all of them. Students come to terms with their own subjugated histories and find ways to tell their stories so that all may benefit. It is through the telling of stories that students discover their connections and work toward liberation, equality, and justice.

With the preceding comments in mind, students are never categorized as remedial or developmental or in other similarly pejorative terms. Student services are not designed to repair or change students to make them more acceptable to faculty as is discussed in our case study of Vocational Community College. Differences are honored and respected and students are encouraged to offer their own experiences as legitimate forms of knowledge in the context of the college community.

Concerns about Multiple Demands Like other community colleges, Demo struggles to balance commitments to transfer, vocational, and community education. The relevance of each is continuously debated at Demo as faculty, staff, and students struggle to enact the college's multiple roles around a democratic vision.

In terms of transfer education, a central goal of Demo is to create opportunities for students who desire a four-year degree. The college has worked hard to establish articulation agreements with four-year colleges throughout the state. As a result, a number of courses have been revised over recent years in an effort to meet the standards of four-year institutions. Because of the democratic processes embraced by Demo, students learn the importance of participating in class and interacting with professors on an equal basis. The education students get at Demo helps them to take an active role in structuring their own learning experience. Such a learning outcome proves helpful to transfer students, who face new obstacles as they progress through their postsecondary education.

Vocational education at Demo is not confined to specific career options. Instead, it revolves around general skills often required in the work setting. For example, a student who desires to go into auto mechanics may take courses in physics, mathematics, and business. The courses seek to combine academic preparation with practical aspects in order to provide students with the basic skills and abilities to pursue their education at another level if desired. Creativity and problem solving are stressed throughout the vocational tracks. In many cases, the courses in the vocational tracks are transferable to four-year institutions. A commitment to democracy challenges Demo to present students with a variety of career and educational options and to think about the choices they have made and continue to make that shape their economic futures. College officials regularly meet with employers in the area. Discussions not only focus on how Demo might do a better job of preparing students for the work settings, but also stress how companies might modify their work settings to tap the strengths of Demo's students. After hiring Demo graduates, some employers have complained about the lack of *specific* job skills of the students. But, in time, the vast majority of employers have come to appreciate the initiative, creativity, and flexibility Demo students bring to the workplace.

Democratic Community College has struggled to enact more collaborative and participatory administrative and pedagogical processes. Such changes have not occurred in a vacuum and Demo has struggled to involve its community, local businesses, and state four-year institutions in the changes. Some changes have come more easily than others and many complaints and problems have yet to be solved. The college seems chaotic at times and some members of the academic community complain about the college's inability to make quick and forceful decisions. Everything is open to questioning and criticism, and for some this is troublesome. However, the changes at Demo have excited many faculty, staff, and students about the chance to have a voice in how the college operates. For these individuals, Demo has become a place of personal, professional, and educational commitment and they take pride in being an active part of administrative and pedagogical processes.

General Principles

Our example of Democratic Community College is a fictitious one that highlights only a few of the issues that critical multiculturalism calls forth. The culture of each college or university varies and demands attention in different areas. With this said, we offer the following general principles as considerations for community college faculty, staff, and students concerned with restructuring more democratic and multicultural academic communities. The principles derive from what we have learned from the case studies presented in this book and from theoretical insights related to a critical multicultural view of college and university life.

Principle 1:
Community college officials committed to multiculturalism and democracy promote greater collaboration and more participatory management processes.

Community colleges committed to the practice of democracy make every effort to be collaborative and seek feedback from a wide spectrum of campus and community members. Good ideas are not the sole province of official institutional leaders, but may come from anyone affiliated with the organization. This includes students, who should have significant opportunities to provide input into organizational decision making.

Principle 2:
A commitment to multiculturalism requires that community college officials create opportunities for others to assume leadership.

Like good ideas, leadership ability is possessed by many organizational participants. The strengths and personal qualities of individuals vary widely. In different settings and in different contexts, the strengths or qualities needed by individuals to provide direction for the organization and for others also will vary. Therefore, opportunities must be created that enable a variety of members of the college to assume responsibility. Leadership is not a quality possessed only by high-ranking organizational officials.

Principle 3:
Community colleges committed to multiculturalism include culturally diverse students, faculty, and staff in organizational participation and decision making.

Experiences of marginality have rendered many in our society voiceless. Community colleges committed to multiculturalism and the practice of democracy seek to restructure the organization around equal opportunity for all. This means being more inclusive not only in terms of recruitment, but also in terms of how decisions get made at the college. Such a recommendation challenges community colleges to review current practices, policies, and structures that impede equal opportunity for all.

Principle 4:

Community colleges committed to multicultural education encourage teachers to enact critical pedagogical practices within classrooms and in their interactions with students.

A critical multicultural pedagogy presents a challenge to teachers in that they must seek to uncover the unique experiences and forms of knowledge that students bring to the educational process. This involves dealing with some of the complex social conditions and problems that have limited certain groups based on race, class, gender, or sexual orientation. Faculty should be encouraged to establish open and dialogical classrooms as well as share their knowledge and expertise with their peers.

Principle 5:

Community colleges committed to a more democratic education enact collaborative classroom techniques whenever possible.

From the perspective of a critical multicultural pedagogy, teachers are not the sole possessors of knowledge. Students also bring important ideas and experiences to the classroom, as well as diverse ways of knowing. To better tap students' knowledge, greater teamwork and interdependence must be encouraged. Classroom environments that encourage collaborative learning allow students to share experiences and to validate their own border knowledge. Collaborative teaching and learning strategies also encourage students to become active participants in the learning process.

Principle 6:

Community colleges establish both specific programs and broad initiatives to expand the institution's commitment to multiculturalism.

Programs like Nuevos Horizontes serve a key role in helping students to see education in more positive terms. Such programs must be guided by staff who are knowledgeable of cultural differences and who are capable of crossing multiple cultural borders. At the same time, however, community colleges need to challenge all organizational members to learn more about culturally diverse students and to work to better meet their needs. Therefore, all faculty and staff, regardless of their institutional role, must strive to be border crossers.

Principle 7:
Community colleges, as democratic educational centers, are committed to preparing students to be socially responsible and active participants in communities and society.

When community colleges make a commitment to democratic pedagogies and administrative practices, students learn to think of themselves as active participants in their own education and growth as citizens. This means students must be continually challenged to participate in the college as well as the local community. With such learning comes an expectation that they will be active participants in public life beyond their college years.

Principle 8:
Transfer education is fundamental to a democratic vision of the community college and the goal of education as a vehicle for social mobility.

An educational institution grounded in democracy and multiculturalism seeks to overcome the historical, political, and cultural forces that have limited the achievement of members of marginalized groups. This means a community college committed to democracy must intentionally seek to advance the educational opportunities of underrepresented students. Stressing an academic component to the curriculum that encourages student transfer is therefore fundamental to a democratic vision. Relatedly, community colleges must work to eliminate structural barriers and provide sufficient information and preparation to students who wish to transfer to four-year institutions.

Principle 9:
Community colleges committed to democracy embrace a broad vision of vocational education.

Community colleges have an important role to play in preparing students for the world of work. But such preparation should deal with important transferable skills that once acquired enable students to adjust to labor market changes. Basic skills such as analytical and creative thinking, communication abilities, reading, writing, and mathematics should be central to any vocational track. Vocational education should not involve the mastering of repetitive tasks that are easily learned on the job site. Community colleges must avoid becoming the training centers for nonprofessional positions.

Principle 10:
Community colleges committed to democracy reach out and involve local community members in lifelong educational opportunities.

A well-educated citizenry is vital to the life of a democratic society and community colleges play a central role in this process. Community members have diverse educational needs and community education programs must address such needs. This requires that community colleges be closely connected to their communities and that they continually monitor community issues and concerns. Meeting local needs also should involve ongoing collaboration with the community. Such collaboration ought to reflect the democratic processes which govern the institution.

Principle 11:
Community colleges need to work with prospective employers to build more democratic work environments and thus create greater synergism between the world of work and the educational sector.

In challenging students to become active and participatory learners and citizens, employers must be prepared for a new breed of worker committed to and capable of playing an active role in organizational decision making. Community colleges committed to a democratic vision must therefore work with local and regional companies to challenge work arrangements and educate companies about the benefits of a more creative and involved work force. In many cases, companies have already suggested such actions in their criticism of the lack of general skills of today's graduates.

Principle 12:
Democratic community colleges offer academic support to less prepared students primarily by providing additional classroom assistance and, in some cases, by offering preparatory courses.

Developmental education must be restructured so that students are not seen as deficient in knowledge. The knowledge and strengths of students must be recognized, and academic skills must build on the student's previous knowledge. Efforts must be made to include students in college-credit courses as soon as possible, and to discourage the separation of students into developmental tracks. Collaboration and caring are central to the democratic classroom and advanced students should be encouraged to provide assistance to other students.

Principle 13:
Democratic community colleges establish partnerships with local and regional businesses and educational institutions as a means to create greater opportunities for students.

In seeking to expand the opportunities for community college students, institutions often face the reality of minimal financial resources. One way to deal with limited resources is to organize cooperative efforts with other organizations and at the same time reduce expenses by eliminating duplication. Democratic community colleges recognize that organizational boundaries must be viewed as dynamic and ever-changing, and take advantage of potential partnerships within their local communities and regions.

Principle 14:
Democratic community colleges embrace change as a way of life in the ongoing quest to achieve greater equality, justice, and freedom.

Democracy is an ideal. It is something seen on the horizon but never fully reached. With this in mind, community colleges committed to democratic processes must continually strive to enact new and more inclusive and collaborative practices. This involves continually revising and rethinking what the organization is trying to accomplish. From this perspective, change becomes an ongoing and normal part of organizational life.

We offer these principles as a general framework for rethinking community college education. The suggestions offered here and throughout this book are based on a view that multiculturalism involves establishing democratic educational communities committed to inclusiveness, equal opportunity, and justice and freedom for all. Behind much of our thinking is the realization that in our society exclusivity, inequity, and injustice are firmly entrenched within our understandings of cultural differences. This is why a commitment to education as the practice of democracy must come to terms with issues of culture and identity. In other words, what has kept our country from achieving a more democratic educational system and society is tied to a large degree to cultural identity differences and our inability to understand and respect such differences. In concluding, we return to the underlying theme of this work.

Education and Identity

Kenneth Gergen (1991) suggests that postmodernism is "marked by a plurality of voices vying for the right to reality—to be accepted as legitimate expressions of the true and the good" (p. 7). Because educational institutions play a central role in defining the "true and the good," it is easy to see why the struggle for identity (the essence of multiculturalism) is so closely linked to educational processes. Multiculturalism calls attention to the fact that educational institutions must come to terms with how identities are legitimized or denigrated and the role schooling plays in identity development. For too many years, educators have failed to understand or have ignored the fact that knowledge is culturally derived and therefore has significant implications for which groups achieve academic and economic rewards and which groups are denied. Multiculturalism challenges educational institutions such as community colleges to broaden their vision of knowledge embraced within the curriculum, pedagogy, and administrative practice.

Education as the practice of democracy epitomizes the kind of ideals multiculturalism calls forth. Democratic practices encourage inclusiveness, not only in terms of visibility, but in terms of participation. A commitment to education as the practice of democracy demands that institutions be collaborative both in the classroom and in the board room. In particular, such a vision seeks to include those groups who have historically been denied full participation.

To accomplish more democratic community colleges, institutions must come to terms with the diverse and multiple understandings students bring to the educational process. Including the border knowledge of culturally diverse students must be a central concern of community college educators. The challenge is to balance the kinds of knowledge needed to succeed in society as it is, with the kinds of knowledge diverse students bring that offer opportunities to transform society. Such a process involves a bidirectional view of socialization in which both students and educational institutions change as a result of learning from the other.

For the most part, educational settings reflect a rigid view of students and a narrow understanding of student identities. As a result, most students are expected to enact white, middle- and upper-class, male cultural models. Little leeway is accorded to different ways of knowing and experiencing one's social world. Embracing border knowledge is about providing greater flexibility and legitimating a broader conception of identity. In fact, the democratic vision suggested throughout this book ultimately seeks to eliminate border knowledge through the development of an inclusive and accepting educational environment that no longer situates certain ways of knowing on society's margins.

Community colleges, as social institutions, do not stand alone. And they cannot resituate border knowledge and border identities without assistance and cooperation from other institutions in this society. This is why collaboration and partnerships with communities, businesses, and other educational institutions is imperative to achieving the democratic, multicultural vision suggested in this book.

Community college education as the practice of democracy challenges individuals to confront the relationship between self and society, and the role of power in the construction of cultural identities. Education as the practice of democracy forces students to rethink their place in institutions, communities, and society, and advances social transformation around the ideals of justice, freedom, and equality.

Conclusion

Community colleges have long been known as democracy's college. While their open-door policies and blue-collar image have made them seem less elitist than their four-year counterparts, community colleges have failed in their promise to provide social mobility to all students. Community colleges have certainly opened their doors to the masses, but to what result? Lower- and working-class students and minorities who enter the community college continue to march toward low-paying and working-class jobs, while middle- and upper-class students attending four-year institutions progress toward higher-level roles and more lucrative careers. The cycle is regenerated and democracy remains an often-mouthed myth.

Community colleges most likely will continue to be the institution of choice for minority, lower-, and working-class students. More than fifty percent of minority students enrolled in postsecondary education attend community colleges, and more than fifty percent of all students begin their college careers in a community college. Many of America's poor seek a pathway to a better life through the community college. They believe that higher education will provide the way for them, and the "open door" is seen as an opportunity to achieve their version of the American dream. Community colleges can truly become democracy's college by assuring that all groups have a central place in the organizational life of the institution. Education as the practice of democracy offers a philosophical and practical framework from which to structure community college life. Such a vision rests on the view that democracy is best achieved by practicing it—in all our social institutions.

References

Adelman, Clifford. (1992). *The way we are: The community college as American thermometer*. Washington, DC: United States Department of Education.

Almanac, The. (1994, August). *The Chronicle of Higher Education*.

American Council on Education. (1988). *One-third of a nation*. A Report of the Commission on Minority Participation in Education and American Life. Washington, DC: American Council on Education.

American Council on Education. (1991). *Setting the national agenda: Academic achievement and transfer*. Washington, DC: American Council on Education.

Anyon, Jean. (1981). Social class and school knowledge. *Curriculum Inquiry, 11*(1), 3–42.

Apple, Michael. (1988). *Teachers and texts: A political economy of class and gender relations in education*. New York: Routledge.

Aronowitz, Stanley, & Giroux, Henry A. (1991). *Postmodern education: Politics, culture and social criticism*. Minneapolis: University of Minnesota Press.

Bagg, Lyman H. (1871). *Four years at Yale*. New Haven, CT: Charles C. Chatfield & Company.

Belenky, Mary F., Clinchy, Blythe M., Goldberger, Nancy R., & Tarule, Jill M. (1986). *Women's ways of knowing: The development of self, voice, and mind*. New York: Basic Books.

Bennett, William J. (1984). *To reclaim a legacy: A report on the humanities in higher education*. Washington, DC: National Endowment for the Humanities.

Bensimon, Estela M. (Ed.). (1994). *Multicultural teaching and learning*. University Park, PA: National Center on Postsecondary Teaching, Learning, & Assessment.

Bensimon, Estela M., & Tierney, William G. (1992/93). Shaping the multicultural campus: Strategies for administrators. *The College Board, 166*, 4–7, 30.

Berger, Renee, & Ruiz, Aida M. Ortiz. (1988). The crucial role of faculty in transfer articulation. In C. Prager (Ed.), *Enhancing articulation and transfer* (pp. 39–47). New Directions for Community Colleges, No. 61. San Francisco: Jossey-Bass.

Birnbaum, Robert. (1988). *How colleges work*. San Francisco: Jossey-Bass.

Bloom, Allan. (1987). *The closing of the American mind*. New York: Simon & Schuster.

Bloom, Harold. (1994). *The western canon: The books and the school of the ages*. New York: Harcourt Brace & Company.

Board of Governors. (1993). *The California middle college high school program*. A report of the California Community Colleges, Office of the Chancellor, Sacramento, CA.

Bourdieu, Pierre. (1977). *Outline of a theory of practice*. New York: Cambridge University Press.

Bourdieu, Pierre. (1986). The forms of capital. In J. G. Richardson (Ed.), *Handbook of theory and research in the sociology of education* (pp. 241–258). New York: Greenwood Press.

Bourdieu, Pierre, & Passeron, Jean-Claude. (1990). *Reproduction in education, society and culture* (2nd ed.). London: Sage.

Bowles, Samuel, & Gintis, Herbert. (1976). *Schooling in capitalist America*. New York: Basic Books.

Boyer, Ernest L. (1983). *High school: A report on secondary education in America*. New York: Harper & Row.

Breneman, David W., & Nelson, Susan C. (1981). *Financing community colleges*. Washington, DC: Brookings Institute.

Brint, Steven, & Karabel, Jerome. (1989). *The diverted dream: Community colleges and the promise of educational opportunity in America, 1900–1985*. New York: Oxford University Press.

Burbules, Nicholas C. (1986). A theory of power in education. *Educational Theory, 36*(2), 95–114.

Burbules, Nicholas C., & Rice, Suzanne. (1991). Dialogue across differences: Continuing the conversation. *Harvard Educational Review, 61*(4), 393–416.

Bureau of the Census. (1990). *1990 Census of the population*. Washington, DC: U.S. Government Printing Office.

Burns, James MacGregor. (1978). *Leadership*. New York: Harper & Row.

Burrell, Gibson. (1988). Modernism, postmodernism and organizational analysis 2: The contribution of Michel Foucault. *Organization Studies, 9*(2), 221–235.

Cain, Maureen. (1993). Foucault, feminism and feeling: What Foucault can and cannot contribute to feminist epistemology. In C. Ramazanoglu (Ed.), *Up against Foucault: Explorations of some tensions between Foucault and feminism* (pp. 73–96). London: Routledge.

Cherryholmes, Cleo. (1988). *Power and criticism: Poststructural investigations in education*. New York: Teachers College Press.

Clark, Burton R. (1960). The cooling-out function in higher education. *American Journal of Sociology, 65*(6), 569–576.

Clowes, Darrel A., & Levin, Bernard H. (1989). Community, technical, and junior colleges: Are they leaving higher education? *Journal of Higher Education, 60*, 349–355.

Cohen, Arthur M., & Brawer, Florence B. (1989). *The American community college* (2nd ed.). San Francisco: Jossey-Bass.

Cooper, Robert. (1989). Modernism, postmodernism and organizational analysis 3: The contribution of Jacques Derrida. *Organization Studies, 10*(4), 479–502.

Cooper, Robert, & Burrell, Gibson. (1988). Modernism, postmodernism and organizational analysis: An introduction. *Organization Studies, 9*(1), 91–112.

Cullen, Cecelia. (1991). Membership and engagement at Middle College High School. *Urban Education, 26*(1), 83–93.

Dawes, Robyn M. (1993). Racial norming: A debate. *Academe, 79*(3), 31–34.

DeLoughry, Thomas. (1989, April 26). At Penn State: Polarization of the campus persists amid struggles to ease tensions. *The Chronicle of Higher Education*, A30.

Denzin, Norman. (1989). *The research act* (3rd ed.). New York: Prentice-Hall.

Dewey, John. (1916). *Democracy and education*. New York: Macmillan.

Dewey, John. (1927). *The public and its problems*. New York: Henry Holt and Company.

Dougherty, Kevin J. (1994). *The contradictory college: The conflicting origins, impacts, and futures of the community college*. Albany: State University of New York Press.

D'Souza, Dinesh. (1991). *Illiberal education: The politics of race and sex on campus*. New York: The Free Press.

Eaton, Judith S. (Ed.). (1992). *Faculty and transfer: Academic partnerships at work*. Washington, DC: American Council on Education.

Eaton, Judith S. (1994a). *Strengthening collegiate education in community colleges*. San Francisco: Jossey-Bass.

Eaton, Judith S. (Ed.). (1994b). *Strengthening transfer through academic partnerships*. Washington, DC: American Council on Education.

Eaton, Judith S. (1994c). The fortunes of the transfer function: Community colleges and transfer 1900–1990. In G. A. Baker III (Ed.), *A handbook on the community college in America: Its history, mission, and management* (pp. 28–40). Westport, CT: Greenwood Press.

Eckert, Penelope. (1989). *Jocks & burnouts: Social categories and identity in the high school*. New York: Teachers College Press.

El-Khawas, Elaine. (1992). *Campus trends*. Washington, DC: American Council on Education.

Estrada, Kelly, & McLaren, Peter. (1993). A dialogue on multiculturalism and democratic culture. *Educational Researcher, 22*(3), 27–33.

Ferguson, Kathy E. (1984). *The feminist case against bureaucracy*. Philadelphia: Temple University Press.

Ferguson, Ronald F. (1991). Racial patterns in how school and teacher quality affect achievement and earnings. *Challenge, 2*(1), 1–35.

Fifty-six protestors arrested at Berkeley sit-in. (1990, March 28). *The Chronicle of Higher Education*, A3.

Fine, Michelle. (1991). *Framing dropouts: Notes on the politics of an urban high school*. Albany: State University of New York Press.

Foucault, Michel. (1978). *The history of sexuality, volume I: An introduction* (R. Hurley, trans.). New York: Vintage.

Foucault, Michel. (1980). *Power/Knowledge* (C. Gordan et al., trans.). New York: Vintage.

Fraser, Nancy. (1990). Rethinking the public sphere: A contribution to the critique of actually existing democracy. *Social Text, 25/26*, 56–80.

Freire, Paulo. (1970). *Pedagogy of the oppressed*. New York: Continuum.

Gaff, Jerry G. (1992). Beyond politics: The educational issues inherent in multicultural education. *Change, 24*(1), 31–35.

Galarza, Ernesto. (1971). *Barrio boy*. Notre Dame, IN: University of Notre Dame Press.

Geertz, Clifford. (1973). *The interpretation of cultures*. New York: Basic Books.

Gergen, Kenneth J. (1991). *The saturated self: Dilemmas of identity in contemporary life*. New York: Basic Books.

Gergen, Kenneth J. (1992). Organization theory in the postmodern era. In M. Reed & M. Hughes (Eds.), *Rethinking organization: New directions in organization theory and analysis* (pp. 207–226). Newbury Park, CA: Sage.

Giddens, Anthony. (1991). *Modernity and self identity*. Stanford, CA: Stanford University Press.

Gilligan, Carol. (1982). *In a different voice*. Boston: Harvard University Press.

Giroux, Henry A. (1983). *Theory & resistance in education: A pedagogy for the opposition*. South Hadley, MA: Bergin & Garvey.

Giroux, Henry. (1992). *Border crossings: Cultural workers and the politics of education*. New York and London: Routledge.

Giroux, Henry A. (1993). *Living dangerously: Multiculturalism and the politics of difference*. New York: Peter Lang.

Gleazer, Edmund J. (1980). *The community college: Values, vision, and vitality*. Washington, DC: American Association of Community and Junior Colleges.

Goodwin, Gregory. (1971). *The historical development of the community—junior college ideology*. Doctoral dissertation. University of Illinois at Urbana.

Gordan, Edmund W., & Bhattacharyya, Maitrayee. (1992). Human diversity, cultural hegemony, and the integrity of the academic canon. *Journal of Negro Education 61*(3), 405–418.

Gore, Jennifer. (1993). *The struggle for pedagogies: Critical and feminist discourses as regimes of truth*. New York: Routledge.

Greenberg, Arthur R. (1991). *High school-college partnerships: Conceptual models, programs and issues*. ASHE-ERIC Higher Education Report No. 5. Washington, DC: Association for the Study of Higher Education.

Greenfield, Thomas B. (1980). The man who comes back through the door in the wall: Discovering truth, discovering self, discovering organizations. *Educational Administration Quarterly, 16*(3), 26–59.

Griffith, Marlene, & Connor, Ann. (1994). *Democracy's open door*. Portsmouth, NH: Boynton/Cook Publishers, Inc.

Grubb, W. Norton. (1989). The effects of differentiation in educational attainment: The case of community colleges. *The Review of Higher Education, 12*(4), 349–374.

Grubb, W. Norton. (1991). The decline of transfer rates: Evidence from national longitudinal surveys. *Journal of Higher Education, 62*(2), 194–217.

Hall, Stuart. (1990). Cultural identity and diaspora. In J. Rutherford (Ed.), *Identity: Community, culture, difference* (pp. 222–237). London: Lawrence & Wishart.

Hanson, Sandra L. (1994). Lost talent: Unrealized educational aspirations and expectations among U.S. youths. *Sociology of Education, 67*(3), 159–183.

Hartman, Mary S. (1990, July 5). Mills students provided eloquent testimony to the value of women's colleges. *The Chronicle of Higher Education*, A40.

Hill, Patrick J. (1991). Multiculturalism: The crucial philosophical and organizational issues. *Change, 23*(4), 38–47.

Hirsch, Jr., E. D. (1987). *Cultural literacy.* New York: Vintage Books.

Hodgkinson, Harold L. (1985). *All one system.* Washington, DC: The Institute for Educational Leadership, Inc.

Holland, Dorothy C., & Eisenhart, Margaret A. (1990). *Educated in romance: Women, achievement, and college.* Chicago: University of Chicago Press.

hooks, bell. (1992). *Black looks: Race and representation.* Boston: South End Press.

hooks, bell. (1994a). *Outlaw culture: Resisting representations.* New York: Routledge.

hooks, bell. (1994b). *Teaching to transgress: Education as the practice of freedom.* New York: Routledge.

Horowitz, Helen Lefkowitz. (1987). *Campus life: Undergraduate cultures from the end of the eighteenth century to the present.* New York: Alfred A. Knopf.

Iannello, Kathleen P. (1992). *Decisions without hierarchy: Feminist interventions in organization theory and practice.* New York: Routledge.

Karabel, Jerome. (1972). Community colleges and social stratification. *Harvard Educational Review, 42,* 521–562.

Karabel, Jerome. (1986). Community colleges and social stratification in the 1980s. In L. S. Zwerling (Ed.). *The community college and its critics.* New Directions for Community Colleges, No. 54. San Francisco: Jossey-Bass.

Kerkhoff, Alan C. (1992). *Diverging pathways: Social structure and career reflections.* Cambridge: Cambridge University Press.

Kester, Donald. (1993). *An instructional guide concerning the highly successful teaching & motivational practices of Jaime Escalante.* Los Angeles: Los Angeles County Office of Education.

Kimball, Roger. (1990). *Tenured radicals: How politics has corrupted our higher education.* New York: Harper & Row.

Kincheloe, Joe. (1995). *Toil and trouble: Good work, smart workers, and the integration of academic and vocational education.* New York: Peter Lang.

Kozol, Jonathan. (1991). *Savage inequalities: Children in America's schools.* New York: Harper Perennial.

La Belle, Thomas J., & Ward, Christopher R. (1994). *Multiculturalism and education: Diversity and its impact on schools and society.* Albany: State University of New York Press.

Lara, Juan F., & Mitchell, Ruth. (1986). The seamless web: The interdependence of educational institutions. *Education and Urban Society, 19*(1), 24–41.

Lareau, Annette. (1987). Social class in family-school relationships. *Sociology of Education, 63,* 178–193.

Larrabee, Mary Jeanne. (Ed.). (1993). *An ethic of care: Feminist and interdisciplinary perspectives.* New York: Routledge.

Levine, Arthur, & Cureton, Jeanette. (1992). The quiet revolution: Eleven facts about multiculturalism and the curriculum. *Change, 24*(1), 25–29.

Lieberman, Janet E. (1985). Combining high school and college: LaGuardia's Middle College High School. In W. T. Daly (Ed.), *College school collaboration: Appraising the major approaches* (pp. 47–57). New Directions for Teaching and Learning, No. 24. San Francisco: Jossey-Bass.

Lieberman, Janet E. (1989). Turning losers into winners: Integrating structural change. *The College Board Review, 153,* 14–19, 53.

Lieberman, Janet E., & Callagy, Anne K. (1990). Reach them and teach them: The International High School program. *Urban Education, 24*(4), 376–390.

Lincoln, Yvonna, S. & Guba, Egon G. (1986). But is it rigorous? Trustworthiness and authenticity in naturalistic evaluation. In D. D. Williams (Ed.), *Naturalistic evaluation* (pp. 73–84). New Directions for Program Evaluation, No. 30. San Francisco: Jossey-Bass.

London, Howard B. (1978). *The culture of a community college.* New York: Praeger.

Lyotard, Jean-François. (1984). *The postmodern condition.* Minneapolis: University of Minnesota Press.

MacLeod, Jay. (1987). *Ain't no makin' it.* Boulder, CO: Westview.

Magolda, Marcia B. Baxter. (1992). *Knowing and reasoning in college: Gender-related patterns in students' intellectual development.* San Francisco: Jossey-Bass.

McCurdy, Jack. (1990, May 16). Mills College trustees may reconsider their decision to admit men. *The Chronicle of Higher Education,* A2.

McCurdy, Jack. (1993, May 19). UCLA's "no" on Chicano studies dept. brings violent protest. *The Chronicle of Higher Education,* A16.

McGrath, Dennis, & Spear, Martin B. (1991). *The academic crisis of the community college.* Albany: State University of New York.

McKenna, Teresa. (1988). "Immigrants in our own land": A Chicano literature review and pedagogical assessment. *ADE Bulletin, 91,* 30–38.

McLaren, Peter. (1986). *Schooling as a ritual performance.* London: Routledge.

McLaren, Peter. (1989). *Life in schools.* New York: Longman.

McLaren, Peter. (1995). *Critical pedagogy and predatory culture.* New York: Routledge.

McNeil, Maureen. (1993). Dancing with Foucault: Feminism and power-knowledge. In C. Ramazanoglu (Ed.), *Up against Foucault: Explorations of some tensions between Foucault and feminism* (pp. 147–175). London: Routledge.

McRobbie, Angela. (1978). Working class girls and the culture of femininity. In Centre for Contemporary Cultural Studies (Ed.), *Women take issue* (pp. 96–108). London: Routledge & Kegan Paul.

Medsker, Leland L. (1960). *The junior college.* New York: McGraw-Hill.

Mehan, Hugh. (1978). Structuring school structure. *Harvard Educational Review, 48*(1), 32–64.

Mehan, Hugh. (1992). Understanding inequality in schools: The contribution of interpretive studies. *Sociology of Education, 65,* 1–20.

Mehan, Hugh, Hubbard, Lea, & Villanueva, Irene. (1994). Forming academic identities: accommodation without assimilation among involuntary minorities. *Anthropology & Education Quarterly, 25*(2), 91–117.

Meznek, James, McGrath, Patricia, & Garcia, Felix. (1989). *The Puente Project.* Report for the Board of Governors, California Community Colleges. Sacramento: Office of the Chancellor.

Middaugh, Michael F. (1984, May). *An empirical evaluation of boundary spanning as a conceptual framework for examining the organizational roles of offices of institutional research.* Paper presented at the Annual Forum of the Association for Institutional Research, Fort Worth, TX.

Minh-ha, Trinh T. (1991). *When the moon waxes red: Representation, gender and cultural politics.* New York: Routledge.

Mittelstet, Stephen K. (1994). A synthesis of the literature on understanding the new vision from community college culture: The concept of community building. In G. A. Baker III (Ed.), *A handbook on the community college in America* (pp. 549–564). Westport, CT: Greenwood Press.

Moed, Martin G., & Greenberg, Arthur. (1982). College with its own high school. *Community and Junior College Journal, 52*(5), 33–35.

Moore, Kathryn McDaniel. (1978). The war with the tutors: Student-faculty conflict at Harvard and Yale, 1745–1771. *History of Education Quarterly, 18*(2), 115–127.

Morgan, Gareth. (1986). *Images of organizations.* Beverly Hills, CA: Sage.

Nicholson, Linda J. (Ed.). (1990). *Feminism/postmodernism.* New York: Routledge.

Noddings, Nel. (1984). *Caring: A feminine approach to ethics and moral education.* Berkeley: University of California Press.

Nora, Amaury. (1993). Two-year colleges and minority students' educational aspirations: Help or hindrance? In J. C. Smart (Ed.), *Higher education: Handbook of theory and research* (pp. 212–247). New York: Agathon Press.

Nora, Amaury, & Rendon, Laura. (1988). Hispanic student retention in community colleges: Reconciling access with outcomes. In L. Weis (Ed.), *Class, race, and gender in American education* (pp. 126–143). Albany: State University of New York Press.

Novak, Steven J. (1977). *The rights of youth: American colleges and student revolt, 1798–1815.* Cambridge, MA: Harvard University Press.

Olivas, Michael. (1979). *The dilemma of access: Minorities in two-year colleges.* Washington, DC: Howard University Press.

Orfield, Gary, & Ashkinaze, Carol. (1991). *The closing door: Conservative policy and Black opportunity.* Chicago: University of Chicago Press.

Ortego, Philip D. (Ed.). (1973). *"We are Chicanos": An anthology of Mexican-American literature.* New York: Washington Square Press.

Palmer, James C., Ludwig, Meredith, & Stapleton, Laura. (1994). *At what point do community college students transfer to baccalaureate-granting institutions.* Washington, DC: American Council on Education.

Parker, Martin. (1992). Post-modern organizations or postmodern organization theory? *Organization Studies, 13*(1), 1–17.

Parsons, Talcott. (1959). The school class as a social system: Some of its functions in American society. *Harvard Educational Review, 29*(4), 297–318.

Patton, Michael Q. (1980). *Qualitative evaluation methods.* Beverly Hills, CA: Sage.

Pincus, Fred L. (1980). The false promises of community colleges: Class conflict and vocational education. *Harvard Educational Review, 50*(3), 332–361.

Pincus, Fred L. (1983). Class conflict and community colleges: Vocational education during the Reagan years. *The Review and Proceedings of the Community Colleges Humanities Association, 4,* 3–18.

Pincus, Fred L. (1986). Vocational education: More false promises. In L. S. Zwerling (Ed.), *The community college and its critics* (pp. 41–52). New Directions for Community Colleges, No. 54. San Francisco: Jossey-Bass.

Ratcliff, James L. (1994). Seven streams in the historical development of the modern American community college. In G. A. Baker III (Ed.), *A handbook on the community college in America: Its history, mission, and management* (pp. 3–16). Westport, CT: Greenwood Press.

Ravitch, Diane. (1990). Multiculturalism: E Pluribus Plures. *The American Scholar, 59*(3), 337–354.

Reed, Michael, & Hughes, Michael. (Eds.). (1992). *Rethinking organization: New directions in organization theory and analysis.* Newbury Park, CA: Sage.

Rendon, Laura I., (1993). *The university and community college paradox: Why Latinos do not transfer.* A report prepared for the University of California Latino Eligibility Study, Spring Symposium.

Rendon, Laura I., & Valadez, James R. (1993). Qualitative indicators of Hispanic student transfer. *Community College Review, 20*(4), 27–37.

Rhoads, Robert A. (1994). *Coming out in college: The struggle for a queer identity.* Westport, CT: Bergin & Garvey.

Rhoads, Robert A., & Tierney, William G. (1992). *Cultural leadership in higher education.* University Park, PA: National Center for Postsecondary Teaching, Learning, and Assessment.

Richardson, Laurel. (1991). Postmodern social theory: Representational Practices. *Sociological Theory, 9*(2), 173–179.

Rist, Ray. (1977). *The urban school: A factory for failure.* Cambridge: MIT Press.

Rodriguez, Richard. (1982). *Hunger of memory.* Boston: David R. Godine.

Roueche, John E., Baker, George A. III, & Rose, Robert R. (1989). *Shared vision: Trans-*

formational leadership in American community colleges. Washington, DC: Community College Press.

Schwartz, Robert. (1992). A systemwide approach to school-college collaboration. *The School Administrator,* November, 14–17.

Scott, Richard W. (1987). *Organizations: Rational, natural, and open systems* (2nd ed.). Englewood Cliffs, NJ: Prentice-Hall.

Seidman, Steven. (1991). The end of sociological theory: The postmodern hope. *Sociological Theory, 9*(2), 131–146.

Shor, Ira. (1987). *Critical teaching & everyday life.* Chicago: University of Chicago Press.

Smircich, Linda. (1983). Concepts of culture and organizational analysis. *Administrative Science Quarterly, 28,* 339–358.

Smircich, Linda. (1985, August). *Toward a woman centered organization theory.* Paper presented at the Annual Meeting of the Academy of Management, San Diego, CA.

Smircich, Linda, & Morgan, Gareth. (1982). Leadership: The management of meaning. *The Journal of Applied Behavioral Science, 18*(3), 257–273.

Sotello, Caroline, & Turner, Viernes. (1992). It takes two to transfer: Relational outcomes and educational outcomes. *Community College Review, 19*(4), 27–33.

Stage, Frances K., & Manning, Kathleen. (1992). *Enhancing the multicultural campus environment: A cultural brokering approach.* New Directions for Student Services, No. 60. San Francisco: Jossey-Bass.

Sternberg, Robert J. (1988). *The triarchic mind: A new theory of human intelligence.* New York: Viking Press.

Tierney, William G. (1988). Organizational culture in higher education. *Journal of Higher Education, 59*(1), 2–21.

Tierney, William G. (1992). *Official encouragement, institutional discouragement: Minorities in academe—The Native American experience.* Norwood, NJ: Ablex.

Tierney, William G. (1993). *Building communities of difference: Higher education in the 21st century.* Westport, CT: Bergin & Garvey.

Tierney, William G., & Rhoads, Robert A. (1993a). *Enhancing promotion, tenure and beyond: Faculty socialization as a cultural process.* ASHE-ERIC Higher Education Report No. 6. Washington, DC: Association for the Study of Higher Education.

Tierney, William G., & Rhoads, Robert A. (1993b). Postmodernism and critical theory in higher education: Implications for research and practice. In J. C. Smart (Ed.), *Higher education: Handbook of theory and research* (pp. 308–343). New York: Agathon.

Valli, Linda (1986). *Becoming clerical workers.* Boston: Routledge & Kegan Paul.

Van Maanen, John. (1983). Doing new things in old ways: The chains of socialization. In J. L. Best (Ed.), *College and university organization: Insights from the behavioral sciences* (pp. 211–247). New York: New York University Press.

Vaughan, George B. (Ed.). (1980). *Questioning the community college role.* New Directions for Community Colleges, No. 32. San Francisco: Jossey-Bass.

Vaughan, George B. (1989). *Leadership in transition: The community college presidency.* New York: American Council on Education and Macmillan.

Velez, William. (1985). Finishing college: The effects of college type. *Sociology of Education, 58,* 191–200.

Weis, Lois. (1985). *Between two worlds.* Boston: Routledge.

Weis, Lois. (1990). *Working class without work: High school students in a de-industrializing economy.* New York: Routledge.

Welch, Sharon D. (1990). *A feminist ethic at risk.* Minneapolis: Fortress Press.

West, Cornell. (1993a). *Keeping faith: Philosophy and race in America.* New York: Routledge.

West, Cornell. (1993b). *Race matters.* New York: Vintage Books.

Willis, Paul E. (1977). *Learning to labor.* Aldershot: Gower.

Yin, Robert K. (1989). *Case study research: Design and methods* (rev. ed.). Newbury Park, CA: Sage.

Young, Iris M. (1990). *Justice and the politics of difference*. Princeton, NJ: Princeton University Press.

Zwerling, L. Steven. (1976). *Second best: The crisis of the community college*. New York: McGraw-Hill.

Zwerling, L. Steven. (1980). The new "new student": The working adult. In G. B. Vaughan (Ed.), *Questioning the community college role* (pp. 93–100). New Directions for Community Colleges, No. 32. San Francisco: Jossey-Bass.

Zwerling, L. Steven. (1986). Lifelong learning: A new form of tracking. In L. S. Zwerling (Ed.), *The community college and its critics* (pp. 53–60). New Directions for Community Colleges, No. 54. San Francisco: Jossey-Bass.

Index